Who, Where and When:
The History & Constitution
of the University of Glasgow

Who, Where and When:

The
History
&
Constitution
of the
University of Glasgow

Compiled by
Michael Moss, Moira Rankin and Lesley Richmond

UNIVERSITY
of
GLASGOW

© University of Glasgow, Michael Moss, Moira Rankin and Lesley Richmond, 2001
Published by University of Glasgow, G12 8QQ
Typeset by Media Services, University of Glasgow
Printed by 21 Colour, Queenslie Industrial Estate, Glasgow, G33 4DB
CIP Data for this book is available from the British Library
ISBN: 0 85261 734 8

Contents

Introduction

The *History and Constitution* is designed to provide a brief overview of the history of the University, its constitution, management, faculties, administration chairs, and endowed lectureships. Lists of the incumbents of chairs since foundation, personal professorships since 1995 and honorary graduates since 1978 are included. Anyone wishing to know more about the history of the University should consult A L Brown and Michael Moss, *The University of Glasgow 1451 - 2001*, *(Edinburgh University Press, 2001)*, and Michael Moss, J Forbes Munro, and Richard H Trainor, *University, City and State - The University of Glasgow since 1870*, *(Edinburgh University Press, 2001)*. Statistical information is published annually on the University website as *Facts and Figures*. A more extensive bibliography can be found on page 209.

Every attempt has been made to ensure the accuracy of the information but due to its sheer volume minor errors are inevitable. The editors extend their apologies to anyone omitted or wrongly designated.

The information contained in this volume is scheduled to appear on the University website in late 2001. Corrections for the Web version should be sent to the University Archivist. A mechanism for updating sections will also be provided online. Additional historical information, such as lists of the Professors at predecessor institutions will be compiled and posted in the longer term. Suggestions for useful additions are welcomed. Throughout this work reference to 'the University' is the University of Glasgow.

This edition of the History and Constitution could not have been produced without the assistance of numerous members of the University community. Of particular help were the staff of the Senate Office, the Faculty Clerks, the Court Office, Human Resources, Media Services, the Registry and our colleagues in Archive Services, especially Archie Leitch.

Michael Moss
Moira Rankin
Lesley Richmond

A Brief History

The University of Glasgow

The University of Glasgow was founded by Pope Nicholas V in a letter dated 7 January 1451 and authenticated with a lead seal or 'bull'. It erected a *studium generale* or university for all future time in Glasgow - in theology, canon and civil law, in arts and in all lawful faculties with all the privileges, liberties, honours, exemptions and immunities enjoyed by the *studium* at Bologna, Italy, and it is still the authority by which the University awards degrees. Although the letter states that it was issued at the request of King James II, the real founder of the University was William Turnbull, Bishop of Glasgow from 1447 to 1454. With experience of St Andrews and several continental universities, he no doubt expected that a university would enhance the reputation of his diocese and provide much needed education for his clergy.

Like other universities of the time, only undergraduate Arts degrees were available. The Master of Arts was awarded after five years of study in Latin, Greek, Logic, Moral Philosophy, Natural Philosophy (Physics) and/or Mathematics. At first the teaching was by regents who took their charges through the whole course of study. A Bachelor of Arts could be obtained after three years' study, providing a licence to teach, but only Masters of Arts were officially members of the University with a right to vote at the election of the Chancellor. Students studying in Arts were divided according to their place of birth into four nations originally Clydesdale, Teviotdale, Albany and Rothesay. These students, known as *togati* or gowned, voted for the Rector by their nation, a practice which was not abolished until 1977. Few students chose to study in higher faculties and in practice there was only teaching in Theology and Canon Law. These were known as *non-togati*, as they were not required to wear the undergraduate red gown since they were supposed to have already graduated, but not necessarily at Glasgow.

Throughout its first century, the University enjoyed a close affinity with the Cathedral, being located near by, and was part of the efforts to reform the church by improving the education of both the clergy and laity. Education was also dear to the heart of the Protestant reformers, who believed that the University should fulfil a similar role but with more emphasis on the training of parochial schoolmasters. However, they failed to provide any endowments and it was not until Andrew Melville (1545-1622) became Principal in 1574 that the problem was addressed. He reformed the curriculum by placing greater emphasis on liberal arts and made the teaching of Greek and Hebrew more stable. In so doing he attracted more students, which enabled him to secure a new charter from James VI in 1577. Known as the *Nova Erectio*, this provided an endowment (albeit leased from the Crown) and established the mode of governance for almost 300 years. The Principal, who was to be an ordained minister and to teach Divinity, was placed in overall charge of the University's affairs. Three regents were to be subject to his authority and were to teach a definite group of subjects, Greek and Rhetoric; Dialectic, Morals and Politics; and Arithmetic and Geometry. Although the professor with a chair in a specific discipline was to grow out of this innovation, it proved difficult to sustain and the old system of unspecified regenting was reintroduced in 1642 and continued until 1727.

Despite this setback, the quality and range of teaching improved. A bold decision was taken to erect a new building around two quadrangles facing the High Street. Work began in 1631 and continued as money allowed through the difficult times of the civil war. A donation of £200, promised by Charles I, was honoured by Oliver Cromwell. The handsome new buildings were virtually complete by the time of the restoration of the monarchy in 1660 when the royal coat of arms was added above the main entrance.

In more settled times the University grew quickly from some 150 students in 1660 to 400 by 1702. In the course of the next thirty years, seven professorships were either created or restored, often with endowments from the Crown, as part of a wider programme of university reform. Teaching in Medicine, which had been briefly attempted between 1637 and 1646, was revived in 1714 and the Faculty of Medicine came to embrace all the life sciences, Botany, Zoology and Chemistry. For the first time since the Reformation, Law became a recognised faculty with its own regius professor.

Under the terms of the Act of Uniformity all professors and graduates were required to sign the Westminster Confession. There were, however, no religious tests at matriculation and students from a variety of confessional backgrounds attended the University. Tests on graduation seem to have been abandoned by the end of the eighteenth century and those for professors were finally abolished in 1853.

Although there was no barrier to matriculation, few students took the trouble as there was no need unless they wished to graduate, vote in a rectorial election, or use the library. Attendance at lectures was recorded by the individual regents or professors, who issued class tickets for satisfactory performance and awarded most prizes. In 1717, the professors disenfranchised the students of their rights to vote at rectorials. The students resisted and their rights were restored in 1726, but professors continued to vote until 1858. In 1727, three of the nations were renamed. Clydesdale, Teviotdale and Albany became Glottiana, Loudonina and Transforthiana. *(See also the History of Matriculation on page 69)*.

By the end of the eighteenth century there was increasing tension between the 'Faculty' which consisted of the Principal (also holder of the Chair of Divinity) and the twelve other professors appointed before 1761. Holders of chairs created thereafter by the Crown were only considered to be members of Senate and therefore had no role in the governance of the University. The treatment of some of these new appointments by the Faculty was shameful. They were denied the use of the best classrooms and in one case of even a blackboard. Despite public disagreement, it was not until 1858 that an Act of Parliament abolished the Faculty and replaced it with the University Court composed of lay members whose main responsibility was the oversight of the fabric and finances. This legislation also made matriculation compulsory for the first time for all students irrespective of faculty and restricted the franchise in rectorial elections to the students. The Rector *ex officio* was to chair the Court. The distinction between *togati* and *non-togati* students was also abolished and the General Council was set up, comprising members of the University Court, professors and graduates. The Students Representative Council was not given formal recognition until the Universities (Scotland) Act of 1889.

By the 1840s the buildings in the High Street were no longer adequate and the whole area had become run down as the city had expanded westwards. After an abortive attempt to move to Woodlands Hill in the late 1840s, the University finally left its original home for a splendid new edifice on Gilmorehill in the west end in 1870. It had been foreseen that the move would impact on clinical teaching and funds were also raised to build a new hospital, the Western Infirmary, on adjacent ground. In 1889, under a new Act of Parliament, the balance of responsibilities between the Court and Senate was altered and the professors became fully salaried instead of depending for much of their income on class fees. One consequence of this legislation was that in 1892 all Scottish universities were permitted to admit women and consequently Queen Margaret College *(see histories of Predecessor Institutions on page 12)* merged with the University. In the following year the Science faculty was established independent of both Arts and Medicine. Engineering was part of the Science Faculty until it became a separate faculty in 1923.

The Faculty of Medicine was enlarged in 1947 to include the two independent medical schools, St Mungo's College and Anderson's College of Medicine, along with the Glasgow Dental School. The following year Glasgow Veterinary College also joined the Medical Faculty, eventually becoming the Faculty of Veterinary Medicine in 1966. A new Act of Parliament, the Universities (Scotland) Act of 1966, gave Scottish universities much greater autonomy in the content and design of courses. Eleven years later the Faculty of Social Science was created out of the Faculty of Arts. The Law Faculty was renamed Law and Financial Studies in 1984. The Faculty of Education was established in 1999 when St Andrew's College of Education merged with the University. The Faculty of Science was again restructured in 2000 to form three new faculties, Biomedical and Life Sciences, Physical Sciences, and Computing Science, Mathematics and Statistics.

Predecessor Institutions

Anderson's College of Medicine

John Anderson, MA, FRS, the founder of Anderson's Institution, was born at Rosneath, Dunbartonshire, in 1726, the eldest son of James Anderson, minister of Rosneath. He studied at the University of Glasgow and was appointed Professor of Oriental Languages in 1756, and Professor of Natural Philosophy in 1760. During his tenure of the latter chair, he realised that an acquaintance with the principles of natural philosophy would be invaluable to mechanics, and this led him to establish, in addition to his usual class, one of a more popular character, for those whose pursuits did not allow them to follow the routine of academic study. These lectures were illustrated by numerous experiments and could be understood by those who did not have the advantage of a mathematical education. He continued to hold this class every Tuesday and Thursday during the session to the close of his life. About this time he commenced making a private collection of scientific apparatus and natural history specimens, which formed the nucleus of the Andersonian Museum, now dispersed.

John Anderson died on 13 January 1796, bequeathing by his will, of 7 May 1795, the whole of his property, with a few trifling exceptions, 'to the public, for the good of mankind, and the improvement of science, in an institution to be denominated 'Anderson's University'. Initially, however, the institution established under this will, was known as Anderson's Institution. In 1828, it changed its name to Anderson's University.

The origins of Anderson's Medical School date from 1800 when Dr John Burns commenced lectures on anatomy and surgery. In 1819, Botany was added; in 1828, the Chairs of Midwifery, Materia Medica, and the Practice of Medicine were set up, followed by Medical Jurisprudence in 1831, Institutes of Medicine or Physiology in 1849, Ophthalmic Medicine and Surgery in 1869, Hygiene and Public Health in 1878 and Aural Surgery in 1879. The Chairs of Physics, Zoology, Diseases of the Throat and Nose, and Mental Diseases were established in 1891 and Diseases of the Skin in 1914. The Medical School long held a foremost position as an extra-mural school, and provided a medical education at a cost suited to the circumstances of many who would not otherwise have been able to pursue the study of medicine. The School did not award its own qualifications and students often used their class tickets towards either University degrees or licences from the various Faculties of Physicians and Surgeons in Scotland, England and Ireland.

Anderson's College succeeded Anderson's University following the passing in 1877 of the Anderson's College (Glasgow) Act (40 Vic., c.xii). In 1887, under the Educational Endowments (Scotland) Act of 1884, the College was split in two. Its medical school was incorporated as a separate and distinct institution, as Anderson's College Medical School.

The rest of the College was amalgamated with the College of Science and Arts, Allan Glen's Institution, the Young Chair of Technical Chemistry and Atkinson's Institution to form the Glasgow and West of Scotland Technical College (later the Royal College of Science and Technology).

Anderson's Institution was initially located in John Street, but in 1828 it moved into new premises in George Street. From 1889, the buildings of the Anderson's College Medical School were situated in Dumbarton Road close to the Western Infirmary and the main University campus. In 1947, Anderson's College of Medicine was absorbed into the University. The buildings now house the Department of Medical Genetics.

Glasgow Dental Hospital and School
Formed as the School of Dental Surgery and Dental Hospital of Glasgow in 1879, it was initially located within Anderson's College but as Anderson's could not award its own medical qualifications, the students sat examinations set by the Faculty of Physicians and Surgeons of Glasgow. The Glasgow Dental Hospital and School became a voluntary hospital in 1885 when it moved to 56 George Square. It moved again in 1889, to 4 Chatham Place, in 1896, to 5 St Vincent Place, and in 1903 to 15 Dalhousie Street. It became a limited company in 1904. A purpose-built dental hospital and school was completed in Renfrew Street in 1931. In 1947, the Dental School became affiliated to the University of Glasgow and incorporated into the Faculty of Medicine. In 1948, the Glasgow Dental Hospital became part of the National Health Service, with its own board of management. The present buildings in Sauchiehall Street were completed in 1970. Following the National Health Service reforms of the early 1990s, the Glasgow Dental Hospital and School National Health Service Trust was formed. In 1999 this was replaced by the larger North Glasgow University Hospitals NHS Trust which also includes the Royal Infirmary, the Western Infirmary, Gartnavel General, and Stobhill Hospital.

Glasgow Veterinary College
The origins of veterinary medicine in Glasgow can be traced back to 1832 when Anderson's College of Medicine appointed a professor of veterinary education. However this was a part-time appointment and the formal training of most vets in Scotland from 1823 until 1863, was carried out through the Dick Veterinary College, Edinburgh. The Glasgow Veterinary College was established in 1862 by James McCall, a lecturer at the Edinburgh College, as result of a profound disagreement with William Dick, the College principal, over the best way to tackle the *Rinderpest* cattle plague that was sweeping Europe. McCall was committed to slaughter whereas Dick believed recuperation was possible.

Formal establishment came by Royal Warrant in 1863, although Dick had already been teaching Glasgow based Dick Veterinary College students for some years using premises in Sauchiehall Lane. In 1863, McCall moved to larger premises at 397 Parliamentary Road and in 1873 a new building, which previously had been a water-pumping station, was acquired at 83 Buccleuch Street. After refurbishment the new premises were opened on 28 October 1874. Following the College's incorporation in 1909, it purchased its premises in Buccleuch Street from James McCall. After the merger of the College with the University of Glasgow in October 1945, the Buccleuch Street site continued to be used until 1969. A new veterinary hospital for clinical and research facilities was built in 1950 on the Garscube Estate, a veterinary field station had been established on the Cochno Estate in 1954, and new teaching buildings for both pre- and para-clinical departments were built at Garscube in the 1960s. *(See also the Faculty of Veterinary Medicine history on page 53).*

Queen Margaret College

Queen Margaret College was established in 1883 by the incorporation of the Glasgow Association for the Higher Education of Women. The Association had been formed in 1877 to offer educational opportunities for women, following the 'lectures for ladies' given by University professors initiated in 1868 by Mrs Jessie Campbell of Tullichewan, a pioneer of the higher eduction of women in Scotland. In 1892, the College merged with the University of Glasgow, following the Scottish Universities Commissioners Ordinance empowering Scottish Universities to make provision for the instruction and graduation of women.

The College was based at North Park House (now the Queen Margaret Drive offices of BBC Scotland), which were gifted by the philanthropist, Mrs Isabella Elder. Following the merger with the University, the building, grounds and a £25,000 endowment were handed over to the University on the understanding that they were kept for the teaching of women only. The building was sold in 1935.

Initially, the College only offered subjects in Arts but after laboratories were built in 1888, Science subjects were taught. By 1890, classes were being conducted in Classics, Mathematics, Physics, Philosophy, English Literature, Chemistry, Zoology, Botany, Physiology, Geology and Physical Geography, History, Political Economy, French and German Language and Literature, Music, and Painting. In October that year, the College opened its own medical school, its students receiving clinical instruction at the Royal Infirmary and the Maternity and Sick Children's Hospitals.

The College had no authority to issue degrees but their medical students could acquire licences to practice medicine and surgery from the Triple Qualification Board of the Faculty of Physicians and Surgeons of Glasgow and the Royal Colleges of Physicians and Surgeons of Edinburgh and their Irish or English equivalents. The Queen Margaret College medical curriculum was equivalent to that of the University and after the merger medical students could sit their professional examinations at the University. Marion Gilchrist graduated with a high commendation in 1894 and was the first woman to receive a degree from the University of Glasgow. She was also the first woman to receive a medical degree from any Scottish University.

Due to the non-equivalency of the arts and science curriculum, existing Queen Margaret College students wishing to qualify for a degree form the University could not present their earlier examination passes, but had to take the new University classes, taught at the College. The first woman to graduate with an MA was Isabella Blacklock in 1895 and the first female BSc graduate was Ruth Pirret in 1898.

Royal Scottish Academy of Music and Drama

The Royal Scottish Academy of Music and Drama's association with the University formally dates from 1929 when a joint appointment of Principal of the Academy and Professor of Music in the University was made. This association continued until 1994 with the University validating the Academy's degrees.

The Royal Scottish Academy of Music and Drama began as the Glasgow Atheneum in 1847 with the purpose of providing, not only commercial skills, but philosophy, literature and languages as well as music. It drew on the Glasgow Educational Association ideas of giving opportunities for training to young men engaged in commercial pursuits. It was established in rented premises in the Glasgow Assembly Rooms in Ingram Street and opened to the public on 13 October 1847 with an inaugural address delivered by Charles Dickens. On 15 September 1890 the Glasgow Atheneum (Ltd) School of Music was founded and its first principal was Allan Macbeth. The next major change was in 1929 with the establishment of a Scottish National Academy of Music when the vestiges of non-musical activities were swept away. The driving force behind this was Sir Daniel Macaulay Stevenson who at the same time raised funds for a Chair of Music at the University of Glasgow. The Academy was recognised by the Scottish Education Department as a central institution qualifying for government funding in 1939. In July 1944 King George VI granted the prefix "Royal".

The academy became known as the Royal Scottish Academy of Music and Drama in 1968. Its first qualifications in Drama were Diplomas in either Dramatic Art or Speech and Drama. The latter required educational qualifications on entry and was given in conjunction with a Certificate in Dramatic Studies awarded by the University. In 1983, the Diploma in Speech and Drama was validated as the BA (Dramatic Studies).

The Academy moved into new premises at 100 Renfrew Street in 1987. In 1994, the Privy Council granted the Academy powers to award its own degrees.

St Andrew's College of Education

St Andrew's College of Education was established in 1981 and was the result of the merger of Notre Dame College of Education and Craiglockhart College of Education. Notre Dame College was set up in 1895 as Dowanhill Training College, by the sisters of Notre Dame de Namur, and Craiglockhart College opened in 1919. Both were Roman Catholic teacher training institutions initially for women students only. Men were admitted to Notre Dame College from 1967 and the College moved to its Bearsden site in 1968. On 11 April 1999 St Andrew's College of Education merged with the University of Glasgow to form the University's Faculty of Education. *(See also the Faculty of Education history on page 46).*

St Mungo's College of Medicine

St Mungo's College of Medicine was established in 1888 as a new independent medical college, although it incorporated the Glasgow Royal Infirmary School of Medicine which had been set up in 1876 to counteract the effect of the opening of the Western Infirmary which had deprived the Royal of all its clinical chairs. The college was housed in the buildings of the Royal Infirmary.

St Mungo's continued the policy of the Glasgow Royal Infirmary School of Medicine of allowing women to matriculate for a complete course of medical study and, during the period 1890-1892, forty-three women received clinical instruction alongside male students although classes were separated thereafter. St Mungo's was, however, always struggling to get enough students to enrol, as it was not affiliated to a university and could not award its own degrees. As with Anderson's College of Medicine, the students used their class tickets towards University degrees or Faculty of Physicians and Surgeons licenses.

The college always hoped that it would become an extra-mural college of the University of Glasgow, but an attempt to affiliate in 1905 failed. As the class sizes at the Western Infirmary got larger, however, the University became keen to re-establish links with the Royal Infirmary and in 1910 the Chairs of Clinical Medicine and Clinical Surgery were transferred to the Royal Infirmary from the Western. In 1911, the St Mungo Chairs of Surgery and Pathology and the Muirhead Chairs of Medicine and Obstetrics and Gynaecology were created. Arrangements were made to have classes at the Royal Infirmary on venereal disease, diseases of the ear, diseases of the throat and nose and skin diseases. By 1930, five more clinical lectureships had been attached to the Royal Infirmary and St Mungo's College of Medicine became the centre for clinical and systematic instruction during the last two years of the University of Glasgow's medical curriculum.

In 1947, St Mungo's College of Medicine was amalgamated with the University's Medical Faculty and its property was transferred to Glasgow Royal Infirmary.

Trinity College

Trinity College, in Lynedoch Street, Woodlands Hill, designed by the Glasgow architect, Charles Wilson, was opened as the Glasgow Free Church College in 1857. A memorial to open a theology college in Glasgow had been presented in 1855 to the General Assembly of the Free Church by a group of Glasgow laymen. Teaching began on 4 November 1856 in a building in Thistle Street prior to the opening of the college building. Following the union of The Free Church and the United Presbyterian Church in 1900, it became the Glasgow College of the United Free Church of Scotland. The professors of the College were amongst the most distinguished theologians of their time.

Following the union of the United Free Church and the Church of Scotland in 1929 the College adopted the name Trinity and further rationalisation took place in the training and teaching of ministers. In Glasgow, the outcome, in operation from 1935, was to combine the teaching strength of the University and that of the College to make an enlarged Faculty of Divinity.

By 1970, with declining enrolments, it had been obvious that the College building could not be adapted economically for the needs of the Faculty. By Easter 1973 all classes formerly held in the College had been transferred to the University campus, and later that year the Church of Scotland resolved that Trinity College should be disposed of and the library offered to the University. The college building was sold and subsequently transformed into residential accommodation. The College remains a corporate entity within the Faculty of Divinity with its own constitution and endowments.

The Constitution

The University of Glasgow was founded by Papal Bull in 1451, however, its modern constitutional framework derives from the Universities (Scotland) Acts 1858 to 1966. These Acts make provision for the main statutory bodies and officers: the Court, the Senate, the General Council; the Chancellor, the Principal and Vice Chancellor, and the Rector, and set out the powers and duties of those statutory bodies, as well as specifying their composition. From 1858 until 1966 the instruments by which the University exercised its powers were Ordinances. These were drafted by the University but given legal authority by the Privy Council after approval by the General Councils of the other Scottish Universities. The Universities (Scotland) Act of 1966 gave the power to make legal instruments back to the Universities themselves - these being known as Resolutions. The University Court issues the Resolutions having consulted widely with the University community. In a few restricted areas, mainly of constitutional import, Ordinances are still required.

The Papal Bull

Bull by Pope Nicholas V, ordaining a University to be founded in the City of Glasgow. Rome, 7 January 1450/1.

NICHOLAS the Bishop, servant of the servants of God, for perpetual memory of the fact. Amongst other blessings which mortal man is able in this transient life by the gift of God to obtain, it is to be reckoned not among the least, that by assiduous study he may win the pearl of knowledge, which shows him the way to live well and happily, and by the preciousness thereof makes the man of learning far to surpass the unlearned, and opens the door for him clearly to understand the mysteries of the Universe, helps the ignorant, and raises to distinction those that were born in the lowest place. And therefore, the Apostolic See, the prudent administrator of spiritual as well as temporal things, and the steady and unfailing friend of every commendable undertaking, to the end that men may be moved more readily to win so lofty a height of human condition, and when won, dispense it again to others, always with increase thereof, encourages some, prepares places for others, aids and fosters others, and loads them with gracious favours. Forasmuch, therefore, as it was lately shown to us on behalf of our dearest son in Christ, James, the illustrious King of Scots, that the said King, laudably intending not only the weal of the commonwealth, and indwellers and inhabitants of the country subject to him, but also the other parts neighbouring thereto, was very desirous that a university, with every lawful faculty, should be set up and ordained by the Apostolic See in his city of Glasgow, as being a place of renown and particularly well fitted therefor, where the air is mild, victuals are plentiful, and great store of other things pertaining to the use of man is found, to the end that there the Catholic faith may be spread, the simple instructed, equity in judgement upheld, reason flourish, the minds of men illuminated, and their understandings enlightened. We, having carefully considered the premises, and also the uncommon sincerity of faith and devotion which the said king is known to bear towards us and the Roman Church, are moved with fervent desire that the said city may be adorned with the gifts of the sciences, so that she may produce men distinguished for ripeness of judgement, crowned with the ornaments of virtue and erudite with the dignities of the various faculties and that there may be an overflowing fountain of the sciences, out of whose fullness all that desire to be imbued with the lessons of knowledge may drink. Having, therefore, with careful deliberation, deeply weighed all these things, and especially the suitableness of this city, which, as we have heard, is said to be particularly meet and well fitted for multiplying the seeds of learning and bringing forth of salutary fruits, not only for the advantage and the profit of the said city, but also of the indwellers and inhabitants of the whole kingdom of Scotland, and the regions lying round about, we, being moved with fatherly affection, and inclined by the supplications of the said king in that behalf, to the praise of God's name, and propagation of the orthodox faith, erect, by apostolical authority a university in the said city in all times to come for ever, as well in theology and cannon and civil law as in arts, and every other lawful faculty. And that the doctors, masters, readers, and students there may brook and enjoy all and sundry privileges, liberties, honours, exceptions, and immunities granted by the apostolic see, or otherwise in any manner of way to the masters, doctors and students in the university of our city of Bologna: And that our reverend brother, William, bishop of Glasgow, and his successors for the time being, bishops of Glasgow, shall be rectors of the schools of the said university of Bologna have. And that those who in process of time shall merit to obtain a diploma in the faculty in which they study, and licence to teach, that they may be able to instruct others; and also that those who seek the honour of master or doctor to be conferred on them, shall be presented by the doctor or doctors and master or masters of the faculty in which the examination is to be held, to the Bishop of Glasgow now and for the time being, and if the church of Glasgow lack the solace of a pastor, to the vicar or official in spiritual things of our beloved sons of the chapter of the said church. Which bishop, or vicar, or official, having called together the other doctors and masters then teaching there, shall diligently attend by himself or another to the examination of those that are to be promoted in those things which in any way are requisite for the degree of master or doctor, according to the wont and custom commonly observed in other universities, and shall bestow on them such licence, or confer such honour of mastership, if they shall be found fit and qualified for the same. And those who shall have been examined and approven in the said university of the city of Glasgow, and shall have got such licence to teach and degree, as aforesaid, shall thenceforth, without any other examination and approval, have full liberty to be regents and to teach, as well in the said city as in each and all other universities in which they shall choose to rule and teach, notwithstanding of any statues and customs, even although strengthened by oath, apostolic conformation, or any other guarantee, and whatsoever else there may be in the contrary, Let none therefore in any wise infringe this writing of our erection, constitution and appointment, or with foolhardy daring go in the contrary thereof; but if any one shall presume to attempt this, let him know that he shall incur the wrath of Almighty God, and of the blessed apostles Peter and Paul. Given at Rome, at St Peter's, the year of our Lords incarnation, one thousand four hundred and fifty, the seventh of the ides of January, and the fourth year of our pontificate.

Note on the date of the Bull: Throughout the middle ages, Western Europe used the Julian calendar, consisting of 365 days with an extra day every fourth year. By this calendar New Year's Day was 25 March, i.e. 24 March 1450 was followed by 25 March 1451. This, the Feast of the Blessed Virgin Mary, was precisely 9 months before Christmas Day. Pope Gregory XIII began his reformation of the calendar in 1582 and his 'Gregorian' calendar is still the one most popularly used in the western world today. His reforms included a loss of ten days, adopted in Scotland and England in 1751 and the beginning of a new year on 1 January. In Scotland, 31 December 1599 was followed by 1 January 1600 but the change did not take place in England until 1 January 1752. Therefore in dating the University's Papal Bull, it is 1450 by the Julian calendar but 1451 by the Gregorian one. By modern reckoning this makes the University 550 years old in 2001.

The Story of the Papal Bull

The University has been without its original Bull, issued by Pope Nicholas V in 1451, since the mid-sixteenth century. In 1560, during the political unrest accompanying the Scottish Reformation, the then chancellor, Archbishop James Beaton, a supporter of the Marian cause, fled to France taking with him for safe-keeping many of the archives and valuables of the Cathedral and the University, including the Mace and the Bull. Although the Mace was sent back in 1590 the archives were not. Principal Dr James Fall told the Parliamentary Commissioners of Visitation on 28 August 1690, that he had seen the Bull at the Scots College in Paris, together with the many charters granted to the University by the Kings and Queens of Scotland from James II to Queen Mary. The University enquired of these documents in 1738 but was informed by Thomas Innes and the superiors of the Scots College, that the original records of the foundation of the University were not now to be found. If they had not been lost by this time they certainly went astray during the French Revolution when the Scots College was itself under threat and its records and valuables were moved for safe-keeping out of the city of Paris. Nevertheless, the Bull remains the authority by which the University awards degrees.

The Coat of Arms

The University of Glasgow's crest depicts the legend of St Kentigern or St Mungo, with the addition of the Book of Learning and a representation of the University Mace. The Mace is the symbol of the University's corporate dignity, it has a silver shaft and a hexagonal head of gold and enamel work. It was made for the University in France in 1465. The Latin motto on the ribbon - 'Via, Veritas, Vita' - is 'the Way, the Truth, the Life'.

The story of the life of St Kentigern is vague and of the many legends the following is generally accepted. He was born at Culross on the north shore of the Firth of Forth in the early years of the sixth century, the son of Urien, Prince of Cumbria, and Thenew, daughter of the King of Lothian. He was educated and trained as a priest of the Celtic Church at the monastery of St Serf at Culross, Fife. The name Kentigern means 'High Lord' but St Serf was very fond of him and called him Mungo, meaning "my dear friend".

In about 550 Mungo finished his training and went to the house of a holy man named Fergus at Kernach. Fergus died the night he arrived and Mungo placed his body on a cart yoked by two wild bulls commanding them to convey it to the place ordained by the Lord. They stopped at Cathures where Fergus was buried and Mungo established a church. Mungo refered to this spot as 'Glasgu' or the beloved green place. This became Glasgow and the church developed into Glasgow Cathedral. Mungo lived an ascetic and holy life until his death in 603. He was canonised and became the patron saint of Glasgow with a feast day on 13 January.

The legend of St Mungo depicted on the University crest consists of:

'Here's the Bird that never flew' - the wild robin which St Serf tamed. It was accidentally killed by some of his disciples who blamed it on Mungo. He took the dead bird in his hands and prayed, restoring it to life, whereupon it flew to its master.

'Here's the Bell that never rang' - the bell may have been given to St Mungo by the Pope but there is no definite information as to how he obtained it. By the fifteenth century St Mungo's handbell had become a notable Glasgow symbol. Handbells were common in the Celtic church and were used by Holy men to call the flock to worship. In 1450, John Stewart, 'the first provost that was in Glasgow", left, as did many others, an endowment to have the bell tolled throughout the city to call the inhabitants to pray for his soul. The fate of the original bell is unknown although it was known still to exist in 1578. A replacement was purchased by Town Magistrates in 1641 and this bell is still in the People's Palace Museum.

'Here's the Tree that never grew' - the tree is now depicted as an oak but it started in the legend as a hazel branch. As a boy in the monastery Mungo was left in charge of the holy fire in the refectory. He fell asleep and some of the other boys, being envious of him, put out the fire. When he woke and found what had happened, Mungo broke off some frozen branches from a hazel tree and caused them to burst into flames by praying over them.

'**Here's the Fish that never swam**' - the fish with a ring in its mouth is a salmon and the ring was a present from Hydderch Hael, King of Cadzow, to his Queen, Languoreth. The Queen gave the ring to a knight and the King, suspecting an intrigue, took it from him while he slept during a hunting party and threw it into the River Clyde. On returning home the King demanded the ring and threatened Languoreth with death if she could not produce it. The Queen appealed to the knight who, of course, could not help and then confessed to St Mungo who sent one of his monks to fish in the river, instructing him to bring back the first fish caught. This was done and St Mungo extracted the ring from its mouth.

Management

Chancellor

The Chancellor is the titular head of the University and has the function of conferring degrees on persons found qualified and presented to him by the Senatus Academicus. The Chancellor is now elected by the General Council, of which he is president, and holds office for life. He nominates an Assessor who is a member of the University Court and he is empowered to appoint a Vice-Chancellor to discharge, in his absence, the function of conferring degrees. The office of Vice-Chancellor has usually been, and now is, held by the Principal, but other senior professors, usually the Dean of Faculties or the Clerk of Senate, may be appointed Depute Vice-Chancellors to officiate at degree ceremonies. (Resolution 442 of 1997). Although technically elected by the Masters of the University, from 1451 to 1692 all Chancellors were Bishops or Archbishops of Glasgow except those elected in 1642, 1658 and 1660.

1451	William Turnbull	1661	Andrew Fairfowl
1455	Andrew de Durisdeer	1664	Alexander Burnet
1474	John Laing	1672	Robert Leighton
1483	Robert Blackadder	1674	Alexander Burnet
1508	James Beaton I	1679	Arthur Ross
1524	Gavin Dunbar	1684	Alexander Cairncross
1551-1560	James Beaton II	1687	John Paterson
1571	John Porterfield	1692	John, Second Lord Carmichael
1572	James Boyd	1714	James, First Duke of Montrose
1581	Robert Montgomery	1743	William, Second Duke of Montrose
1585	William Erskine	1781	James, Third Duke of Montrose
1587	Walter Stewart, First Lord Blantyre	1837	James, Fourth Duke of Montrose
1598	James Beaton	1875	Sir William Stirling Maxwell of Pollok
1603	John Spottiswoode	1878	Walter Francis, Fifth Duke of Buccleuch
1615	James Law		
1633	Patrick Lindsay	1884	John, Tenth Earl of Stair
1642	James, Third Marquis of Hamilton	1904	William, First Baron Kelvin of Largs:
1658	John Thurloe		*previously Professor of*
1660	William, Eighth Earl of Glencairn		*Natural Philosophy and*
			Dean of Faculties

1908	Archibald Philip, Fifth Earl of Rosebery, and Midlothian: *previously Rector*	1972	Sir Alexander Kirkland Cairncross: *previously Professor of Applied Economics*
1929	Sir Donald MacAlister of Tarbert: *later Principal*	1996	Sir William Kerr Fraser: *previously President of the Students' Representative Council and Principal*
1934-1944	Sir Daniel Macaulay Stevenson		
1946	John Boyd Orr, First Baron Boyd Orr of Brechin: *previously Rector and Member of Parliament for the Scottish Universities*		

Rector

As in other universities of medieval foundation, the Rector was originally the active head of the University, exercising jurisdiction over all it members and elected by the votes of their nations. Under the *Nova Erectio* he was made president of the Senatus Academicus but was not a member of the Faculty. The office gradually became an honorary one, although until the end of the eighteenth century the Rector occasionally exercised visitorial functions. Since 1858, the Rector has been elected trienially by matriculated students. Originally the date of election was fixed by the original statutes for St Crispin's Day, October 25: it may now be held on any day in the Candlemas Term fixed by the University Court after consultation with the Senatus. The Rector is president of the University Court, and holds office for three years. For a list of Rectors from 1451 to 1600 see Durkan and Kirk, *The University of Glasgow 1451-1577* (Glasgow, 1977). No authoritive list of Rectors has yet been compiled for the period 1601 to 1689.

1690	David Boyle of Kelburn: *later First Earl of Glasgow*	1726	George Ross, Master of Ross: *later Thirteenth Lord Ross*
1691	Sir John Maxwell of Nether Pollok	1729	Francis Dunlop of Dunlop
		1731	John Orr of Barrowfield
1718	Mungo Graham of Gorthie	1733	Colin Campbell of Blythswood
1720	Robert Dundas the Younger of Arniston	1738	George Bogle of Daldowie
		1740	John Graham of Dugalston
1723	James Hamilton of Aikenhead	1742	John Orr of Barrowfield
1725	Sir Hugh Montgomerie of Hartfield	1743	George Bogle of Daldowie
		1746	Sir John Maxwell of Pollok

1748	George Bogle of Daldowie	1803	Robert Dundas of Arniston:
1750	Sir John Maxwell of Pollok		*Chief Baron of Exchequer*
1753	William Mure of Caldwell	1805	Henry Glassford of Dugalston
1755	John, Third Earl of Glasgow	1807	Archibald Colquhoun
1757	Patrick Boyle, Lord Shewalton		of Killermont
1759	James Milliken of Milliken	1809	Archibald Campbell
1761	James, Fifteenth Earl of Errol		of Blythswood
1763	Sir Thomas Miller of Barskimmen	1811	Lord Archibald Hamilton
1764	William Mure of Caldwell	1813	Thomas Graham,
1767	Dunbar, Fourth Earl of Selkirk		Lord Lynedoch
1768	Sir Adam Ferguson of Kilkerran	1815	David Boyle, Lord Boyle
1770	Robert Ord:	1817	George, Fourth Earl of Glasgow
	Chief Baron of Exchequer	1819	Kirkman Finlay:
1772	Sir Frederick Campbell:		*later Dean of Faculties*
	Lord Clerk Register	1820	Francis Jeffrey, Lord Jeffrey
1773	Charles, Ninth Baron Cathcart	1822	Sir James Mackintosh
1775	Sir James William Montgomerie:	1824	Henry Peter Brougham:
	Chief Baron of Exchequer		*later First Baron Brougham*
1777	Andrew Stewart of Torrance		*and Vaux*
1779	James, Seventh Earl	1826	Thomas Campbell
	of Lauderdale	1829	Henry Thomas, Fourth
1781	Henry Dundas:		Marquis of Lansdowne
	later First Viscount Melville	1831	Henry Thomas Cockburn,
1783	Edmund Burke		Lord Cockburn
1785	Robert Graham of Gartmore	1834	Edward George Geoffrey Smith,
1787	Adam Smith:		Lord Stanley:
	previously Professor of Moral		*later Fourteenth Earl of Derby*
	Philosophy and Professor	1836	Sir Robert Peel
	of Logic and Rhetoric	1838	Sir James Robert George Graham
1789	Walter Campbell of Shawfield	1840	John, Second Marquis
1791	Thomas Kennedy of Dunure		of Breadalbane
1793	William Mure of Caldwell	1842	Fox Maule:
1795	William McDowell of Garthland		*later First Earl of Dalhousie*
1797	George Oswald of Auchencruive	1844	Andrew Rutherford
1799	Sir Ilay Campbell of Succoth,	1846	Lord John Russell:
	Lord Succoth		*later First Earl Russell*
1801	William Craig, Lord Craig	1847	William Mure of Caldwell:
			later Dean of Faculties

1848	Thomas Babington Macaulay: *later Baron Macaulay*		1908	George Nathaniel, First Marquess of Curzon
1850	Sir Archibald Alison		1911	Augustine Birrell
1852	Lord Archibald William, Thirteenth Earl of Eglinton: *previously Dean of Faculties*		1914	Raymond Poincaré: *President of the French Republic*
			1919	Andrew Bonar Law
1854	George Douglas, Eighth Duke of Argyll		1922	Frederick Edwin, First Earl of Birkenhead
1856	Sir Edward George Earle Lytton Bulwer-Lytton: *later First Baron Lytton*		1925	Sir Austen Chamberlain
			1928	Stanley Baldwin: *later First Earl Baldwin*
1859	James, Eighth Earl of Elgin		1931	Sir Compton Mackenzie
1862	Henry John, Third Viscount Palmerston		1934	Sir Iain Colquhoun of Luss
			1937	Hugh Richard Lawrie Sheppard: *Canon of St Paul's*
1865	John Inglis, Lord Glencorse		1938	Sir Archibald Henry Macdonald Sinclair of Ulbster
1868	Edward Henry, Fifteenth Earl of Derby			
1871	Benjamin Disraeli: *later First Earl of Beaconsfield*		1945	Sir John Boyd Orr: *later Lord Boyd Orr of Brechin and Chancellor*
1877	William Ewart Gladstone			
1880	John Bright		1947	Walter Elliot Elliot: *previously Member of Parliament for the Scottish Universities*
1883	Henry Fawcett			
1884	Edmund Law Lushington: *previously Professor of Greek*			
			1950	John Macdonald MacCormick
1887	Edward Robert Bulwer, First Earl of Lytton		1953	Tom John Honeyman: *Director of Glasgow Museums and Art Galleries*
1890	Arthur James Balfour, First Earl Balfour			
1893	Sir John Eldon Gorst		1956	Richard Austen Butler: *later Baron Butler of Saffron Walden*
1896	Joseph Chamberlain			
1899	Archibald Philip, Fifth Earl of Rosebery and Midlothian: *later Chancellor*		1959	Quintin McGarel Hogg, Second Viscount Hailsham
1902	George Wyndham		1962	Albert John Lutuli
1905	Herbert Henry Asquith: *later First Earl of Oxford and Asquith*		1965	John Charles Walsham, First Baron Reith of Stonehaven
			1968	George Fielden, Baron Macleod of Fuinary

1971	James Reid	1990	Patrick Kane
1974	Arthur Montford	1993	Johnny Ball
1977	John Lamberton Bell	1996	Richard Wilson
1980	Reginald Bosanquet	1999	Ross Kemp
1984	Michael Kelly	2001	Greg Hemphill
1987	Winnie Mandela		

Principal and Vice-Chancellor

The office of Principal Regent, or Principal of the College, dates from the beginning of the University when he was responsible for the day-to-day administration of the College, whereas the Rector had overall responsibility. The office has changed many times over the centuries. For example, under the *Nova Erectio* of 1577 the role was reconstituted and the Principal had to preach at the church of Govan every Sunday as the College enjoyed the revenues of the parish. The Principal was at that time forbidden to take any extended journey without the permission of the Rector, Dean and regents and being absent for three consecutive days without permission was tantamount to resignation. This practice soon became burdensome and in 1621 the Principal was freed from the arrangement. Although for centuries the Principal was nominated by the Crown, the appointment is now made by the University Court to whom the Principal is responsible for the running of the University. The role of Principal today can be likened to that of chief executive of the University. The Principal sits on the University Court and is President of the Senate. In modern times the Principal has also been Vice Chancellor and carries out the task of conferring degrees in the Chancellor's absence, although this power may also be delegated to Depute Vice-Chancellors.

1451	Alexander Geddes, STL:	1490	John Doby, MA
	Cistercian, senior regent	1498	Patrick Coventry, MA, BDec,
1460	Duncan Bunch, MA, STB		STB
1475	Walter Bunch, STB:	1510	Thomas Coutts, MA
	Cistercian	1514	David Melville, MA
1478	John Goldsmith, MA, BDec	1517	David Abercromby, MA
	and John Doby:	1518	John Mair (Major), MA, STD
	joint Principals	1526	James Lindsay, MA
1480	John Brown, MA, DDec	1536	Alexander Logan, MA:
1483	Walter Leslie, MA		*senior regent*
1485	John Goldsmith, MA, BDec	1540	Alexander Hamilton, MA:
1485	George Crichton, MA		*senior regent*

1547	John Hamilton, MA:	1858	Thomas Barclay, MA, DD

1547 John Hamilton, MA:
     senior regent
1555 John Houston, MA:
     senior regent
1556 John Davidson, MA
1560 John Davidson, MA
1574 Andrew Melville, MA:
     later Principal of St Mary's
     College, St Andrews
1580 Thomas Smeaton, MA
1585 Patrick Sharp, MA
1615 Robert Boyd, MA
1622-1623 John Cameron, MA:
     previously regent
1626 John Strang, MA, DD
1651 Robert Ramsay, MA
1653 Patrick Gillespie, MA
1660 Robert Baillie, Jnr, MA:
     previously regent, Professor
     of Divinity and Librarian
1662 Edward Wright, MA
1684 James Fall, MA
1690 William Dunlop, MA:
     Historiographer Royal for
     Scotland and previously
     regent
1701 John Stirling, MA
1728 Neil Campbell, MA
1761 William Leechman, MA, DD:
     previously Professor of Divinity
1785 Archibald Davidson, MA, DD:
     Dean of the Thistle
1803 William Taylor, MA, DD
1823 Duncan MacFarlan, MA, DD:
     previously Dean of Faculties

1858 Thomas Barclay, MA, DD
1873 John Caird, MA, DD, LLD:
     previously Professor of Divinity
1898 Robert Herbert Story, MA,
     DD, LLD:
     previously Professor of
     Ecclesiastical History
1907 Sir Donald Macalister of
     Tarbert, KCB, MA, MD, DCL,
     LLD, DSc, PhD:
     later Chancellor
1929 Sir Robert Sangster Rait,
     MA, LLD:
     Historiographer Royal for
     Scotland and previously
     Professor of Scottish History
     and Literature
1936 Sir Hector James Wright
     Hetherington, GBE, DL, MA,
     LLD, DLitt, D-es-L:
     previously Professor
     of Moral Philosophy and
     Principal of the University
     of Liverpool
1961 Sir Charles Haynes Wilson,
     MA, LLD, DLitt, DCL
1977 Sir Alwyn Williams, PhD, DSc,
     LLD, FRS, FRSE, MRIA, FGS
1988 Sir William Kerr Fraser, GCB,
     MA, LLD, FRSE:
     later Chancellor
1995 Sir Graeme John Davies, BE,
     MA, PhD, ScD, FREng, FRSE,
     FIM, FIMEchE, FRSA, CBIM

Vice-Principals

In 1972, Court Resolution 168 made provision for the office of Vice-Principal. This office was created in response to the ever growing administrative pressures on the Principal although from 1969 to 1970 a Principal's Assessor undertook many of the duties now associated with Vice-Principals. Vice-Principals must be appointed from among the Senatus and serve for a period of three years which may be renewed at the discretion of the Court. The duties of the Vice-Principals are assigned by the Principal. Vice-Principals may deputise for the Principal as president of the Senate. Initially the Vice-Principals held territorial roles but in 1995 they were given functional responsibilities. In 2001 there were five Vice-Principals with responsibility for Estates, External Relations and Marketing, Learning and Teaching, Research, and Staffing.

Principal's Assessor
1969-1970 Donald Robertson, MA: *Professor of Industrial Relations*

Vice-Principals
1972-1977 John Currie Gunn, CBE, MA: *Professor of Natural Philosophy*

1972-1976 William Walker Chambers, MBE, MA, PhD, L-ès-L: *Professor of Modern Languages and later Dean of Faculties*

1976-1979 Rodney Julian Hirst, MA: *Professor of Logic and Rhetoric*

1977-1980 John Lamb, DSc, PhD: *Professor of Electrical Engineering*

1979-1982 Allen Meyers Potter, MA, PhD: *Caird Professor of Politics*

1980-1983 William Mulligan, MSc, PhD: *Professor of Veterinary Physiology*

1981-1985 David Flint, TD, MA, BL, CA: *Johnstone Smith Professor of Accountancy*

1982-1986 Sir Laurence Colin Hunter, CBE, MA, DPhil, FRSE: *Professor of Applied Economics*

1983-1991 John Spence Gillespie, MB ChB, PhD, FRCP, FRSE: *Professor of Pharmacology and later Dean of Faculties*

1985-1990 Alfred Lawson Brown, MA, DPhil, FRHistS: *Edwards Professor of Medieval History*

1986-1997 Sir Michael Richard Bond, MD, PhD, FRCS, FRCPsych, FRCP, DPM, FRSE: *Professor of Psychological Medicine*

1991-2001 Arthur C Allison, BSc, PhD, DipNumMath, FBCS: *Professor of Computing Science*

1991-1995 Sir James Armour, CBE, PhD, DVMS, FRCUS, FRSE: *Titular Professor of Veterinary Parasitology and later Dean of Faculties*

1991-1996 Andrew Stewart Skinner, MA, BLitt, FRSE: *Adam Smith Professor of Political Economy*

1995-2000 J Drummond Bone, MA: *Professor of English Literature and later Principal of Royal Holloway, University of London*

1996-2000 Richard H Trainor, BA, MA, DPhil, FRHistS: *Professor of Social History and later Vice-Chancellor of the University of Greenwich*

1997-2001 David R Green, MSc, PhD, CEng, FIStructE: *Professor of Structural Engineering*

1997 Peter H Holmes, BVMS, PhD, MRCVS: *Professor of Veterinary Physiology*

1998 Ronald V Emanuel, BSc, PhD, CChem, FRSC

1999 Malcolm D McLeod, MA BLitt, FRSE: *Professor of African Studies*

2000 Christopher D Morris, BA, DipEd, MIFA, FSA, FSAScot, FRSE, FRHistS, FRSA: *Professor of Archaeology*

2001 Robin E Leake, MA, DPhil (from August): *Professor of Endocrine Oncology*

2001 Joseph M Thomson, LLB, FRSE (from August): *Regius Professor of Law*

Dean of Faculties

In the pre-Reformation University, the Dean of Faculties was elected annually by the Masters to exercise a general superintendence over studies. After the Reformation the Dean acted as an auditor of the college accounts and Visitor of the College. The office is now honorary and the Dean is elected by the Senatus for a period of three years.

Deans from 1800

1800 James Couper, MA, DD: *Professor of Astronomy, later Clerk of Senate and Keeper of the Hunterian Museum*

1802 Archibald Campbell of Succoth

1804 Gavin Gibb, MA, DD, LLD: *later Professor of Oriental Languages*

1806 Duncan MacFarlan, MA, DD: *later Principal*

1808 Gavin Gibb, MA, DD, LLD: *later Professor of Oriental Languages*

1810 Duncan MacFarlan, MA, DD: *later Principal*

1812 Gavin Gibb, MA, DD, LLD: *later Professor of Oriental Languages*

1814 Stevenson Macgill, MA, DD: *also Professor of Divinity*

1815 Archibald Campbell, MP

1817 Sir John Connel

1819 Archibald Campbell, MP

1821 Sir John Connel

1823 Archibald Campbell, MP

1825 Sir John Connel

1827 Archibald Campbell, MP

1829 Sir John Connel

1833 Archibald Campbell, MP

1837 Archibald Campbell, MP

1839 Kirkman Finlay: *previously Rector*

1841	James, First Baron Dunfermline
1843	Sir Thomas Makdougall Brisbane
1845	Alexander Maconochie, Lord Meadowbank: *later Rector*
1847	Lord Archibald William, Thirteenth Earl of Eglinton: *later Rector*
1849	William Mure of Caldwell, MP: *previously Rector*
1851	William Lockhart, MP
1853	William Mure of Caldwell, MP: *previously Rector*
1857	William Stirling of Keir, MP
1860	James Moncrieff: *later First Baron Moncrieff and Member of Parliament for the Universities of Glasgow and Aberdeen*
1863	Sir Archibald Campbell of Succoth
1865	Henry Glassford Bell
1868	Sir James Fergusson of Kilkerran
1869	Sir Thomas Edward Colebrooke, MP
1872	Archibald Orr Ewing, MP
1876	Alexander Bennett McGrigor, LLD
1879	Sir James King, LLD: Lord Provost of Glasgow
1882	Robert William Cochran-Patrick, BA, LLD, MP
1885	Alexander Crum, MP
1888	Robert Berry, MA, LLD: *previously Regius Professor of Law*
1896	William Purdie Dickson, MA, DD, LLD: *previously Professor of Divinity*
1901	William Thomson, Baron Kelvin of Largs, GCVO, MA, DCL, LLD, FRS: *previously Professor of Natural Philosophy and later Chancellor*
1904	Sir James King, LLD
1911	William Stewart, MA, DD, LLD: *previously Clerk of Senate*
1919	George Gilbert Ramsay, MA, LLD, LittD: *previously Professor of Humanity*
1921	Sir Hector Clare Cameron, CBE, MD, LLD: *previously Professor of Clinical Surgery*
1929	Frederick Orpen Bower, MA, ScD, LLD, FRS: *previously Regius Professor of Botany*
1940	John Duncan Mackie, CBE, MC, MA, LLD: *previously Professor of Scottish History and Literature*
1945	Sir Arthur Trueman, KBE, DSc, LLD, FRS: *previously Professor of Geology*
1946	Sir Robert Muir, MA, MD, ScD, LLD, DCL, FRS: *previously Professor of Pathology*
1949	William Rennie, CBE, MA, LLD, LittD: *previously Professor of Humanity and Professor of Greek*
1953	William Barron Stevenson, MA, DLitt, DD, LLD: *previously Professor of Hebrew and Semitic Languages*
1954	Ritchie Girvan, MA, LLD: *previously Professor of English Language*
1958	Thomas Murray MacRobert, MA, DSc, LLD: *previously Professor of Mathematics*

1961	John Duncan Mackie, CBE, MC, MA, LLD: *previously Professor of Scottish History and Literature*
1964	Charles Arthur Campbell, MA, DLitt: *previously Professor of Logic and Rhetoric*
1967	John Walton, MA, DSc, ScD, D-es-Sc, LLD: *previously Professor of Botany*
1970	Daniel Fowler Cappell, CBE, MD, LLD: *previously Professor of Pathology*
1973	Christian James Fordyce, MA, LLD: *previously Clerk of Senate and Professor of Greek*
1974	Alec Lawrence Macfie, MA, DLitt, LLD: *previously Professor of Political Economy*
1978	Sir Charles Frederick William Illingworth, CBE, MD, ChM, DSc, LLD: *previously Regius Professor of Surgery*
1981	Sir William Lee Weipers, BSc, DUniv, FRCVS, DVSM: *previously Professor of Veterinary Surgery*
1984	William Walker Chambers, MBE, MA, PhD, L-es-L: *previously Professor of Modern Languages and Vice-Principal*
1985	Robert Alexander Rankin, MA, PhD, ScD: *previously Clerk of Senate and Professor of Mathematics*
1988	Sir John Currie Gunn, CBE, MA, DSc, DUniv, FRSE, FInstP, FIMA: *previously Cargill Professor of Natural Philosophy and Vice-Principal*
1992	Edward McCombie McGirr, CBE, BSc, MD, FRSE: *previously Professor of Administrative Medicine and Muirhead Professor of Medicine*
1995	John S Gillespie, MB ChB, PhD, FRCP, FIBiol, FRSE: *previously Professor of Pharmacology and Vice-Principal*
1998	Archibald Alexander McBeth Duncan, MA, FBA, FRHistS, FRSE: *previously Clerk of Senate and Professor of Scottish History and Literature*
2001	Sir James Armour, CBE, PhD, DVMS, FRCUS, FRSE: *previously Titular Professor of Veterinary Parasitology and Vice-Principal*

University Court

The Court is a body corporate with perpetual succession and a common seal. The powers of the Court, which are fully set out in the Universities (Scotland) Acts 1858 to 1966, may be stated briefly to be: to administer the whole property and revenue of the University; to review any decision of the Senatus, appealed against by a member of the Senatus or other interested member of the University; to receive representations and reports from the Senatus and General Council; to appoint chairs which are in patronage of the University; to appoint examiners and lecturers; to recognise as qualifying towards graduation the teaching of any college or individual teacher; to take proceedings against a principal or professor, lecturer, assistant, recognised teacher or examiner, or any other person employed in teaching or examining; to fix fees; to found new professorships; and, on the recommendation of the Senatus, to prescribe regulations for degree courses. The Court's powers are exercised, according to their nature, either outright or by resolution under the 1966 Act. In a few restricted areas, mainly of constitutional import, they are recognised by ordinance.

The University Court consists of the Rector; the Principal; the President of the Students' Representative Council; an assessor nominated by the Chancellor; an Assessor nominated by the Students' Representative Council; an Assessor nominated by the City of Glasgow Council; five Assessors elected by the General Council; seven Assessors elected by the Senatus Academicus, of whom at least three are readers or lecturers; two employee representatives; and up to five co-opted members. The Assessors continue in office for four years except the Students' Representative Council Assessor, who serves for one year by virtue of the nature of the office. The Rector, and in his absence the Chancellor's Assessor, is chairman and seven members constitute a quorum. The Court meets regularly throughout the year, receiving papers from a variety of committees, as well as from Senate.

Secretary of Court
Originally the Secretary of Court was a Glasgow lawyer who held the position part-time. In 1944, the Secretary became a full time member of the University staff and was combined with the post of Registrar, although the posts were separated from 1983 and 1996.

1860	Andrew Bannatyne, LLD
1865	Revd Andrew Sym, MA, DD
1870	Revd James Pearson, DD
1874	Anderson Kirkwood, LLD: *previously Professor of Conveyancing*
1887	George D Mclellan, MA, LLB
1888	Alan Ernest Clapperton, BL, LLD
1931	Sir John Spencer Muirhead, DSO, MC, BA, LLD
1944	Robert Thomson Hutcheson, OBE, JP, MA, PhD, LLD
1974	James McCargow, JP, MA
1985	Robert Ewen, OBE, TD, MA
1995	Dugald Mackie, MA, FRSA

Senatus Academicus
The Senatus is charged with the regulation and superintendence of the teaching and the discipline of the University and the promotion of research. The *ex officio* members of the Senatus are the Principal, who is its president, and the Professors, both established chairholders and personal professors, together with a number of other officers, including the Clerk of Senate. Readers and lecturers who are members of the Faculties may be

elected to membership of the Senate to a number equal to one third of its members *ex officio* by virtue of the Universities (Scotland) Act of 1858. Members of Senate are also elected from the following constituencies: library staff - three members, research staff - six members and other related staff - three members. Membership of Senate has also been extended to a number of matriculated students: the Students' Representative Council President, Senior Vice-President, Vice-President for University Affairs, and one representative from each of the Faculties. The Principal has a deliberative and casting vote. One third of the Senatus constitutes a quorum.

Senate Oath

At induction Professors are required to make a verbal oath and sign as a permanent record of their promise:

> *I, (Name, Degrees and Honours) and Professor of (Subject) in this University faithfully promise in the presence of the Senate here assembled, that I shall fulfil the duties of the office entrusted to me here, in the service of learning as my abilities shall best allow.*

The new Senator is then welcomed by his/her peers.

Vice-Principal (Learning and Teaching)/Clerk of Senate

A review of the role of the Clerk of Senate led to the decision in February 2001 that the Clerkship should be combined with the Vice-Principalship (Learning and Teaching), in anticipation of the new post of Vice-Principal (Learning and Teaching)/Clerk of Senate being fully operational with effect from August 2002.

The Vice-Principal (Learning and Teaching)/Clerk of Senate is a member of the University Management Group with responsibilities for the preparation of Senate business; the implementation of the University's strategy and policy in learning and teaching; the profile of educational provision; admissions and access; the approval of course and programmes; the implementation of regulations; student appeals, complaints and discipline; graduations and other ceremonial occasions.

Clerks of Senate

1728	Robert Simson, MA, MD: *Professor of Mathematics*
1762	Joseph Black, MD: *Professor of Chemistry*
1783	Patrick Wilson, LLD: *Professor of Astronomy*
1795	Patrick Cumin, MA, LLD: *Professor of Oriental Languages*
1796	Patrick Wilson, LLD: *Professor of Astronomy*
1799	James Mylne, MA: *Professor of Moral Philosophy and later University Chaplain*

1803	William Meikleham, MA, LLD: *Professor of Natural Philosophy*
1806	William McTurk, MA, DD: *previously Librarian, and Univeristy Chaplain, later Professor of Ecclesiastical History*
1810	James Couper, MA, DD: *Professor of Astronomy, Keeper of the Hunterian Museum and previously Dean of Faculties*
1814	James Jeffray, MD: *Regius Professor of Anatomy*
1815	James Millar, MA: *Professor of Mathematics*
1820	James Couper, MA, DD: *Professor of Astronomy, Keeper of the Hunterian Museum and previously Dean of Faculties*
1828	William Meikleham, MA, LLD: *Professor of Natural Philosophy*
1831	William Meikleham, MA, LLD: *Professor of Natural Philosophy*
1846	James Seaton Reid, MA, DD: *Professor of Ecclesiastical History*
1851	Allen Thomson, MA, MD, LLD, DCL, FRS: *Regius Professor of Anatomy*
1855	Duncan Harkness Weir, MA, DD: *Professor of Oriental Languages*
1876	William Stewart, MA, DD, LLD: *Professor of Divinity and Biblical Criticism and later Dean of Faculties*
1911	George Milligan, MA, DD, DCL: *Professor of Divinity and Biblical Criticism*
1930	John Ronald Currie, MA, MD: *Henry Mechan Professor of Public Health*
1940	Christian James Fordyce, MA, LLD: *Professor of Humanity*
1971	Robert Alexander Rankin, MA, PhD, ScD: *Professor of Mathematics and later Dean of Faculties*
1978	Archibald Alexander McBeth Duncan, MA, FBA, FRHistS, FRSE: *Professor of Scottish History and Literature and later Dean of Faculties*
1983	Andrew Stewart Skinner, MA, BLitt, FRSE, FBA: *Daniel Jack Professor of Political Economy and later Professor of Political Economy (Adam Smith Chair) and Vice-Principal*
1991	John Forbes Stables Munro, MA, PhD, FRHistS: *Titular Professor of Economic History*
1996	Rex R Whitehead DSc, PhD, FRSE: *Professor of Theoretical Physics*

Vice-Principal (Learning and Teaching)/Clerk of Senate

2001	Joseph M Thomson (from August): *Regius Professor of Law*

Management Group

The Management Group was originally formed in 1983 as the Planning and Resources Committee. It had been established as a result of the Jarratt Committee Report to be responsible for the co-ordination of the University's strategic planning and its presentation to Court and Senate. It was renamed in 1996.

Management Group's main purpose is to advise the Principal, as chief executive officer of the University, on matters of policy, to advise Court and Senate on matters of strategic policy, academic and resource, and to act on a day-to-day basis to implement the policies of Court and Senate. The members are the Principal, Vice-Principals, the Secretary of Court, Clerk of Senate, the Directors of Estates and Buildings, Finance, Human Resources and Information Services.

General Council

The General Council was constituted by the Universities (Scotland) Act of 1858, as one of two supervisory bodies (the other, being the University Court) to take into consideration all questions affecting the well-being of the University, and to make recommendations to the University Court, which was required to respond to the Council. In common with the General Council of the other Scottish Universities, it was required to approve the ordinances of other institutions. Disputes were to be referred to a committee of the Privy Council. While the regulatory powers of the Court were increased by the Universities (Scotland) Act of 1889, the Council continued in a consultative role. Its composition is now regulated under the Universities (Scotland) Act of 1966 by Ordinance 200 of 1997 and comprises all persons on whom the University has conferred degrees other than honorary degrees and have paid the statutory registration fee as a requirement of graduation, all persons on whom the University has conferred certain degrees in the Glasgow School of Art and the former St Andrew's College of Education and have elected to pay the statutory registration fee, the Chancellor of the University, the members of the University Court, the holders of Chairs in the University, and all readers, senior lecturers and lecturers in the University, and those former members of Court and former professors who have elected to pay the statutory registration fee.

In terms of Ordinance 183 of 1978 the University is required to keep a register of members of the General Council which is authenticated annually as the electoral roll for election of the Chancellor (in accordance with Ordinance 199 of 1995) and five Assessors on the University Court (in accordance with Ordinance 193 of 1986). The election of Assessors takes place every two years, with two and three Assessors being elected alternately to serve for four years at a time and no member of the Senate having any part in the elections. The register of members is required to be open for inspection at reasonable times in the office of the Registrar.

The Council meets twice a year on the fourth Saturday in January and June and may hold special meetings in addition. It elects twenty members to its Business Committee, on which the Principal and the five Assessors also serve, to carry forward the work of the Council. The Business Committee appoints sub-committees covering educational policy, finance and statistics, communications, and social affairs. The University Court is required by the 1966 Act to report annually to the Council and to lay before it for comment all changes in the regulations of the University that are effected by Resolutions and Ordinances under the Act. The chairman of the Council is the Chancellor; whom failing, the Principal; whom failing, the Rector; whom failing, the Chancellor's Assessor; whom failing, the Chairman is elected by the Meeting *(see also the Registry history on page 69)*.

Clerks to the General Council
1987   Andrew Hardie Primrose, BA, LLB
1990   George Ronald Gibson Graham, CBE, MA, LLB
1996   John Michael Black, BA: *previously Registrar*

Until 1918 the General Councils of the Universities of Glasgow and Aberdeen jointly returned one representative to Parliament. Under the Representation of the People Act of 1918, the General Councils of the four Scottish Universities jointly returned three representatives. By the Representation of the People Act of 1948 the University constituencies were abolished.

Members of Parliament for the Universities of Glasgow and Aberdeen
1868   James Moncrieff, LLD: *previously Dean of Faculties and later Lord Advocate and First Baron Moncrieff*
1869   Edward Strathearn Gordon, LLD: *Dean of the Faculty of Advocates, later Baron Gordon*
1876   William Watson, LLD: *Lord Advocate*
1880   James Alexander Campbell Campbell, LLD
1906   Sir Henry Craik, KCB, MA, LLD
1910   Sir Henry Craik, KCB, MA, LLD

Members of Parliament for the Scottish Universities
1924   Sir Henry Craik, KCB, MA, LLD
1924   Sir George Andreas Berry, MB, LLD, FRSE
1924   Dugald McCoig Cowan, MA
1927   John Buchan, CH, MA, LLD: *later First Baron Tweedsmuir*
1931   Archibald Noël Skelton, BA
1934   George Alexander Morrison, MA, LLD
1935   Sir John Graham Kerr, MA, LLD, FRS: *previously Regius Professor of Zoology*
1936   James Ramsay Macdonald, LLD: *previously Prime Minister, Lord President of the Council*
1938   Sir John Anderson, GCB, GCSI, GCIE, MA, LLD, FRS
1945   Sir John Boyd Orr, MD, DSc, LLD, FRS: *later First Baron Boyd Orr of Brechin and Rector and Chancellor of the University*
1946   Walter Elliot Elliot, MC, MB ChB, DSc, LLD, FRS: *later Rector*

Students' Representative Council

Glasgow University Students' Representative Council of the University of Glasgow was instituted in January 1885, with the stated aims of representing the students in such matters as affect their interests; affording a recognised means of communication between the students and the University authorities; and promoting social and academic unity among the students. Under Section 14 (12) of the Universities (Scotland) Act of 1889, the Council was given officially recognised status. The appointed University Commissioners were authorised to make Ordinances 'to lay down regulations for the Constitution and functions of a Students' Representative Council in each University, and to frame regulations under which that Council shall be entitled to make representations to the University Court'. The Council, which is affiliated to the Scottish Union of Students and the National Union of Students, comprises elected representatives from each faculty and from student clubs and societies. All matriculated students of the University are eligible to vote in the election of representatives to the Council.

Presidents of the Students' Representative Council

1885	Robert Mark Wenley	1906	J C Watson
1886	Gavin Lambie	1907	R E Lee
1887	Charles Edward Robertson	1908	J B Galbraith
1888	John Hunter Harley	1909	J Hendry
1889	Robert Gordon Bell	1910	Robert Gibson
1890	W Newlands	1911	J Boyd
1891	J White	1912	I D Grant
1892	Robert Stevenson Horne	1913	R H Williamson
1893	John Hamilton Pagan	1914	Archibald Rae
1894	W M R Pringle	1916	A S Strachan
1895	J Scoular Thomson	1918	T S Sargent
1896	Hyam Goodman	1919	J W C McDougall
1897	Arthur Stanley Middleton	1920	R E Davie
1898	J M Black	1921	R L McKay
1899	Ivy MacKenzie	1922	J M Stirling
1900	J Muir	1923	G McCallum
1901	E R Mitchell	1924	J Thomson
1902	D A Dick	1925	J C Stewart
1903	G F Spreull	1926	H R Leishman
1904	F W Saunders	1927	A F McLeod
1905	R H Napier	1928	W A Smellie

1929	G W Robertson	1964	M J McManus
1930	R Dollar	1965	J J Murray
1931	W G Cowan	1966	N C J Fraser
1932	J McCaig	1967	T C S Marr
1933	J Good	1968	D A McKay
1934	R Hillman	1969	G Ross McKay
1935	Harold H Munro	1970	Martin Caldwell
1936	John Montgomery	1971	Thomas Wilson
1937	J MacKechnie	1972	Elaine McGregor
1938	H G Howie	1973	David Crowe
1939	Charles D Rigg	1974	John L Bell
1940	G B Shaw	1975	John Deykin
1941	R M Archiebald	1976	R Porter
1941	D Campbell	1977	W Seith S Ireland
1942	W M McDonald	1978	(M J) Terrance F Williams
1942	J P Carruthers	1979	Tim Heath
1943	W M McDonald	1980	Jimmy Black
1944	D G Landells	1981	Patricia Bell
1945	A McArthur	1982	Robert E Stevenson
1946	W D Crombie	1983	Paul Madill
1947	A M L McFarlane	1984	Malcolm R Clark
1948	D Gourlay	1985	Austin Lally
1949	D J McKay	1986	David Rennie
1950	D McMillan	1987	Murdo MacDonald
1951	William Kerr Fraser	1988	Robert Pollock
1952	C A Boyle	1989	Michael Kellet
1953	Hugh M Reilly	1990	Craig Cathcart
1954	T Kiltie	1991	Angela Constance
1955	(John) Ross Harper	1992	Gillian Shirreffs
1956	W (Kenneth) Fee	1993	Amanda Aiken
1957	Douglas N Alexander	1994	Stephen F McCloy
1958	Meta M Ramsay	1995	Alberto C Costa
1959	Campbell B Burns	1996	Stephen Rixon
1960	John M M McArthur	1997	Gavin A Muir
1961	D N McDonald	1998	(Alexander) Ewan Lamont
1962	David G Holmes	1999	Andre L C de Almeida
1963	J S Campbell	2000	Marilyn Croser

Faculties

In 2001, there were over 100 academic departments, interdisciplinary centres and institutes grouped together into eleven faculties. Each faculty was presided over by an appointed dean and conducts appropriate academic administration, including degree and course development, admissions and appeals, and the financial administration of its own resources. Scrutiny of new course proposals was conducted by relevant faculty committees (boards of studies), but there was provision for interdisciplinary boards of studies (Information Technology and Managerial and Administrative Studies) to report directly to the Education Committee of Senate.

Arts

This is the senior faculty in the University as it was the only one at the time of the University's foundation which taught undergraduates. It originally provided teaching in Latin, Greek, Moral Philosophy, Logic, Mathematics and Natural Philosophy (Physics). During the nineteenth century other modern subjects were added including English Literature, French, German, Political Economy, and History. With the growth of new social science disciplines, several new departments were formed in the 1960s including Economic History, Politics, Psychology, and Sociology. In 1977, the Faculty divided to form the Faculty of Social Science.

For a list of Deans of the Faculty of Arts from 1451 to 1600 see Durkan and Kirk, *The University of Glasgow 1451-1577* (Glasgow, 1977). No authoritative list for 1601 to 1896 has yet been compiled.

Deans

1896	George Gilbert Ramsay, MA, LLD, LittD: *Professor of Humanity*
1898	William Jack, MA, LLD: *Professor of Mathematics*
1902	Sir Henry Jones, CH, MA, LLD, LittD, FBA: *Professor of Moral Philosophy*
1905	John Swinnerton Phillimore, MA, LLD, LittD: *Professor of Greek*
1908	Dudley Julius Medley, MA, LLD: *Professor of Modern History*
1910	Robert Latta, MA, DPhil, LLD: *Professor of Logic and Rhetoric*
1915	William Macneile Dixon, MA, LLD, LittD: *Regius Professor of English Language and Literature*
1916	Gilbert Austin Davies, MA: *Professor of Greek*
1920	Sir Robert Sangster Rait, MA, LLD: *Professor of Scottish History and Literature and later Principal*
1924	Herbert Smith, MA, PhD: *William Jacks Professor of Modern Languages*

1928	Archibald Allan Bowman, MA, LittD: *Professor of Moral Philosophy*
1931	William Rennie, CBE, MA, LLD, LittD: *Professor of Humanity*
1935	Herbert James Paton, MA, DLitt: *Professor of Logic and Rhetoric*
1937	John Duncan Mackie, CBE, MC, MA, LLD: *Professor of Scottish History and Literature*
1941	Andrew Browning, MA, DLitt, FBA: *Professor of History*
1945	William Christopher Atkinson, MA: *Professor of Hispanic Studies*
1946	Andrew Browning, MA, DLitt, FBA: *Professor of History*
1947	William Christopher Atkinson, MA: *Professor of Hispanic Studies*
1948	Christian James Fordyce, MA, LLD: *Professor of Humanity*
1952	Peter Alexander, CBE, MA, FBA: *Regius Professor of English Language and Literature*
1955	Alan Martin Boase, MA, PhD: *Marshall Professor of Modern Romantic Languages*
1958	Charles Arthur Campbell, MA, DLitt: *Professor of Logic and Rhetoric*
1961	William Walker Chambers, MBE, MA, PhD, L-es-L: *William Jacks Professor of Modern Languages and later Vice-Principal*
1965	Stanley Donald Nisbet, MA, MEd: *Professor of Education*
1968	Donald James Allan, MA, FBA: *Professor of Greek*
1971	Rodney Julian Hirst, MA: *Professor of Logic and Rhetoric*
1974	Archibald Alexander McBeth Duncan, MA, FBA, FRHistS, FRSE: *Professor of Scottish History and Literature*
1977	Allan Meyers Potter, MA, PhD: *Caird Professor of Politics*
1979	Ernest Kenneth Charles Varty, BA, PhD, DLitt, FSA, Chevalier dans l'Ordre des Palmes Académiques: *Stevenson Professor of French Language and Literature*
1983	Roderick J Lyall, MA, PhD: *Titular Professor of Scottish Literature*
1986	Patrick Gerard Walsh, MA, PhD, DLitt, FRSE: *Professor of Humanity*
1989	Colin Smethurst, MA, BLitt, DipEd, Officier dans l'Ordre des Palmes Académiques: *Marshall Professor of French Language and Literature*
1992	J Drummond Bone, MA: *Professor of English Literature*
1996	Mark G Ward, BA: *Professor of German Language and Literature*
1999	John M Caughie, MA: *Professor of Film and Television Studies*

Biomedical and Life Sciences

The Institute of Biomedical and Life Sciences was formed in 1994 through the merger of the departments of Anatomy, Botany, Biochemistry, Cell Biology, Genetics and Biotechnology, Microbiology, Pharmacology, Physical Education and Sports Science, Physiology, Virology, and Zoology. In 2000, the Institute was granted faculty status with departments formally leaving the Faculty of Science.

Dean
2000   John R Coggins, MA, PhD, FRSE: *Professor of Molecular Enzymology*

Computing Science, Mathematics and Statistics

The Faculty was formed in 2000 out of the Science Faculty from the departments of Computing Science, Mathematics and Statistics.

Dean
2000   Ian Ford, BSc, PhD: *Professor of Biostatistics/Biometrics*

Divinity

This was originally a higher faculty, only offering postgraduate degrees to those who had already taken an Arts degree. In practice however, undergraduates attended classes in the Faculty. Originally there was only one professor in Divinity, but in the early eighteenth century chairs were added in Hebrew and Semitic Languages and Ecclesiastical History. Although officially teaching in the faculty was only available to members of the Church of Scotland, the University was sympathetic to seceders and allowed them to use the College Fore Hall for their own classes and to share in University teaching. At the time of the union of the United Free Church and the Church of Scotland in 1929, Trinity College became part of the Divinity Faculty. *(See also the entry for Trinity College on page 17)* . No authoritative list of Deans prior to 1896 has yet been compiled.

Deans
1896   William Stewart, MA, DD, LLD: *Professor of Divinity and Biblical Criticism*
1911   Henry Martyn Beckwith Reid, MA, DD: *Professor of Divinity*
1912   James Cooper, MA, DD, LittD, DCL: *Professor of Ecclesiastical History*
1915   William Barron Stevenson, MA, DLitt, DD, LLD: *Professor of Hebrew and Semitic Languages*
1918   George Milligan, MA, DD, DCL: *Professor of Divinity and Biblical Criticism*
1921   Henry Martyn Beckwith Reid, MA, DD: *Professor of Hebrew and Semitic Languages*
1924   William Barron Stevenson, MA, DLitt, DD, LLD: *Professor of Hebrew and Semitic Languages*
1928   Archibald Main, MA, DD, DLitt, LLD: *Professor of Ecclesiastical History*
1931   William Fulton, MA, BSc, DD, LLD: *Professor of Divinity*
1936   George Hogarth Carnaby MacGregor, MA, DLitt, DD: *Professor of Divinity and Biblical Criticism*
1939   William Fulton, MA, BSc, DD, LLD: *Professor of Divinity*

1942	William Dickie Niven, MA, DD, LLD: *Professor of Ecclesiastical History*
1945	John Gervase Riddell, MA, DD: *Professor of Divinity*
1948	John Mauchline, MA, DD: *Professor of Old Testament Language and Literature*
1951	Cecil James Mullo Weir, MA, DPhil, DD: *Professor of Hebrew and Semitic Languages*
1954	Ian Henderson, MA, DD: *Professor of Systematic Theology*
1957	John Foster, MA, DD: *Professor of Ecclesiastical History*
1960	Ronald Gregor Smith, MA, ThD, DD: *Professor of Divinity*
1963	John Mauchline, MA, DD: *Professor of Old Testament Language and Literature*
1966	William Barclay, CBE, MA, DD: *Professor of Divinity and Biblical Criticism*
1969	Allan Douglas Galloway, MA, BD, PhD, STM: *Professor of Divinity*
1972	William Hugh Clifford Frend, TD, MA, DPhil, DD, FRSE: *Professor of Ecclesiastical History*
1975	Robert Davidson, DD, MA, BD: *Professor of Old Testament Language and Literature*
1978	Ernest Best, MA, BD, PhD: *Professor of Divinity and Biblical Criticism*
1982	Robert Davidson, DD, MA, BD: *Professor of Old Testament Language and Literature*
1985	Joseph Houston, MA, BD, DPhil, FRSE: *later Professor of Philosophical Theology*
1988	George Mcleod Newlands, MA, BD, PhD: *Professor of Divinity*
1991	Robert P Carroll, MA, PhD: *later Professor of Hebrew and Semitic Studies*
1995	Alastair Hunter, MSc, BD, PhD
1998	David Jasper, MA, BD, PhD: *Professor of Literature and Theology*

Education

The Faculty was established in 1999 on the merger of St Andrew's College of Education with the University. The Departments of Adult and Continuing Education and Education, the Centre for Science Education, and the Teaching and Learning Service were also included in the Faculty. St Andrew's College was itself formed in 1981 by the merger of Notre Dame College of Education in Bearsden and Craiglockhart College in Edinburgh. *(See also the St Andrew's College of Education history on page 16).*

Dean

1999	Bartholomew J McGettrick, BSc, MEd, DHLitt, OBE, KC, HS, FRSA: *Professor of Education*
2001	Hirek S Kwiatowski, MA, MEd, PhD (from August)

Engineering

Although Engineering has been taught at the University since 1840, the Faculty was not formed until 1923. This was partly a consequence of the concordat with the Royal Technical College (now the University of Strathclyde) ratified in 1913. This allowed Royal Technical College students to receive Glasgow degrees in Applied Sciences, particularly engineering. The trigger for the creation of the Faculty was the foundation of two new chairs in Electrical Engineering and in the Theory and Practice of heat engines by the Institute of Engineers and Shipbuilders in Scotland to commemorate the centenary of the death of James Watt. The Faculty originally comprised these chairs along with Civil Engineering, Mining, and Naval Architecture.

Deans

1924	John Dewar Cormack, CMG, CBE, DSc: *Regius Professor of Civil Engineering*
1936	William John Goudie, DSc: *James Watt Professor of Theory and Practice of Heat Engines*
1938	George William Osborne Howe, DSc, LLD: *James Watt Professor of Electrical Engineering*
1943	Gilbert Cook, DSc, FRS: *Regius Professor of Civil Engineering*
1946	James Small, DSc, PhD, MIMechE: *James Watt Professor of Theory and Practice of Heat Engines*
1949	Andrew McCance Robb, DSc, LLD: *John Elder Professor of Naval Architecture and Ocean Engineering*
1953	Bernard Hague, PhD, DSc: *James Watt Professor of Electrical Engineering*
1957	William Jolly Duncan, CBE, DSc, FRS: *Mechan Professor of Engineering*
1961	William Thomas Marshall, BSc, PhD: *Regius Professor of Civil Engineering*
1964	John Farquhar Christie Conn, DSc: *Professor of Naval Architecture and Ocean Engineering*
1967	John Lamb, DSc, PhD: *Professor of Electrical Engineering*
1970	Terence Reginald Forbes Nonweiler, BSc, PhD: *Mechan Professor of Engineering*
1973	John Doughty Robson, MA, PhD: *Rankine Professor of Mechanical Engineering*
1976	Hugh Brown Sutherland, SM, FEng: *Cormack Professor of Civil Engineering*
1979	Douglas Faulkner, BSc, PhD, RCNC, FEng: *John Elder Professor of Naval Architecture and Ocean Engineering*
1981	Alexander Coull, BSc, PhD, FICE: *Regius Professor of Civil Engineering*
1984	Bryan Edward Richards, BSc, PhD: *Mechan Professor of Engineering*
1987	Brian Frederick Scott, BSc, PhD: *James Watt Professor of Mechanical Engineering*
1990	John Isaac Sewell, BSc, PhD: *Professor of Electronic Systems*

1993	David Muir Wood, MA, PhD, MICE: *Cormack Professor of Civil Engineering*
1994	David R Green, MSc, PhD, CEng, FIStructE: *Professor of Structural Engineering*
1996	David J Murray Smith, BSc, MSc, PhD, CEng, FIEE, MInstMC: *Professor of Engineering Systems and Controls*
2001	John W Hancock, BSc, PhD, MIM (from August): *Professor of Mechanical Engineering*

Law and Financial Studies

Like Divinity, this was originally a higher faculty, which only had one Regius Professor. From the eighteenth century the Faculty concentrated on the teaching of Scots Law. By the end of the century, teaching was increasingly directed in conjunction with the Glasgow Faculty of Procurators which established a part time chair in Conveyancing in 1861 towards law apprentices. After the move to Gilmorehill, classes continued to be held in the Procurators' Hall in the City Centre. Gradually a law degree became the main avenue into the profession. In 1925, a part time chair of Accountancy was endowed in the Faculty, offering classes for Law apprentices but mainly taken by accountancy apprentices. In 1967, the Bachelor of Accountancy became the normal entry to the profession. The name of the Faculty was changed to Law and Financial Studies in 1984. No list of Deans before 1896 has yet been compiled.

Deans

1896	Alexander Moody Stuart, LLD: *Regius Professor of Law*
1899	James Moir, LLD: *Professor of Conveyancing*
1901	William Smart, MA, DPhil: *Adam Smith Professor of Political Economy*
1903	John Glaister, Snr, MD, DPH, LLD: *Regius Professor of Forensic Medicine*
1905	James Moir, LLD: *Professor of Conveyancing*
1907	William Murray Gloag, KC, BA, LLD: *Regius Professor of Law*
1909	William Smart, MA, DPhil: *Adam Smith Professor of Political Economy*
1911	John Glaister, Snr, MD, DPH, LLD: *Regius Professor of Forensic Medicine*
1915	William Murray Gloag, KC, BA, LLD: *Regius Professor of Law*
1917	William Robert Scott, MA, DPhil, LLD, LittD, FRBA: *Adam Smith Professor of Political Economy*
1919	John Glaister, Snr, MD, DPH, LLD: *Regius Professor of Forensic Medicine*
1921	William Sharp McKechnie, MA, LLB, DPhil: *Professor of Conveyancing*
1923	Thomas Grieve Wright, LLB: *Professor of Mercantile Law*
1925	William Murray Gloag, KC, BA, LLD: *Regius Professor of Law*
1927	John Glaister, Snr, MD, DPH, LLD: *Regius Professor of Forensic Medicine*
1929	John Loudon, MA: *Johnstone Smith Professor of Accountancy*
1931	John Girvan, LLB: *Professor of Conveyancing*

1933	Sir John James Craik Henderson, BL: *Professor of Mercantile Law*
1935	John Glaister, Jnr, JP, MD, DSc: *Regius Professor of Forensic Medicine*
1937	Andrew Dewar Gibb, MBE, QC, MA, LLD: *Regius Professor of Law*
1939	William Robert Scott, MA, DPhil, LLD, LittD, FRBA: *Adam Smith Professor of Political Economy*
1940	John Glaister, Jnr, JP, MD, DSc: *Regius Professor of Forensic Medicine*
1943	Ian Wilson Macdonald, MA: *Johnstone Smith Professor of Accountancy*
1945	Andrew Dewar Gibb, MBE, QC, MA, LLD: *Regius Professor of Law*
1947	Sir John Boyd, MA, LLD: *Professor of Mercantile Law*
1950	Donald Alexander Stewart McLeish, LLB: *Professor of Conveyancing*
1953	Robert Browning, CBE, MA, LLB: *Johnstone Smith Professor of Accountancy*
1956	David Maxwell Walker, CBE, QC, MA, PhD, LLD, FBA, FRSE: *Professor of Jurisprudence*
1959	John Menzies Halliday, CBE, MA, LLD: *Professor of Conveyancing*
1962	Joseph Anthony Charles Thomas, MA, LLB: *Douglas Professor of Civil Law*
1965	James Bennett Miller, CBE, TD, MA, LLB: *Professor of Mercantile Law*
1968	Alexander Elder Anton, MA, LLB, FBA: *Professor of Jurisprudence*
1971	David Flint, TD, MA, BL, CA: *Johnstone Smith Professor of Accountancy*
1974	William Morrison Gordon, MA, LLB, PhD: *Douglas Professor of Civil Law*
1977	Gordon Strachan Cowie, MA, LLB: *Professor of Public Law*
1980	William Arthur Harland, MD, PhD: *Regius Professor of Forensic Medicine*
1983	Thomas Douglas Campbell, MA, PhD: *Professor of Jurisprudence*
1985	John Paxton Grant, BA, LLB, PhD: *Professor of Public International Law*
1989	John Philip Dickinson, MA, MSc, PhD, AASA: *Professor of Accountancy*
1992	John Paxton Grant, BA, LLB, PhD: *Professor of Public International Law*
1997	Joseph M Thomson, LLB, FRSE: *Regius Professor of Law*
2000	Neil William Garrod, BSc, PhD, ACIS: *Professor of Accountancy*

Medicine

Although the Papal Bull of 1451 provided for the teaching of medicine, formal teaching did not begin on a regular basis until 1714. Then, the Faculty included teaching in Medicine, Botany, and Anatomy, to which were added later Chemistry, Natural History, Surgery, Midwifery, Materia Medica, Physiology, and Forensic Medicine. Since all the life sciences were taught in the Faculty, the MD was the only qualification available for scholars in those disciplines along with veterinary medicine and agricultural science. In 1893, the Science Faculty was formed removing Botany, Zoology and Chemistry from the Faculty. Not all undergraduate medical training in Glasgow was, however, provided by the Faculty. There were two independent medical schools, St Mungo's College and Anderson's College of Medicine. Following government enquiries, these two colleges merged with the University in 1947, along with the Glasgow Dental School. In 1945, the Glasgow Veterinary College also joined the Faculty, becoming a Faculty in its own right in 1966. No list of Deans before 1896 has yet been compiled. *(See also the histories for Anderson's College of Medicine on page 12, St Mungo's College of Medicine page 16, Glasgow Veterinary College page 13 and Glasgow Dental Hospital and School page 13).*

Deans

The Dean of the Medical Faculty was elected until 2000 when the first Executive Dean was appointed by the University Court.

1896	Sir William Tennant Gairdner, KCB, MD, LLD, FRS: *Regius Professor of Practice of Medicine*
1899	John Cleland, MA, MD, FRS: *Regius Professor of Surgery*
1900	Sir Thomas McCall Anderson, MD: *Regius Professor of Practice of Medicine*
1904	Murdoch Cameron, MD: *Professor of Midwifery*
1906	Ralph Stockman, MD, LLD: *Regius Professor of Materia Medica*
1908	John Glaister, Snr, MD, DPH, LLD: *Regius Professor of Forensic Medicine*
1910	Sir Robert Muir, MA, MD, ScD, LLD DCL, FRS: *Professor of Pathology*
1912	Diarmid Noel Paton, MD, BSc, LLD, FRS: *Regius Professor of Physiology*
1915	Thomas Hastie Bryce, MA, MD, FRS: *Regius Professor of Anatomy*
1920	Edward Provan Cathcart, CBE, MD, DSc, LLD, FRS: *Professor of Physiological Chemistry*
1925	John Ronald Currie, MA, MD: *Henry Mechan Professor of Public Health*
1930	Walter King Hunter, MD, DSc: *Muirhead Professor of Medicine*
1935	Carl Hamilton Browning, MD, LLD, FRS: *Professor of Bacteriology*
1938	John Shaw Dunn, MA, MD, MSc: *Professor of Pathology*
1942	George MacFeat Wishart, MD, BSc: *Professor of Physiological Chemistry*
1946	William John Brownlow Riddell, MD: *Professor of Ophthalmology*
1948	George MacFeat Wishart, MD, BSc: *Professor of Applied Physiology*
1959	Geoffrey Balmanno Fleming, MBE, BA, MD: *Samson Gemmell Chair of Child Health*
1971	James Holmes Hutchison, CBE, MD: *Samson Gemmell Chair of Child Health*
1974	Edward McCombie McGirr, CBE, BSc, MD, FRSE: *Muirhead Professor of Medicine*
1981	William Bryan Jennett, MD: *Professor of Neurosurgery*
1987	Sir Donald Campbell, CBE, MB ChB: *Professor of Anaesthesia*
1992	Brian Whiting, MD, FRCP, FFPM, FMedSci: *Professor of Clinical Pharmacology*
2000	Michael John Godfrey Farthing, BSc, MD, FRCP: *Professor of Medicine*

Physical Sciences

The Faculty was formed out of the Faculty of Science in 2000, comprising the Departments of Physics and Chemistry.

Dean

2000   Professor Geoffrey Webb, PhD, DSc, CChem, FRSC, FRSE: *Professor of Catalytic Science*

Science *(1893-2000)*

Although the formation of a Faculty of Science had been discussed from the 1870s, it was not established until 1893 by the Commissioners appointed under the Universities (Scotland) Act of 1889. The Chairs of Mathematics, Natural Philosophy, Geology, Astronomy, Civil Engineering, and Naval Architecture were transferred from the Faculty of Arts and those in Botany, Zoology, and Chemistry from the Medical Faculty. The Science Faculty was replaced on 1 October 2000 with the Faculties of Biomedical and Life Sciences, Computing Science, Mathematics and Statistics and Physical Sciences.

Deans

1894   John Ferguson, MA, LLD, FSA: *Regius Professor of Chemistry*
1896   Frederick Orpen Bower, MA, ScD, LLD, FRS: *Regius Professor of Botany*
1898   Archibald Barr, DSc, LLD, FRS: *Regius Professor of Civil Engineering*
1899   John Young, MD: *Regius Professor of Natural History*
1902   Andrew Gray, MA, LLD, FRS: *Professor of Natural Philosophy*
1905   Sir John Graham Kerr, MA, LLD, FRS: *Regius Professor of Natural History*
1909   John Walker Gregory, DSc, FRS: *Professor of Geology*
1912   Thomas Hastie Bryce, MA, MD, FRS: *Regius Professor of Anatomy*
1915   George Alexander Gibson, MA, LLD: *Professor of Mathematics*
1920   George Gerald Henderson, MA, DSc, LLD, FRS: *Regius Professor of Chemistry*
1923   Thomas Stewart Patterson, DSc, PhD: *Gardiner Professor of Chemistry*
1926   James Montague Frank Drummond, MA: *Regius Professor of Botany*
1929   Edward Taylor Jones, DSc, LLD: *Professor of Natural Philosophy*
1934   Thomas Murray Macrobert, MA, DSc, LLD: *Professor of Mathematics*
1937   John Walton, MA, DSc, ScD, D-es-Sc, LLD: *Regius Professor of Botany*
1940   Thomas Alty, DSc, PhD, LLD: *Cargill Professor of Applied Physics*
1943   Alexander Stevens, MA, BSc, LLD: *Professor of Geography*
1946   William Marshall Smart, MA, BSc, LLD: *Regius Professor of Astronomy*

1949   John Monteath Robertson, CBE, MA, PhD, DSc, LLD, FRS: *Gardiner Professor of Chemistry*

1952   Thomas Neville George, DSc, PhD, ScD, D-es-Sc, LLD, FRS: *Professor of Geology*

1955   Philip Ivor Dee, CBE, MA, FRS: *Professor of Natural Philosophy*

1958   Sir John Currie Gunn, CBE, MA, DSc, DUniv, FRSE, FInstP, FIMA: *Cargill Professor of Natural Philosophy*

1961   Charles Maurice Yonge, CBE, PhD, DSc, FRS: *Regius Professor of Zoology*

1964   Ronald Miller, MA, PhD: *Professor of Geography*

1967   Robert Alexander Rankin, MA, PhD, ScD: *Professor of Mathematics*

1970   Ian Naismith Sneddon, OBE, MA, DSc, FRSE: *Simson Professor of Mathematics*

1973   Peter Alan Sweet, MA, PhD: *Regius Professor of Astronomy*

1976   Dennis Cyril Gilles, BSc, PhD: *Professor of Computing Science*

1980   David Richmond Newth, BSc, PhD: *Regius Professor of Zoology*

1982   David William Arthur Sharp, MA, PhD: *Regius Professor of Chemistry*

1985   Malcolm Barrett Wilkins, PhD, DSc, FRSE: *Regius Professor of Botany*

1988   Ernest W Laing, MA, PhD: *Titular Professor of Physics*

1990   R Stephen Phillips, BSc, PhD: *Professor of Parasitology*

1993   Rex R Whitehead, DSc, PhD, FRSE: *Professor of Theoretical Physics*

1996-2000 Geoffrey Webb, PhD, DSc, CChem, FRSC, FRSE: *Professor of Catalytic Science*

Social Sciences

After a long and hotly contested debate, the Faculty was established in 1977 by removing Social Science departments from the Faculty of Arts. The development of Social Science teaching and research had been one of the goals of Sir Hector Hetherington, Principal 1936-61. This had been encouraged by the University Grants Committee in the 1960s with the establishment of a number of new departments. Initially, the Faculty comprised Political Economy, Psychology, Applied Economics, Economic History, Politics, Sociology, Town and Regional Planning, Social Administration, and the Business School.

Deans

1978   Frederick Morris Martin, BA, PhD: *Professor of Social Policy and Social Work*

1979   Gordon Campbell Cameron, BA: *Professor of Town and Regional Planning*

1980   Andrew Stewart Skinner, MA, BLitt, FRSE, FBA: *later Daniel Jack Professor of Political Economy*

1984   Patrick J O'Donnell, MA

1987   John Forbes Stables Munro, MA, PhD, FRHistS: *Titular Professor of Economic History*

1989   William V Wallace, MA

1992   Richard H Trainor, MA, DPhil, FRHistS: *Professor of Social History*
1996   Anthony Slaven, MA, BLitt, FRHistS: *Professor of Business History*
2000   V Anton Muscatelli, MA, PhD, FRSA: *Daniel Jack Professor of Political Economy*

Veterinary Medicine

The Faculty has its origins in the Veterinary College, Glasgow, which itself was formally founded in 1863. Veterinary Medicine became a University discipline within the Medical Faculty in 1949. Since 1966, it has been a separate Faculty in its own right, more popularly known as Glasgow Vet School. The first Dean was officially appointed when the School moved to its current site at Garscube in 1969. The Faculty of Veterinary Medicine was the first to appoint a woman as Dean in 1999. *(See also the Glasgow Veterinary College history on page 13).*

Deans
1969   Sir William Lee Weipers, BSc, DUniv, FRCVS, DVSM: *Professor of Veterinary Surgery*
1974   William Ian Mackay McIntyre, PhD, MRCVS: *Professor of Veterinary Medicine*
1977   William Mulligan, MSc, PhD: *Professor of Veterinary Physiology*
1980   Donald Douglas Lawson, BSc, MRCVS: *Professor of Small Animal Clinical Studies*
1983   Thomas Alexander Douglas, BSc, PhD, MRCVS: *Titular Professor of Veterinary Clinical Biochemistry*
1986   Sir James Armour, CBE, PhD, DVMS, FRCUS, FRSE: *Titular Professor of Veterinary Parasitology*
1991   Norman G Wright, BVMS, PhD, DVM, MRCVS, FIBiol, FRCATH: *Professor of Veterinary Anatomy*
1999   Andrea M Nolan, MVB, PhD, DVA: *Professor of Veterinary Pharmacology*

Administration

The majority of the administration of the University is carried out centrally, but faculties, the larger departments and a few groups of departments also have their own administrators. The central part of the administration is divided into two groupings for managerial and budgetary purposes - they are named Central Administration and Information Services. Only histories of the oldest offices within Central Administration and Information Services are provided in this volume. Additional information on all the administrative departments can be found on the University's website.

Archive Services

Glasgow University Archive Services is the central place of deposit for records documenting the history of the University. Effective record keeping has been an important function of the head of the University since at least 1490 when it was noted in the *Annales Universitatis Glasguensis 1451 - 1558* that 'in accordance with a proposition of the Lord Rector, a parchment book is ordered to be procured, in which important writs, statutes, and lists of the University, are to be engrossed: and also a paper book, for recording judicial proceedings.' The Rector continued to be concerned with safe storage of the University's vital records as it was recorded in 1522 that the 'Rector deposits the Royal Charters and other writs of the University in the Common Chest, which he locks with four keys, and delivers these to four Masters'. The Clerk to the Faculty, and subsequently the Clerk of Senate, maintained the records of the University due to the continuing requirement to ensure that the privileges, rights, policies and finances of the University were kept in good order. The Clerk's Press, now on display in the Hunterian Museum, is the oldest surviving piece of University furniture and was acquired in 1634 to hold such records. Since 1955, when the first professional University Archivist was appointed, the collections have grown to be more than just the official corporate memory of the University. They now include documents that provide an insight into the history of the University which official administrative records do not convey such as material created by individual staff and students or groups and societies, as well as those of cross-institutional Higher Education bodies.

The University Archives holds the records of the University back to its foundation in 1451, with its earliest dating from 1304, and continues to advise on effective record-keeping practice and the identification of current records for selection as the historical records of the future. These institutional records are primary resources for Scotland's educational, intellectual and cultural history. The collections include those for predecessor and affiliated bodies, such as Anderson's College of Medicine, Glasgow Veterinary College,

Glasgow Dental Hospital and School, Queen Margaret College, Royal Scottish Academy of Music and Drama, St Andrew's College of Education, St Mungo's College of Medicine, and Trinity College. There are large collections of photographs relating to University personnel and buildings and Scottish topography and plans of University buildings and land.

Archive Services also manage internationally important collections of business records covering the whole of Scotland and beyond, dating from the eighteenth century to the present. These reflect the contribution and breadth of activity that Scotland's business, industry, and enterprise has made past and present to the world economy. The collections were inaugurated in 1959 by Sydney Checkland, the first Professor of Economic History, and have been managed by Archive Services since 1975. The collection of shipbuilding records, many held on behalf of the National Archives of Scotland, is unrivalled and includes those of John Brown of Clydebank, the builders of the *Queen Elizabeth* and *Queen Mary*, William Denny of Dumbarton, Lithgows of Port Glasgow and Scotts of Greenock, the world's senior shipbuilder. Also included are the records of important national and international companies such as North British Locomotive Co, the world's largest locomotive works in 1900; James Finlay and Sons, East India merchants; Gourock Ropeworks Co and their New Lanark Mills, now a world heritage site; J and P Coats, world dominant Paisley thread manufacturers; the House of Fraser department store group; Anchor Line, cruise and emigrant passenger shipping company; Ivory and Sime, Edinburgh investment trust managers; Babcock and Wilcox, boiler-makers; Lloyds TSB, Scotland, and the major Scottish brewing and distilling companies. There are papers of individual and families of entrepreneurs like Viscount William Weir (1877-1959), Sir James Lithgow (1883-1952), and the Napier Family including their shipping, automobile, and textile interests. Altogether there are over five hundred individual collections.

The prime purpose of collecting original and unique archival records is to support teaching and research in the University of Glasgow and the wider community. The records are open to the public five days a week and are well used by both the local and international academic community as well as enthusiasts, local and family historians and many others.

University Archivists
1955   David Reid of Robertland, MA, FSA
1974-2001 Michael S Moss, MA

Bedellus

The office of Bedellus (or Beadle) dates from foundation. The function of the Bedellus was to keep the students in order, and on the days of public functions he arranged the seats for dignitaries. He posted notices of academic and public nature and proclaimed masses, festivals, and holidays. He administered the oath to licentiates, and himself took oath on appointment to be obedient to the Dean of Faculties and mindful of the welfare of the University. He also attended the Rector and on ceremonial occasions carried the Mace. The statutes required the Bedellus to serve any student of the Faculty of Arts who paid him sixpence at the feast of All Saints. He was also allowed eight pence from each student before admission to trial for the BA and eighteen pence at graduation.

The duties of the Bedellus have varied greatly over the centuries and the post has on occasion been merged with that of Janitor. For example, in the seventeenth and eighteenth centuries the incumbent was required to regulate bonfire setting, purchase College supplies, and keep time during the Blackstone Chair examinations.

The work of the modern Bedellus includes the planning of day-to-day janitorial duties which involves liaising with many departments such as Registry and Central Room Booking. The Bedellus also administers the examination venues. The most prominent role continues to be on ceremonial occasions, leading the academic procession carrying the fifteenth century University Mace. At Commemoration Day and Graduations, the Bedellus places the hood over each graduand's head after they have been capped.

The Depute Bedellus assists the Bedellus and on ceremonial occasions carries the Rector's Mace.

1451	John Moffat	1775	John Mclachlan
1451	Archibald McNelsone	1822	James Tyre
1519	William Huchesoune	1832	John Calder
1521	Thomas Crauffurd	1862	Lachlan McPherson
1534	James Schaw	1899	George Gibson
1546	David Kirkland	1907	William Finlayson
1665	John Graham	1923	Frederick H Ramsay
1669	William Ferguson	1944	George Macdonald
1693	Thomas Young	1948	Henry Mayne
1729	John Mcaula	1972	Hugh Boyle
1732	Dugald Weir	1998	Joe McIlroy
1739	John Bryce		

Chaplaincies

The Chaplain to the University

The Blackfriars Church, formerly the church of the adjoining Dominican Priory which had been closely connected with the University since its foundation, became the property of the University after the Reformation and was used as the College Church. In 1635, it was handed over to the Town Council, but the University continued to attend services in it, reserved the right to use it, as it had been used since 1451 for University ceremonies, and contributed to the cost of rebuilding it in 1702. After a petition from the students in 1764, services were instituted in the College Hall and a Chaplain was appointed. Seats were subsequently reserved for the College in St Paul's parish church and the services in the College Hall were then abandoned. They were resumed after the migration to the new buildings in 1870 firstly in the Hunterian Museum and then in the Bute Hall. Work began on building a new chapel in 1914 and in late 1929 it was completed and dedicated as a memorial to the members of the University who fell in the Great War of 1914-1918. Their names are recorded on the tablets at the east end. Other tablets on the walls immediately to the east of the stalls contain the names of the members of the University who are known to have given their lives in the war of 1939-1945. The office of Chaplain was revived in 1930. The chapel services, which are held in accordance with the forms of the Church of Scotland, are under the charge of a Joint Committee of Court and Senate. Services are held on Sundays in term at 11am and there is a daily service at 8.45am.

University Chaplains

1765	William Wight, MA, DD
1773	John Wright, MA
1774-1794	Archibald Arthur, MA: *also Librarian and later Professor of Moral Philosophy*
1809	William McTurk, MA, DD: *previously Librarian, also Clerk of Senate and Professor of Ecclesiastical History*
	James Mylne, MA
1821	William Fleming, MA
1826	John Ferrie
	Robert Johnston
1827	Ebeneezer Russell
1829	William Mair
	John Park, MA
1832	William Fleming, MA, DD
1840	George Gray, MA, DD

1845   James Aitken, DD
        Robert Graham
1847   Robert Reid Rae, MA
1930   Archibald Campbell Craig, MC, MA, DD
1939   James Fraser McLuskey, MC, MA, BD
1947   Hamish McIntosh, MC, MA, BD
1955   David Gourlay, MA, BD
1963   Alexander John Boyd, OBE, MA, DD
1964   David Alexander Ramage Millar, MA
1971   Lionel Alexander Ritchie, MA, BD
1982   David Alexander Ramage Millar, MA
1989   Colin Anderson, BA, BD, STM
1995-2001 Fiona Mathieson, BEd, BD

Roman Catholic Chaplaincy

The Roman Catholic Chaplaincy had its roots in the University Students Sodality formed at the beginning of the twentieth century by Father Parry, SJ. In 1925 the name of the organisation was changed to the Glasgow University Catholic Men's Society. In 1919, a separate association of women students - the Glasgow University Catholic Women's Association - was set up by Sister Mary of St Wilfred, Principal of Dowanhill Training College, with spiritual advice from the Rectors of St Peter's College, Bearsden. The need for a meeting place on campus was great by 1930 and 53 Southpark Avenue was purchased by the Archbishop of Glasgow. The societies flourished under the direction of Rev William Eric Brown, who, in 1930, became the first officially appointed Chaplain to the Roman Catholic Students. That year the societies merged to become the Glasgow University Catholic Society. In 1945, the premises at 53 Southpark Avenue became inadequate and the Archbishop assisted in the purchase of three adjoining houses which became Turnbull Hall, officially opened in 1951.

Chaplains to Roman Catholic Students

1930-1945 William Eric Brown, MC, MA, BSc, DD
        J Ryland Whitaker, SJ
        Matthew Dooley, SJ
1967   Gerard W Hughes, SJ
1976   Kenneth Nugent, SJ
1979   Michael Conway, BA, MSc
1993   Robert Hill, BSc, CertEd
2000   John Keenan, LLB, PhL, STB

Anglican Chaplaincy

A Chaplain to Episcopalian students was first appointed in 1947. In 1963, a Chaplaincy was established at 43 Oakfield Avenue and the chapel dedicated to St Michael being known as Michaelhouse. The Chaplaincy developed as a centre not just for the University of Glasgow but also for all institutions of higher education in Glasgow. In 1989, the Michaelhouse services transferred to the shared University of Glasgow Chaplaincy offices on campus.

Chaplains to Anglican Students

1947	Alexander Philip Barrie, MA
1949	Geoffrey Stewart Whyte Henderson, MA, BSc
1952	Cyril Leighton, BA
1955	George Minshull Sessford, MA
1958	Alexander Stevenson Black, MA
1962	James Raffan Anderson, MA
1970	Cameron Walker, MA
1974	Raymond David Lloyd, BA, MTL
1976	Ian Edward Walter, MA
1979	Michael Richard Knight, MA
1987	John Girvan Turner, MA
1995	Donald Reid, LLB, MPhil, BD
2000	Russell Frederick Jones, BA, BD

Other Chaplaincies

Chaplaincies to the Baptist, Free Church, International, Jewish and Methodist students have also been established along with a Chaplaincy for Overseas Students shared with Glasgow Caledonian University and the University of Strathclyde.

Hunterian Museum and Art Gallery

The University's Museum and Art Gallery are named after William Hunter, the distinguished physician, anatomist, and medical teacher, born in 1718 at East Kilbride, who in 1783 bequeathed to the University, where he had studied, the contents of the museum which he had built up over a number of years in his house in Great Windmill Street, London. 'To acquire knowledge and to communicate it to others has been the pleasure, the business and the ambition of my life.' A fine domed building, with classical facade, was erected in the grounds of the Old College and opened to the public in 1807. The Hunterian is thus Scotland's oldest museum.

Hunter's collections included books and manuscripts, coins, paintings and prints, geological, zoological and botanical specimens, and anatomical preparations related to his medical work. All areas have grown enormously since Hunter's time, and are regularly deployed in undergraduate teaching and in postgraduate research, as well as by curators and other University staff, and are the subject of study by scholars and researchers worldwide. The main subject areas today are fine art, archaeology and ethnography, numismatics, geology, zoology, and scientific instruments. There is a very active education programme for school pupils and indeed for groups of all ages and backgrounds.

After the University move to Gilmorehill in 1870, the entire collections were initially housed within the main museum in the Gilbert Scott Building (where the archaeological, ethnographic, numismatic, and geological displays are still to be found), but over the years the books and manuscripts were transferred to the University Library where they fall within the remit of the Special Collections department, the zoology collections are in the Graham Kerr Building and the anatomy collections in the Allen Thomson Building, and the pathology collections are at the Royal Infirmary. The art collection is housed in the Hunterian Art Gallery in Hillhead Street.

Geology Collections

The Museum has internationally important geological collections, covering almost the whole range of geological science. Particular strengths among the minerals and rocks include William Hunter's own mineral collection (with accompanying eighteenth century lists, bills and invoices), ocean island rocks especially Jan Mayen, and Antarctic islands; J W Gregory rocks and mine suites from Australia, China and elswhere; Playfair and Webb Seymour's specimens illustrating Hutton's work; Connemara metamorphic rocks; South American silver and copper minerals; Dalradian sulphide mineralisation; greenockite; minerals of the Leadhills-Wanlockhead mining district; Scottish Carbonifeous zeolite minerals; gemstones; and meteorites, including the High Possil meteorite which fell on Glasgow in 1804.

The fossil collections comprise both research and display specimens of world-wide significance, with a high proportion of type and figured specimens. Some fossils are local to Scotland including trilobites from the Girvan district, rare Silurian fish from Lesmahagow; Carboniferous shrimps, fish and sharks with soft tissue preservation from Bearsden; footprints from early tetrapods from the Glasgow Carboniferous and the Elgin Permian; the remains of Scottish dinosaurs and their tracks; as well as mammoth teeth; and an extensive palaeobotanical collection.

Archaeology, Ethnography and History Collections

William Hunter's own collection did not include many antiquities, but he had acquired important 'first contact' ethnographic material brought back by Captain Cook and his officers in the 1770s from New Zealand, Oceania, and the north-west coast of North America. Many other ethnographic items have been presented by students, graduates and members of staff of the University who had travelled abroad, and by missionaries. The holdings in prehistoric archaeology owe much to a substantial donation, in 1914 and 1951, by a local collector, A Henderson Bishop, including Lower Palaeolithic artefacts from Southern England, Upper Palaeolithic objects from the Dordogne area of France, and fine Mesolithic collections excavated in Argyllshire; material from Swiss Neolithic 'lake villages' is especially unusual. Scottish Iron Age pottery and artefacts have been obtained more recently though excavations by the Museum's staff. Other material derives from the Mediterranean area, including Greece and Italy, and the Middle East, including much interesting Egyptian material from El Amarna, the Eighteenth Dynasty capital of the Pharaoh Akhnaten.

Locally found Roman material dating to the first and second centuries AD, a period during which the Roman government was attempting to add Scotland to its Empire, includes altars, gravestones, commemorative tablets and sculpted figures; special mention may be made of the Distance Slabs, erected by the Roman legions to mark the construction of the Antonine Wall between Forth and Clyde in AD 142; some stones were acquired by the University well before the Hunterian Museum was founded. Excavated material from more than twenty Roman forts in central and south-western Scotland includes several hundred fragments of shoes and other leatherwork, stone capitals and columns, and a complete wooden wheel from Bar Hill, near Kirkintilloch.

Historical material includes Scottish and English pewter and glass, examples of Scottish nineteenth and twentieth century ceramics presented by Henry E Kelly, besides other objects of mediaeval date or later. Under this heading come memorials of William Hunter and of the past history of the University.

Scientific and medical instruments

The collection has its origins in teaching apparatus purchased by Glasgow professors from the seventeenth century onwards, including the model Newcomen 'Atmospheric' steam engine that in 1765 inspired James Watt, then employed as the University's 'scientific instrument maker', to invent the 'separate condenser' which made the industrial revolution possible, the model 'Stirling engine' which inspired Lord Kelvin to postulate the Second Law of Thermodynamics, and Oersted's compression bottle with which he proved it.

Important contributions to the fields of electrical engineering, marine engineering and thermodynamics by William Thomson, later Lord Kelvin, who was Professor of Natural Philosophy 1846-1899, are reflected in a substantial body of apparatus and instruments, many of which were invented and patented by him for industrial use.

Other great names of science and medicine represented include the civil engineer and builder of the Forth and Clyde Canal John Smeaton, the popular educationalist, John Anderson; the discoverer of vaccination Edward Jenner; the botanist George Bentham; the inventor of the electric clock Alexander Bain; the thermodynamicist James Prescott Joule; the father of antiseptic surgery Joseph Lister; the pioneer of x-ray cinematography John MacIntyre; the inventor of the thermionic valve and father of electronics John Ambrose Fleming; the nuclear physicist and Nobel prizewinner Frederick Soddy and the inventor of television, John Logie Baird.

The Hunter Coin Cabinet

At the time of Hunter's death, his Coin Cabinet was second only to that of the King of France. Although more than doubling in size since coming to the University, its core remains William Hunter's own coins and medals and it continues to be regarded as one of the world's great numismatic collections.

Hunter's accounts of the coins, which he bought, still preserved in the original cabinet, show that between 1770 and 1783 he spent more than £22,000 on such purchases. As a result the Cabinet contains an outstanding series of Ancient Greek and Roman coins as well as comprehensive collections of the medieval coins of the British Isles and important groups of Renaissance, Papal and British medals.

Recent additions include the Coats Collection of Greek, Roman and British coins; the Lockie collection of Modern British and World coins; the Lockie and Maclean collections of communion tokens; and the Cuthbert collection of Scottish coins. The Walter Allan bequest allows further additions to be made, noteworthy being a rapidly expanding collection of post-1800 Scottish medals.

The Hunterian Art Gallery

William Hunter's founding bequest included some of the University's most important pictures: Rembrandt's oil sketch for 'The Entombment of Christ'; a 'Panoramic Landscape' by Philips Koninck; 'Head of an Old Man' by Rubens; and three outstanding paintings by Chardin: 'The Cellar Boy', 'The Scullery Maid' and 'A Lady Taking Tea'. Hunter's collection also included important works by Zuccarelli, Philips Wouwerman, Paul de Vos, Lucas van Uden, Alexandre Roslin, Reynolds and Stubbs.

The art collection has continued to grow. In 1963, Ina J Smillie bequeathed seventeenth-century Flemish and Dutch paintings including works by Erasmus Quellinus, Nicolaes Maes, Edwaert Colyer and Pieter Neefs the Younger. The W A Cargill of Carruth collection, presented in 1970, consists of important portraits by Ramsay, Reynolds, Romney and Raeburn, and works by Corot and Pissarro. There is a small holding of modern British pictures and sculptures. Scottish art from the eighteenth century onwards is well represented with particular strengths in the Glasgow Boys and Scottish Colourists. Many of these works were presented by or bought from funds provided by Gilbert Innes and Alec Lawrence Macfie, Adam Smith Professor of Political Economy, 1945-1958.

Two of the most remarkable gifts have been those of the Charles Rennie Mackintosh and the James McNeill Whistler collections. The Mackintosh estate of drawings, designs and archival material was gifted by Sylvan MacNair. It comprises the largest collection anywhere of the architect's work and, as with the Whistler collection, makes the University a major centre for students and scholars interested in 'art nouveau' and the art movements of the latter part of the nineteenth century. The Mackintosh House, the reassembled interiors from Mackintosh's nearby Glasgow home (now demolished), is one of the Gallery's most significant features. The principal interiors of the house - dining room, studio-drawing room and main bedroom - have been meticulously reassembled using fitments salvaged from the original property. The decorative schemes follow the originals as closely as was possible and the rooms are furnished with Mackintosh's personal collection of furniture, all to his design.

The Whistler collection, gifted and bequeathed by the artist's sister-in-law, comprises over seventy oil paintings, a hundred pastels, several watercolours and a large number of etchings and lithographs, supplemented by a group of the artist's possessions and complemented by his personal papers which are housed in the University Library.

The Print Room owed its inception to a series of gifts by Dr James A McCallum in 1939, and periodically until his death in 1949, and the bequest of William Robert Scott, Adam Smith Professor of Political Economy 1915-1940. Together with other gifts and recent purchases the collection contains a representative range of prints of every period from the fifteenth century to the present day and is the largest print collection in Scotland.

Zoology Museum

William Hunter acquired many zoological specimens, the focus of which were his collections of insects, shells and corals. Hunter made this material, especially the insects and corals, available for study to the pre-eminent naturalists of his day and this resulted in many scientifically important type specimens being designated from his collections.

Over the last two hundred years the collections have grown greatly and number over one million specimens today. In 1923, Sir John Graham Kerr, Regius Professor of Zoology, 1902-1935 installed the collections in a fine new gallery reputedly inspired by the design of a Roman bath-house. Graham Kerr himself built up the collections for teaching, reference and research through field collecting, encouraging donations and purchase of specimens. In the 1930s, local naturalists and collectors such as J J F X King and T G Bishop donated their vast collections of insects. Frank Knight, Alexander Frew and Alexander Patience gave collections of molluscs and aquatic arthropods. Kerr himself left important collections of lungfish.

The collection today is particularly strong in entomology, and there are good teaching and research collections across the vertebrates and the common non-insect invertebrate groups. Some of the specimens such as the marsupial wolf, the aye-aye, the elephant bird egg, or the dodo bones represent species that have become extinct or rare and are now irreplaceable.

Visiting the Museum and Art Gallery
The Hunterian Museum in the Gilbert Scott Building and the Art Gallery in Hillhead Street are currently open Monday to Saturday. The Zoology Museum in the Graham Kerr Building can be visited Monday to Friday.

Directors of Hunterian Museum and Art Gallery
From 1809 until 1902 there was one Keeper with overall managerial responsibility. From 1902 until 1977 there was no *one* Keeper, instead Professorial Honorary Keepers took responsibility for the individual collections. In 1977, a Director was appointed with responsibility for the management of the entire collection.

Keepers of the Hunterian Museum
1809   James Pate
1809   James Couper, Jnr
1809-1836 James Couper, Snr *(joint Keeper from 1830)*
1830   William Couper *(joint Keeper to 1836)*
1857   Henry Darwin Rogers
1866-1902 John Young, MD: *Professor of Natural History*

Directors of the Hunterian Museum and Art Gallery
1977   Frank Willett, CBE, MA, DipAnthrop, FRSE, FRAI
1990-1999 Malcolm D McLeod, MA, BLH BLitt, FRSE: *Professor of African Studies*
2001   Evelyn Silber, MA, PhD

Library

The first explicit mention of the University Library was in November 1475 when the first donations by the University's Chancellor, Bishop John Laing, were recorded - a manuscript compendium of Aristotle and Pseudo-Aristotelian texts, and a paper volume of quaestiones. The next gift noted is that of Duncan Bunch, the first Principal of the Auld Pedagogy. This comprised ten volumes, including works by Aristotle, Porphyry, Boethius on logic, Albertus Magnus on physics, and questions by Bunch's teacher at Cologne, John Althilmer. In this fashion of small donations and bequests the Library steadily grew throughout the pre-Reformation period.

The *Nova Erectio* of 1577 also signalled the rebirth of the Library. An early donation of Greek books, Plato, Plutarch, Strabo, Euclid, Aristophanes, mostly with Basel imprints, from the distinguished humanist poet George Buchanan, symbolised the spirit of the new era. From a stock of around 3,500 at the end of the seventeenth century, the Library grew sharply throughout the course of the eighteenth century. This was due largely to the Copyright Act of 1709, which required that it be furnished with a copy of each work entered at Stationers' Hall, London. By 1760 the holdings had extended to about 6,000 and by 1791 this had reached some 20,000. A printed catalogue was published that year by the Foulis Press, compiled by Archibald Arthur, professor of Moral Philosophy, Chaplain and Librarian. The University received the greatest boost to its library holdings in 1807, however, when it inherited the prized collection of books and manuscripts assembled by Dr William Hunter, the distinguished anatomist and Physician Extraordinary to Queen Charlotte. His personal library of some 10,000 printed volumes doubled the library's stock.

Distance from London and the attendant difficulties of acquiring the books required by the teaching staff, rendered the Stationers' Privilege ineffective and consequently in 1836 it was commuted to a fixed sum paid from the Treasury. By 1888, the Library's holdings had risen to some 126,000 volumes.

Today the University Library occupies a twelve storey building in Hillhead Street originally constructed in 1968 and extended in 1983, 1986 and 1997. It is the centre of the University's library system and houses the principal collections in all fields except Chemistry, Dental Medicine, Education, and Veterinary Medicine, which are held in Branch Libraries. There is also a Faculty Library in Social Sciences (the Adam Smith Library), containing mainly duplicate undergraduate texts.

The Director of Library Services, is also the Keeper of the Hunterian Books and Manuscripts. Formal relationships between the Library and the academic community are maintained through the Library Committee, which has representatives from Court, Senate, the Faculties, the Student Representative Council and the Library Staff.

The Library's Special Collections are among the finest in the United Kingdom. They include the aforementioned books and manuscripts of the Hunterian Library, forming part of the Museum bequeathed to the University by William Hunter in 1783. Among the 10,000 volumes are 649 manuscripts, 534 incunabula (including 10 books printed by William Caxton) and upwards of 2,300 sixteenth-century editions.

There are several other notable collections.

The library of William Euing (20,000 volumes), including many fifteenth and sixteenth century books, over 2,000 bibles, 408 black-letter ballads and, by transfer in 1937, his collection of 5,000 music volumes originally bequeathed to Anderson's College. The library of John (Soda) Ferguson (7,500 volumes), consists mainly of items on the history of chemistry, alchemy and the occult. The library of David Murray (23,000 items), is mainly on Glasgow and west of Scotland history. A collection of 2,000 emblem books formed by Sir William Stirling Maxwell, and bequeathed in 1956 by his son, Sir John Stirling Maxwell, is the finest in the world.

The library of Trinity College, Glasgow (75,000 items) was transferred to the University when the Trinity College building closed. Included are several thousand rare early works, 14,000 pamphlets, and the personal collections of John Eadie on biblical studies, Constantin von Tischendorf on Near Eastern topography, biblical codicology and textual studies, and James Mearns on hymnology.

The Scottish Theatre Archive, established in 1981 to collect material from all over Scotland, includes among its largest collections those of the Citizens' Theatre, Edinburgh Festival Fringe, Royal Lyceum Theatre, Wildcat Stage Productions, Scottish Ballet, BBC Radio Scotland scripts, and Jimmy Logan's collection of music-hall memorabilia. Also held are many collections of personal manuscript material including the papers of the artist James McNeill Whistler.

Directors of Library Services

The post was known as University Librarian until 1998.

1641	Andrew Snype
1646	James Huchesoune
1647	Patrick Young: *regent*
1652	John Ross
1655	John Hoggisyard *(elected but not admitted)*
1655	Robert Baillie, Jnr, MA: *regent*
1658	John Bell
1661	James Bell
1667	William Wright, MA: *later regent*
1669	David Oliphant, MA

1671	George Pollok, MA
1673	John Hamilton
1679	James Young: regent
1687	John Young
1692	David Ewing
1694	John Simson: *later Professor of Divinity*
1697	Robert Wodrow, MA
1703	Alexander Dunlop: *Professor of Greek*
1707	Matthew Crawford: *later Professor of Ecclesiastical History in the University of Edinburgh*
1710	William Dunlop: *later Professor of Divinty and Church History in the University of Edinburgh*
1711	John Aird
1716	Alexander Carmichael
1719	Alexander Anderson
1723	John Carmichael
1724	Alexander Carmichael
1725	Frederick Carmichael
1727	Alexander Clerk
1731	Alexander Carmichael
1735	William Craig
1737	Gershom Carmichael, MA
1739	Alexander Dunlop: *later Professor of Oriental Languages*
1743	James Moor, MA, LLD: *later Professor of Greek*
1747	William Patoun, MA
1750	James Wodrow, MA, DD
1755	Andrew Melvil
1757	James Muirhead
1759	Thomas Clark, MA
1763	William Craig, MA, LLD: *later Judge of Court of Session, Lord Craig*
1767	John Finnie, MA
1772	Henry Stevenson
1773	James Jack
1774	Archibald Arthur, MA: *later University Chaplain and Professor of Moral Philosophy*
1794	William McTurk, MA, DD: *later Clerk of Senate, University Chaplain and Professor of Ecclesiatical History*
1795	Lockhart Muirhead, MA, LLD: *later Professor of Natural History*

1823	William Fleming: *later University Chaplain, Professor of Oriental Languages and Professor of Moral Philosophy*
1827	William Park, MA, DD
1845	Nathaniel Jones: *Registrar of General Council*
1863	Robert Scott, MA, FSA
1865	Robert B Spears
1878	James Lymburn
1905-1916	James Lachlan Galbraith
1925	William Ross Cunningham, MA, LLD
1951	Robert Ogilvie Mackenna, MA, ALA
1979	Henry Joseph Heaney, MA, BLitt, FLA
1998-2001	Andrew Wale, BA, ALA

Registry

The Registry arranges the annual matriculation (registration) of all students, and maintains the records of all students and graduates of the University. The office is also responsible for examination arrangements, the distribution of grant and loan cheques, the collection of tuition fees, student financial aid, and the organisation of graduations.

History of Matriculation

Matriculation at the University of Glasgow initially appears to have been known as the incorporation of students, although surviving records from the 1470s onwards also describe the process as being 'admitted' to the University. Later, incorporation became known as matriculation, the name remaining in use to the present time.

Matriculation was not fully comprehensive until 1859. Before that date, only those gowned students (those studying Latin, Greek, Logic, Ethics, and Physics) who wished to proceed to graduation or any student who wished to vote in the Rectorial election, or to use the Library, had to matriculate and even this policy was not rigidly enforced. For many years it was therefore possible for a student to attend the University without ever having matriculated, and, as matriculation at many periods involved the payment of fees, there was incentive for it to be avoided.

In the early days of the University, matriculation could take place at any time during the rectorial year of a student's entry to the University. In I727, however, a Royal Commission laid down, among many other regulations, that the general matriculation of gowned students was to be held annually on the lawful day immediately preceding the rectorial election (held on 15th or 16th of November), although matriculation was still allowed at other times as required. In addition ungowned students were required, when matriculating, to promise to attend their classes for three months at least and to repeat the promise every subsequent year of attendance.

Modern matriculation grew from the system set up by Senate in 1843 to regulate use of the Library when students were required to enter their name in the Library album and pay seven shillings to the Library fund. Matriculation did not truly become compulsory, however until 1859, following the passing of the Scottish Universities Commission Ordinance 3, dated 6 July 1859, which laid down:

'That from and after the fifteenth day of October in this present year, there shall be, in the said University of Glasgow, one matriculation only of each student for each session of attendance; and such matriculation shall, like the matriculation or enrolment now in use at the Library in the said University, be compulsory on all students, and shall, for the session in respect of which it takes place, entitle students to the use of the Library and all the privileges of matriculated students; and the matriculation fee for the winter session shall be ten shillings and for the summer session five shillings.'

Many Ordinances were issued regarding matriculation, the majority altering the amount of fees payable. However, Ordinance 18 of 1889 had a much greater significance. It allowed women to graduate. Women were admitted for the first time as matriculated students of the University of Glasgow in 1892. *(See also the Queen Margaret College history on page 14).*

Lists of matriculated students have been published until 1858. *(See the Select Bibliography on pages 209-210 for details).* For current matriculation regulations see the latest *University Calendar.*

History of Graduation

Since 1451, all graduates have been required to inscribe their names in the graduation album on graduating. These have been published up to 1897. *(See the Select Bibliography on pages 209-210 for details).* Technically from 1688 until 1853 Masters of Arts were also required to sign the Westminster Confession. Until recently it was not possible to graduate *in absentia* and therefore all graduands had to attend the ceremony. Until 1889 graduates were required to pay a fee to each professor who signed their degree parchment. Thereafter graduation fees were set by Ordinance.

Head of Registry

From 1858 until 1944, the Registrar was the most senior administrative officer in the University. When the Secretary of Court became a full-time post in 1944 it was combined with the post of Registrar. The positions were separated once again in 1983. In 1996, the post of Registrar ceased to exist. Day to day administration is undertaken by the Head of Registry but ultimate responsibility for the functions rests with the Secretary of Court.

1858	Nathaniel Jones: *also University Librarian*
1864	Thomas Moir: *also Assistant Clerk*
1886	James Coutts, MA
1906	W Innes Addison
1911	W Innes Addison
1913	Albert Morrison
1922	Robert Brough, JP
1942	Robert Thomson Hutcheson, OBE, JP, MA, PhD, LLD
1974	James McCargow, MA
1983	Farquhar Gillanders, MA
1986	John Michael Black, BA
1996	Christine R Lowther, BA

Affiliated Institutions

Crichton University Campus, Dumfries.

The Crichton University Campus, Dumfries, is the UK's first multi-university campus. In 1996, the University responded to an invitation from Dumfries and Galloway Council about the establishment of a University College in Dumfries. The original intention of the 19th century benefactor Elizabeth Crichton was to establish a university on the site of the Crichton Hospital so as to provide higher education for the region. Her wishes were over-ruled by the government of the day and the benefaction was then used for a mental hospital. Plans for University College were publically announced in July of 1996 and an accord was signed in February 1997 between the University and three other local partners. University of Glasgow Professor of Social Policy and Social Work, Rex Taylor, was appointed the first Director in 1997.

The first students enrolled for a three year BA degree in 1999. The wider campus also accommodates the University of Paisley (offering courses in business, management and computing), Bell College (School of Health Studies) and the Dumfries and Galloway College annexe (offering a range of business and social science courses). Students of the University of Glasgow and the University of Paisley share the library, as well as information technology, and student support services. By 2005, it is envisaged that there will be around 1500 students on the campus.

Glasgow School of Art

Glasgow School of Art has its origins in the Glasgow Government School of Design, which was established in 1845. It changed its name to its present title in 1853. It was given powers to award its own diplomas in 1853 and after the Second World War its own degrees. With the abolition of the Council for National Academic Awards in the early 1990s, the University of Glasgow accredited degrees in fine art and design. From 1885, the School taught architecture and building construction and in 1903 a joint Glasgow School of Architecture was established with the Glasgow and West of Scotland Technical College (later the Royal Technical College). The first diplomas were awarded in 1910. Following the concordat with the Royal Technical College in 1924, the University of Glasgow set up a degree course in architecture which was taught in the School. After the establishment of the University of Strathclyde in 1964, the Glasgow School of Architecture closed. The Mackintosh School of Architecture was established in 1970 within Glasgow School of Art. Its degrees are accredited by the University and the Mackintosh School Director is the University's Professor of Architecture.

Scottish Agricultural College

The College was established as the West of Scotland Agricultural College under the aegis of the Glasgow and West of Scotland Technical College in 1899, with the University being represented on its governing body. Within a year it had a permanent home in Blytheswood Square and sixty-one students. In 1927 the Auchincruive estate in Ayrshire was gifted to the College by John Hannah of Girvan Mains and became the home of the Hannah Dairy Research Institute which had been set up in 1889. Following the recommendations of the Alness Committee in 1943, a degree course in agriculture was established in association with the University of Glasgow. The University took over responsibility for the whole degree programme in 1954 when the Chair of Agriculture, to be held by the Director of the College, was established. The Allness Committee also proposed that all the College's functions should be based at Auchincruive but it was not until 1974 that the Blythswood Square premises were finally abandoned. Following a report of a committee chaired by Sir Alwyn Williams, Principal of the University, the College became in 1990 part of the Scottish Agricultural College formed by the amalgamation of three regional colleges of agriculture, the West of Scotland, the North of Scotland (founded 1904) and the East of Scotland (founded 1901). The Scottish Agricultural College undertakes advanced education and training (up to postgraduate level), research and development, and advisory and consultancy for rural businesses. Its work encompasses a wide range of subjects but there is an emphasis of food, land, environmental science and rural resource, and business management.

Professors of the University

Regents

From the foundation of the University until 1727 the teaching was in the hands of the regents. There were normally four regents, each of whom taught one year of students throughout the curriculum. In 1642, certain subjects were assigned to each regent but the old system was reinstated in 1667. For a list of regents from 1451 to 1573 see Durkan and Kirk, *The University of Glasgow 1451-1577* (Glasgow, 1977).

1573	Peter Blackburn, MA	1618	James Robertson, MA:
1575	James Melville, MA		*later Lord Bedlay*
1577	Blaise Laurie, MA	1619	George Young, MA
1580	Patrick Melville, MA	1623	John Rae, MA
1581	John Bell, MA	1626	Robert Baillie, Jnr, MA:
1586	John Forbes, MA		*later Librarian, Professor*
1586	John Millar, MA		*of Divinity and Principal*
1590	John Gibson, MA	1628	William Wilkie, MA
1592	Archibald Glen, MA	1631	James Forsyth, MA
1594	William Dunlop, MA:	1635	Robert Mayne, MA:
	later Principal		*later Professor of Medicine*
1596	David Sharp, MA	1635	Patrick Maxwell, MA
1599	John Cameron, MA:	1637	David Munro, MA
	later Principal	1637	William Hamilton, MA
1600	Archibald Hamilton, MA:	1639	John Dickson, MA
	later Archbishop of Cashel	1640	David Forsyth, MA
1601	Michael Wallace, MA	1641	James Dalrymple, MA:
1602	Robert Scott, MA		*later First Viscount Stair*
1604	Walter Whiteford, MA	1641	William Semple, MA
1605	Gabriel Maxwell, MA	1645	John Young, MA:
1609	William Blair, MA		*later Professor of Divinity*
1609	Theodore Hay, MA	1646	Hugh Binning, MA
1610	Alexander Boyd, MA	1647	John Kilpatrick, MA
1610	David Dickson, MA:	1648	William Strang, MA
	later Professor of Divinity	1649	Richard Robertson, MA
1614	James Sharp, MA	1650	James Veitch, MA
1616	Robert Blair, MA	1651	Patrick Young, MA
1617	Gavin Forsyth, MA	1653	Robert McCward, MA

1653	Andrew Burnett, MA	1691	John Law, MA
1654	George Sinclair, MA:	1692	James Knibloe, MA
	later Professor of Mathematics	1694	Gerschom Carmichael, MA:
1656	Robert Erskine, MA		*later Professor of Moral*
1662	Walter Forsyth, MA		*Philosophy*
1662	William Blair, MA	1699	John Loudoun, MA:
1666	Thomas Nicolson, MA		*later Professor of Logic*
1669	William Wright, MA	1704	Alexander Dunlop, MA, LLD:
1669	John Tran, MA		*later Professor of Greek*
1672	John Boyd, MA	1706	Andrew Ross, MA:
1682	Thomas Gordon, MA		*later Professor of Humanity*
1682	James Young, MA:	1714	Robert Dick, Snr, MA, MD:
	later Librarian and Professor		*later Professor of Natural*
	of Humanity		*Philosophy*

Established Chairs

The earliest University chairs grew out of the subjects taught under the regenting system. Humanity, Greek, Mathematics, Moral Philosophy, Natural Philosophy, and Logic and Rhetoric all developed this way, having been founded by the University Faculty. However, the earliest recorded *foundation* of a chair was Practice of Medicine (later renamed Medicine and Therapeutics) in 1637. A University meeting on 25 October that year appointed Robert Mayne, one of the regents, to be Professor of Medicine with a stipend of 400 marks. Although in 1713 the chair lapsed, an endowment from Queen Anne allowed its reinstatement. Eleven of the University's Professors in 2001 held chairs that were originally founded or endowed by the Crown. These Regius Chairs were instituted in the period from 1709 (Queen Anne) to 1861 (Queen Victoria). An annual salary from the Crown was orignially attached to some but not all of these chairs. From the 1688 Revolution until 1853 professors on admission to office were required to sign the Westminster Confession before the Presbytery of Glasgow.

From the time of the Universities (Scotland) Act of 1858, chairs were required to be established by Ordinance. The University of Glasgow found this particularly useful as resentments and rivalries had developed between the Faculty and Regius Professors and the Act united them into one body to regulate teaching and discipline. This body was the Senatus Academicus or the Senate. Since the Universities (Scotland) Act of 1966, chairs have been required to be established by Resolution of the University Court.

The following is an alphabetical list of established chairs. An Appendix giving a list of established chairs in chronological order is also provided on page 219.

Accountancy
Founded in 1973 as an additional chair. Patron: the University Court. (Resolution 107).

1975   David Flint, TD, MA, BL, CA: *previously Johnstone Smith Professor of Accountancy and later Vice-Principal*

1985-1992 John Philip Dickinson, MA, MSc, PhD, AASA: *later Principal of King Alfred's College, Winchester*

1995   John B Holland, BSc, MBA, PhD

Accountancy
Founded in 1975. Patron: the University Court. (Resolution 150).

1976   Dennis Henry Patz, MS, PhD
1979   Sidney John Gray, BEc, PhD, FCCA
1993   Neil William Garrod, BSc, PhD, ACIS

Accountancy
Two additional chairs were founded in 1995. Patron: the University Court. (Resolution 409).

1995   Alan Gregory, MSc
1996   William P Rees, MBA

Accountancy (Ernst and Young Chair)
Founded in 1986 as the Arthur Young Chair, the title was amended in 1990 to the Ernst and Young Chair reflecting the change of name of the sponsoring firm. The chair is now solely funded by the University. (Resolution 284, amended 326).

1987   Clive Robert Emmanuel, BSc, MA, PhD

Accountancy (Johnstone Smith Chair)
Founded in 1925 and endowed by David Johnstone Smith, LLD. In 1983, the appointment was made part-time. The funds cannot be used for any other chair or purpose. Patron: a Board of Curators consisting of members of the University Court, the President of the Institute of Accountants and Actuaries in Glasgow, and, during his life or until his resignation the donor of the endowment. The incumbent is appointed for a term of twelve years or such shorter period as the University Court may determine on the occasion of each appointment. (Ordinance 144 and 394-Glasgow 39 and 124, and Resolution 139).

1926   John Loudon, MA
1938   Ian Wilson Macdonald, MA
1950   Robert Browning, CBE, MA, LLB
1964   David Flint, TD, MA, BL, CA: *later Professor of Accountancy and Vice-Principal*
1977   John C Shaw, BL, CA
1983-1989   John Baillie, MA, CA

Accounting
Patron: the University Court. (Resolution pending).

1998   Carol A Adams, BA, MSc, CA

Accounting
Patron: the University Court. (Resolution pending).

2000   Robert Hugh Gray, BSc, MA, FCA, FCCA, FRSA

Administrative Medicine
Founded in 1960. Patron: the University Court. (Ordinance 337-Glasgow 99). The post was suppressed in 1981. (Court minute 214 of 1981).

1960   Charles Mann Fleming, CBE, MA, MD
1971   Alexander John Haddow, CMG, DSc, MD, FRS
1978-1981   Edward McCombie McGirr, CBE, BSc, MD, FRSE: *previously Muirhead Professor of Medicine and later Dean of Faculties*

Aerospace Systems (Shoda Chair)
Founded in 1995, with a gift from family and friends in memory of Paul Taizo Shoda who graduated from the University in 1916 and was awarded a DSc by the University in 1988 for his contribution to engineering in Japan. Patron: the University Court. (Resolution 420).

1995   Roderick A M Galbraith, BSc, PhD

Agriculture
Until 1954 the Principal of the West of Scotland Agricultural College was a Professor at the Royal Technical College. The University of Glasgow Chair was founded in 1954. Patron: the University Court. (Ordinance 299-Glasgow 76).

Principals and Professors at the Royal Technical College
1900   Sir Robert Patrick Wright
1911   William G R Paterson, OBE
1944   John Kirkwood, OBE

Principals and Professors at the University of Glasgow
1954   Donald Stewart Hendrie, BSc
1966   James Snowdon Hall, CBE, BSc
1980   John McCandlish Murdoch Cunningham, CBE, BSc, PhD
1987   Philip Charles Thomas, BSc, PhD, FIBiol, CBiol, FRSE
1999   Karl Alexander Linklater, BVMandS, PhD, FRCVS, FIBiol, CBiol, AgS, FRSE, FRA

Anaesthesia

Founded in 1965 as the Chair of Anaesthetics, it was renamed in 1973. Patron: the University Court. (Ordinance 526-Glasgow 154, amended by Resolution 102).

1967   Alexander Clarkson Forrester, MB ChB
1972   Ronald Alexander Millar, MD, PhD
1976-1992 Sir Donald Campbell, CBE, MB ChB
1996   Gavin N C Kenny, BSc, MD, ChB, FRCA, FANZCA

Anatomy (Regius Chair)

Founded in 1718 under the title of Anatomy and Botany: the province of the chair was restricted to Anatomy in 1818 when the Chair of Botany was founded. Patron: the Crown.

1720   Thomas Brisbane, MD
1742   Robert Hamilton, MD
1756   Joseph Black, MD: *previously lecturer in Chemistry and later Professor of Practice of Medicine and Clerk of Senate in the University, and Professor of Chemistry in the University of Edinburgh*
1757   Thomas Hamilton, MD
1781   William Hamilton, MD
1790   James Jeffray, MD: *later Clerk of Senate*
1848   Allen Thomson, MA, MD, LLD, DCL, FRS: *later Clerk of Senate*
1877   John Cleland, MA, MD, FRS
1909   Thomas Hastie Bryce, MA, MD, FRS
1935-1944 Duncan MacCallum Blair, MB, DSc

1946   William James Hamilton, MD, DSc: *later Professor of Anatomy in the University of London*
1948   George McCreath Wyburn, MB ChB, DSc
1973-1990 Raymond John Scothorne, BSc, MD, FRSE

Applied Dynamics
Founded in 1997. Patron: the University Court. (Resolution 449).

1998   Matthew P Cartmell, BSc, PhD, MASME, MAIAA

Applied Economics
Founded in 1949. Patron: the University Court. (Ordinance 256-Glasgow 64).

1950   Sir Alexander Kirkland Cairncross, KCMG, MA, PhD: *later Chancellor of the University and Master of St Peter's College, Oxford*
1961   Donald James Robertson, MA: *later Professor of Industrial Relations*
1970   Sir Laurence Colvin Hunter, CBE, MA, DPhil, FRSE: *later Vice-Principal*

Applied Geology (James S Dixon Chair)
Founded in 1989 using the endowment of James S Dixon of Bothwell, coalmaster. The funds had previously been applied to the Chair of Mining, permission for the reallocation of the funds having been granted by the Secretary of State in 1981. Patron: the University Court. (Resolution 312).

1989   Michael John Russell, BSc, PhD

Applied Physiology
Founded in 1948. Patron: the University Court. (Ordinance 242-Glasgow 57). Repealed in 1965.

1948-1958 George MacFeat Wishart, MD, BSc: *previously Professor of Physiological Chemistry and later Director of Postgraduate Medical Illustration*

Archaeology
Founded in 1972. Patron: the University Court. (Resolution 85).

1973   Leslie Alcock, MA, FSA, FRHistS, OBE
1990   Christopher David Morris, BA, DipEd, FSA, FRSE, FRHistS, FRSA: *later Vice-Principal*

Architecture
Founded in 1965, the incumbent is based at the Mackintosh School of Architecture. Patron: the University Court. (Ordinance 535-Glasgow 144).

1969	John Harold Westgarth Voelcker, MA, FRIBA
1973	Andrew MacMillan, MA, FRIAS, RIBA, ARSA
1994	Charles HA MacCallum, DA, MCP, RIBA, ARIAS, FRSA
2000	David Porter, BSc, DipArch, RIBA, ARIAS

Astronomy (Regius Chair)
Founded in 1760, under the title Practical Astronomy, with the office of Observer in the University. The title was changed in 1893 by Ordinance 31 of the Universities Commission (1889). Patron: the Crown.

1760	Alexander Wilson, MA, MD
1784	Patrick Wilson, LLD: *later Clerk of Senate*
1799	William Meikleham, MA, LLD: *later Professor of Natural Philosophy and Clerk of Senate*
1803	James Couper, MA, DD
1836	John Pringle Nichol, MA, LLD
1859	Robert Grant, MA, LLD, FRS
1893	Ludwig Wilhelm Emil Ernst Becker, PhD
1937	William Marshall Smart, MA, BSc, LLD
1959	Peter Alan Sweet, MA, PhD
1996	John Campbell Brown, BSc, DSc, PhD, FRSE, FRAS: *Astronomer Royal for Scotland and previously Professor of Astrophysics*

Astrophysics
The appointment to this, a fourth Chair of Natural Philosophy/Astronomy, was approved by the University Court in 1983 on condition that the departments amalgamated.

1984-1996	John Campbell Brown, BSc, DSc, PhD, FRSE, FRAS: *later Regius Professor of Astronomy*

Banking Law
Founded in 1997. Patron; the University Court. (Resolution 444).

1997	Lorne Donald Crerar, LLB

Biochemistry (Cathcart Chair)
Founded in 1965. Patron: the University Court. (Ordinance 522-Glasgow 150).

1966-1987	Robert Martin Stuart Smellie, DSc, PhD: *previously Grieve Lecturer in Physiological Chemistry*
1994	Nicholas B La Thangue, BSc, PhD

Biochemistry (Gardiner Chair)
Founded in 1919 as the Gardiner Chair of Physiological Chemistry and endowed by William Guthrie Gardiner and Sir Frederick Crombie Gardiner, shipowners in Glasgow. In 1958, the title was amended by the substitution of Biochemistry for Physiological Chemistry. Patron: the University Court. (Ordinances 77, 320-Glasgow 24, 90).

1919	Edward Provan Cathcart, CBE, MD, DSc, LLD, FRS: *later Regius Professor of Physiology*
1929	Andrew Hunter, MA, BSc, MB: *later Professor of Pathological Chemistry in the University of Toronto*
1935	George Macfeat Wishart, MD, BSc: *later Director of Postgraduate Medical Education and Professor of Applied Physiology*
1947-1972	James Norman Davidson, CBE, MD, DSc, FRS
1974	Alan Rowe Williamson, BSc, PhD
1984	Miles Douglas Houslay, BSc, PhD, FRSA, FRSE, CBiol, FIBiol

Biostatistics/Biometrics
Founded in 1997. Patron: the University Court. (Resolution 445).

1998	Ian Ford, BSc, PhD, FRSE: *previously Professor of Statistics*

Biotechnology (Robertson Chair)
Founded in 1988 and endowed by bequest of the Robertson Trust. Funds were given simultaneously for the University's Robertson Institute of Biotechnology building. Patron: the University Court. (Resolution 311).

1989	Roger Wayne Davies, BA, MA, PhD

Botany (Hooker Chair)
Founded in 1965. Patron: the University Court. (Ordinance 518-Glasgow 146).

1973   George Bond, PhD, DSc, FRS
1993   Richard J Cogdell, BSc, PhD, FRSE

Botany (Regius Chair)
A Lectureship was instituted in 1704. From 1718 to 1818, the subject was combined with Anatomy. The chair was founded in 1818 by King George III. Patron: the Crown.

Lecturer
1704   John Marshall, MA

Professors
1720-1818 *See under Anatomy*
1818   Robert Graham, MD: *later Professor of Botany in the University of Edinburgh*
1820   Sir William Jackson Hooker, MA, LLD, DCL, FRS: *later Director of the Royal Botanic Gardens, Kew*
1841   John Hutton Balfour, MA, MD: *later Professor of Botany in the University of Edinburgh*
1845   George Arnott Walker Arnott, MA, LLD: *Advocate*
1868   Alexander Dickson, MA, MD: *later Professor of Botany in the University of Edinburgh*
1879   Sir Isaac Bayley Balfour, MA, MD, DSc, FRS: *later Professor of Botany in the University of Oxford*
1885   Frederick Orpen Bower, MA, ScD, LLD, FRS: *later Dean of Faculties*
1925   James Montague Frank Drummond, MA: *later Professor of Botany in the University of Manchester*
1930   John Walton, MA, DSc, ScD, D-es-Sc, LLD: *later Dean of Faculties*
1963   Percy Wragg Brian, BA, PhD, DPhil: *later Professor of Botany in the University of Cambridge*
1968   John Harrison Burnett, MA, DPhil: *later Professor of Botany in the University of Oxford*
1970   Malcolm Barrett Wilkins, PhD, DSc, FRSE
2001   Michael Robert Blatt, BSc, PhD

Business History

Founded in 1988 in response to the foundation of the Centre for Business History in Scotland in the Department of Economic History. The Centre was established with funds from the Aggregate Foundation Charitable Trust, and was the first permanent centre for the study of Business History in Scotland. Patron: the University Court. (Resolution 295).

1988   Anthony Slaven, MA, BLitt, FRHistS

Business Policy

Founded in 1974. Patron: the University Court. (Resolution 126).

1975   Anthony John Eccles, BEng
1978   Andrew William John Thomson, MS, PhD
1988-1990 John Christopher Spender, MA, PhD, FRSA

Cardiac Surgery

Founded in 1974 and funded by the British Heart Foundation in association with the Isidore and David Walton Charitable Trust. Patron: the University Court. (Resolution 129).

1975   Philip Kennedy Caves, MB, BCh, BAO
1979   David John Wheatley, MD, ChM, FRCS, FMedSci

Cell Biology

Founded in 1965. Patron: the University Court. (Ordinance 494-Glasgow 134).

1967   Adam Sebastian Genevieve Curtis, MA, PhD, FRSE

Celtic

In 1881, the Reverend Archibald Kelly McCallum, MA 1849, LLD 1867, provided an endowment for a Lectureship, or a course of not fewer than fifteen lectures, in Celtic Literature. The foundation was placed on a new footing by a Provisional Order made by the Secretary for Scotland and confirmed by the Glasgow University Order Confirmation Act of 1905. In 1910 the University Court resolved to use for the further endowment of the Lectureship the bequest of Alexander Fleming and the Lectureship was named the McCallum-Fleming Lectureship. The Chair was founded in 1956 and partially endowed by the late James Crawford of Glasgow, the Ross Trust, and the University Ossianic Club. Patron: the University Court. (Ordinance 312-Glasgow 84).

Lecturers

1900   Magnus Maclean, DSc

1903   Kuno Meyer, PhD: *later Professor of Celtic in the University of Berlin*

1906   George Henderson, MA, PhD

1912   George Calder, BD, DLitt

1935   James Carmichael Watson, MA: *later Professor of Celtic in the University of Edinburgh*

1938   Angus Matheson, MA

Professors

1956   Angus Matheson, MA

1963   Derek Smith Thomson, MA, FRSE

1991   Donald Macaulay, MA, BA

1995   Cathair N Ó Dochartaigh, MA, PhD

Chemistry (Joseph Black Chair)

Founded in 1961. Patron: the University Court. (Ordinance 370-Glasgow 120).

1962   Durward William John Cruickshank, MA, PhD, ScD: *later Professor of Chemistry in the University of Manchester*

Chemistry (Gardiner Chair)

A Lectureship was instituted in 1898. The Gardiner Chair of Organic Chemistry was founded in 1919 and endowed by the gift of William Guthrie Gardiner and Sir Frederick Crombie Gardiner, shipowners in Glasgow. In 1942, the restriction to Organic Chemistry was removed by Ordinance. Patron: the University Court. (Ordinances 76, 203, 302-Glasgow 23,47, 80).

Lecturers

1898   William Robert Lang, DSc: *later Professor of Chemistry in the University of Toronto*

1901   Matthew Archibald Parker, BSc: *later Professor of Chemistry in the University of Manitoba*

1904   Thomas Stewart Patterson, DSc, PhD

Professors
1919   Thomas Stewart Patterson, DSc, PhD
1942   John Monteath Robertson, CBE, MA, PhD, DSc, LLD, FRS
1970-1990 George Andrew Sim, BSc, PhD
1995   Laurence D Barron, BSc, DPhil, MInstP, FRSE

Chemistry (Ramsay Chair)
Founded in 1966 and named after Sir William Ramsay (1852-1916), winner of the Nobel
Prize in Chemistry. Patron: the University Court. (Ordinance 543-Glasgow 161).

1967-1988 David William Arthur Sharp, MA, PhD
1999   Pavel Kocovsky, MSc, PhD, DSc

Chemistry (Regius Chair)
A Lectureship was established 1747. The Chair was founded in 1817 by King George III.
Patron: the Crown.

Lecturers
1747   William Cullen, MD: *later Professor of Practice of Medicine in the University,*
           and successively Professor of Chemistry and Professor of Medicine in the
           University of Edinburgh
1756   Joseph Black, MD: *later Professor of Practice of Medicine and Clerk of Senate*
           in the University and Professor of Chemistry in the University of Edinburgh
1766   John Robinson, MA: *later Professor of Natural Philosophy in the University*
           of Edinburgh
1769   William Irvine, MD
1787   Thomas Charles Hope, MD, FRS: *later Lecturer in Materia Medica and Professor*
           of Practice of Medicine in the University and Professor of Chemistry in the
           University of Edinburgh
1791   Robert Cleghorn, MD

Professors
1818   Thomas Thomson, MD, FRS
1852   Thomas Anderson, MD
1874-1915 John Ferguson, MA, LLD, FSA
1919   George Gerald Henderson, MA, DSc, LLD, FRS
1937   George Barger, MA, DSc, LLD, FRS

1939   Sir James Wilfred Cook, DSc, ScD, PhD, FRS: *later Vice-Chancellor of the University of Exeter*
1955   Sir Derek Harold Richard Barton, DSc, PhD, FRS: *later Hofmann Professor of Chemistry in Imperial College of Science and Technology, London*
1957   Ralph Alexander Raphael, PhD, DSc, FRS: *later Professor of Chemistry in the University of Cambridge*
1972   Gordon William Kirby, MA, PhD, ScD
1997-2000 Philip J Kocienski, PhD, FRSE, FRS

Child and Adolescent Psychiatry

A Chair of Child Psychiatry was founded in 1973 but never filled (Resolution 110). This chair was founded in 1977 with the incumbent located at the Royal Hospital for Sick Children. With the appointment of Professor Parry-Jones the post moved to Gartnavel Hospital (Academic Development Committee minute 44 of 1986). Patron: the University Court. (Resolution 182).

1977   Frederick Hope Stone, MB ChB
1987-1997 William Llewelyn Parry-Jones, MA, MD, FRCPsych

Child Health (Samson Gemmell Chair)

Founded in 1924 and endowed as the Samson Gemmel Chair of Medical Paediatrics by the bequest of William Gemmell in memory of his brother, Samson Gemmell, Regius Professor of Medicine in the University, 1908-1913. Patron: a Board of thirteen Curators, seven appointed by the University Court, three Directors of the Royal Hospital for Sick Children, and three by the Trustees of William Gemmell. In 1947, the name of the Chair was altered to the Samson Gemmell Chair of Child Health. (Ordinances 124 and 232- Glasgow 34 and 52, amended by Resolution 149).

1924   Leonard Findlay, MD, DSc
1930   Geoffrey Balmanno Fleming, MBE, BA, MD
1947   Stanley Galbraith Graham, MD, LLD
1961   James Holmes Hutchison, CBE, MD
1977   Forrester Cockburn, MD
1996   Lawrence T Weaver, MA, MD, FRCP, FRCPCH, DCH

Christian Ethics and Practical Theology
Founded in 1939. Patron: the University Court acting on the recommendation of the General Assembly of the Church of Scotland. Suppressed in 1945. (Ordinance 199-Glasgow 46).

1939-1945 Arthur John Gossip, MA, DD

Civil Engineering (Cormack Chair)
Founded in 1965. Patron: the University Court. (Ordinance 528-Glasgow 156).

1966	Hugh Brown Sutherland, SM, FEng
1987	David Muir Wood, MA, PhD, MICE
1996	Simon J Wheeler, MA, DPhil

Civil Engineering (Regius Chair)
Founded in 1840 by Queen Victoria. In 1872 the endowment was increased by the bequest of Isabella Elder, (1828-1905) in memory of her husband, John Elder, shipbuilder and marine engineer, (1824-1869). Patron: the Crown.

1840	Lewis Dunbar Brodie Gordon, FRSE
1855	William John Macquorn Rankine, LLD, FRS
1873	James Thomson, MA, DSc, LLD, FRS
1889	Archibald Barr, DSc, LLD, FRS
1913	John Dewar Cormack, CMG, CBE, DSc: *previously James Watt Professor of Electrical Engineering*
1936	Gilbert Cook, DSc, FRS: *later Vice-Chancellor of the University of Exeter*
1952-1975	William Thomas Marshall, BSc, PhD
1977-1992	Alexander Coull, BSc, PhD, FICE
1994	Nenad J D Bicanic, DiplIng, PhD, FICE

Clinical Medicine
Founded in 1874. Patron: the University Court. Suppressed in 1911 on the foundation of the Muirhead Chair of Medicine.

1874	Sir Thomas McCall Anderson, MD: *later Professor of Practice of Medicine*
1900-1908	Samson Gemmell, MD: *later Professor of Practice of Medicine*

Clinical Neuropsychology
Patron: the University Court. (Resolution pending)

1999   Tom McMillan, BSc, PhD, MAppSci

Clinical Physics
Founded in 1973 in furtherance of the association between the University and the Department of Clinical Physics and Bio-Engineering of the Western Regional Hospital Board. Patron: the University Court. (Resolution 101, amended by 238).

1973   John Mark Anthony Lenihan, OBE, MSc, PhD
1983   Joseph McKie, BSc, FInstP
1991   Alexander Thomas Elliott, BA, PhD, DSc, CPhys, FInstP, FIPEM

Clinical Psychology
Founded in 1994. Patron: the University Court. (Resolution 396).

1995   Colin A Espie, BSc, MAppSc, PhD

Clinical Surgery
Founded in 1874. Patron: the University Court. Suppressed in 1911 on the foundation of the St Mungo Chair of Surgery.

1874   George Buchanan, MA, MD, LLD
1900-1910 Sir Hector Clare Cameron, CBE, MD, LLD: *later Dean of Faculties*

Commercial Law (Alexander Stone Chair)
Founded in 1985 with a gift from Sir Alexander Stone (1907-1998), LLD 1986, Glasgow solicitor and bibliophile. Patron: the University Court. (Resolution 262).

1986   David Graham Powles, LLM
1994   Fraser P Davidson, LLB, PhD

Community Care Studies (Nuffield Chair)
Founded in 1992 with a grant from the Nuffield Provincial Hospitals Trust. Patron: the University Court. (Resolution 357).

1993   Alison J Petch, BA, MA, PhD, CQSW

Computing Science
Founded in 1966. Patron: the University Court. (Ordinance 546-Glasgow 164).

1966   Dennis Cyril Gilles, BSc, PhD, FRSE, FIMA
1990-1998 Simon Loftus Peyton Jones, MA, DipCompSci, MBCS, CEng

Computing Science
Founded in 1986. Patron: the University Court. (Resolution 296).

1986   Cornelis Joost van Rijsbergen, BSc, PhD, Dip NAAC, CEng, FIEE, FBCS, FRSE

Computing Science
This additional chair was founded in 1983. Patron: the University Court. (Resolution 240).

1984   Malcolm Philip Atkinson, BSc, MA, DipCompSc, PhD, FBCS, FRSE

Conveyancing
Founded in 1861 and partly endowed by the Faculty of Procurators in Glasgow. Patron: the Dean and Council of the Faculty of Procurators in Glasgow. (Ordinance 20).

1862   Anderson Kirkwood, LLD: *later Secretary of Court*
1867   Sir James Robertson, LLD
1889   James Moir, LLD
1916   William Sharp McKechnie, MA, LLB, DPhil
1927   John Girvan, LLB
1946   Donald Alexander Stewart McLeish, LLB
1955   John Menzies Halliday, CBE, MA, LLD
1979   James Alistair MacFarlane Inglis, CBE, MA, LLB: *simultaneously Professor of Professional Legal Practice*
1993   Robert Rennie, LLB, PhD

Dental Primary Care
Founded in 1971 as the Chair of Conservative Dentistry and amended in 1995. Patron: the University Court. (Resolution 64, amended 418).

1971   James Ireland, BSc, FDS
1980   Robert Craig Paterson, MDS, PhD
1996-2000 F J Trevor Burke, BDS, MDS DDS, MSc

Dental Prosthetics

Founded in 1959. Patron: the University Court. (Ordinance 335-Glasgow 98).

1960   William Malcolm Gibson, MB ChB, FDS
1969-1992 Alistair Roy MacGregor, FDS, PhD

Dermatology

Founded in 1965. Patron: the University Court. (Ordinance 527-Glasgow 155).

1971   John Alexander Milne, MB ChB
1978-2000 Rona Mcleod MacKie, MD, DSc, FRCP, FRCPath, FRSE, FMedSci

Divinity

Theology has been taught since the foundation of the University. Under the *nova erectio* the first Chair of Divinity was founded and its holder was ex-officio the Principal. The last Principal to hold the Chair of Divinity was Robert Herbert Story who held office from 1898 to 1907 In 1640, this, a second Chair of Divinity was instituted and from 1642 to 1661, there was also a third Chair. The patron of the chair is the University Court, since 1935 acting on the recommendation of a Board of Nomination constituted of representatives of the University Court and of the General Assembly of the Church of Scotland. (Ordinance 84 of 1934: amended by Ordinance 284 (General 10) of 1952).

1640-1650 David Dickson, MA: *later Professor of Divinity in the University of Edinburgh*
1642-1661 Robert Baillie, Jnr, MA: *previously regent and later Librarian and Principal*
1653   John Young, MA: *previously regent and later Bishop-designate of Argyll*
1669   Gilbert Burnett, MA: *later Bishop of Salisbury*
1674   David Liddell, MA
1682   Alexander Ross, MA: *later Principal of St Mary's College, St Andrews and Bishop of Moray and of Edinburgh*
1688   James Wemyss, DD
1692   James Wodrow, MA
1705   Alexander Wodrow, MA
1708   John Simson, MA
1740   John Potter, MA
1744   William Leechman, MA, DD: *later Principal*
1761   Robert Trail, MA, DD: *previously Professor of Oriental Languages*
1775   James Baillie, MA, DD
1778   William Wight, MA, DD: *previously Professor of Ecclesiastical History*

1782	Robert Findlay, MA, DD
1814	Stevenson Macgill, MA, DD: *also Dean of Faculties*
1840	Alexander Hill, MA, DD
1862	John Caird, MA, DD, LLD: *later Principal*
1873	William Purdie Dickson, MA, DD, LLD
1895	William Hastie, MA, DD
1903	Henry Martyn Beckwith Reid, MA, DD
1927	William Fulton, MA, BSc, DD, LLD
1947	John Gervase Riddell, MA, DD: *previously Professor of Systematic Theology*
1956	Ronald Gregor Smith, MA, ThD, DD
1969	Allan Douglas Galloway, MA, BD, PhD, STM
1986	George Mcleod Newlands, MA, BD, PhD

Divinity and Biblical Criticism

Founded in 1861. Patron: formerly the Crown, since 1935 the University Court, acting on the recommendation of a Board of Nomination constituted of representatives of the University Court and of the General Assembly of the Church of Scotland. (Ordinances 24 of 1861; 184 of 1934; 284 (General 10) of 1952 and Resolutions 352 and 242).

1863	William Purdie Dickson, MA, DD, LLD
1873	William Stewart, MA, DD, LLD: *later Dean of Faculties and Clerk of Senate*
1910	George Milligan, MA, DD, DCL: *later Clerk of Senate*
1933	George Hogarth Carnaby MacGregor, MA, DLitt, DD
1963	William Barclay, CBE, MA, DD
1974-1982	Ernest Best, MA, BD, PhD
1991	John K Riches, MA

Drama (James Arnott Chair)

Founded in 1972. Patron: the University Court. Renamed the James Arnott Chair in 1996 in memory of the first incumbent, James Fullarton Arnott, (1914-1982). (Resolution 86, amended by 428).

1973	James Fullarton Arnott, TD, MA, BLitt
1979	Janet Brown Inglis McDonald, MA, FRSE

Ecclesiastical History
Founded in 1716 by George I. Patron: formerly the Crown, since 1935 the University Court, acting on the recommendation of a Board of Nomination consisting of representatives of the University Court and of the General Assembly of the Church of Scotland. (Ordinance 184 of 1934; amended by Ordinance 284 (General 10) of 1952).

1721	William Anderson, MA
1752	William Rouet, MA: *previously Professor of Oriental Languages*
1762	William Wight, MA, DD: *later Professor of Divinity*
1778	Hugh Macleod, MA, DD
1809	William McTurk, MA, DD
1841	James Seaton Reid, MA, DD: *later Clerk of Senate*
1851	Thomas Thomson Jackson, MA, DD
1874	William Lee, MA, DD
1886	Robert Herbert Story, MA, DD, LLD: *later Principal*
1898	James Cooper, MA, DD, LittD, DCL
1922-1942	Archibald Main, MA, DD, DLitt, LLD
1946	William Dickie Niven, MA, DD, LLD: *previously Professor of New Testament Language and Literature*
1949	John Foster, MA, DD
1969-1984	William Hugh Clifford Frend, TD, MA, DPhil, DD, FRSE

Economic History
Founded in 1955. Patron: the University Court. (Ordinance 308-Glasgow 82).

1957-1982 Sydney George Checkland, MA, MCom, PhD

Education
In 1894, a Lectureship in Education was instituted by the University. In 1949, the chair was founded. Patron: the University Court. (Ordinance 253-Glasgow 62).

Lecturers

1894	David Ross, MA, BSc, LLD
1899	John Adams, MA, BSc
1902	John Clark, MA
1907	William Boyd, MA, BSc, DPhil, DLitt: *also Reader 1938-1947*
1947	Robert R Rusk, MA, PhD

Professors
1951   Stanley Donald Nisbet, MA, MEd
1978   Nigel Duncan Cameron Grant, MA, MEd, PhD
2000   Michael Adrian Peters, BSc, BA, MA, PhD

Electrical Engineering
Founded in 1965. Patron: the University Court. (Ordinance 530-Glasgow 158).

1967-1969 John Kenneth Lubbock, BSc, MA, PhD

Electrical Engineering (James Watt Chair)
A Lectureship was established in 1898. The chair was founded in 1921 by the Institution of Engineers and Shipbuilders in Scotland in commemoration of the centenary of the death of James Watt (1736-1819), inventor and scientific instrument maker to the University of Glasgow 1756-1773. Patron: the University Court (Ordinance 103-Glasgow 27).

Lecturers
1898   John Dewar Cormack, CMG, CBE, DSc: *later Regius Professor of Civil Engineering*
1901   Sir James Blacklock Henderson, DSc: *later Professor in the Royal Naval College, Greenwich*
1905   John Steel Nicholson, DSc

Professors
1921   George William Osborn Howe, DSc, LLD
1946   Bernard Hague, PhD, DSc
1961   John Lamb, DSc, PhD
1992   Christopher D W Wilkinson, MA, PhD, FRSE

Electronic Systems
Founded in 1983. Patron: the University Court. (Resolution 241).

1985   John Isaac Sewell, BSc, PhD

Engineering (Mechan Chair)
Founded in 1948 and endowed by MEchans Ltd, boatbuilders, Scoutston. In terms of the Ordinance, the University Court, on occasion of each appointment, determines the branch of Engineering Science for which the Professor is responsible (Ordinance 251-Glasgow 61).

1950   William Jolly Duncan, CBE, DSc, FRS *(Aeronautics and Fluid Mechanics)*
1961-1975 Terence Reginald Forbes Nonweiler, BSc, PhD *(Aeronautics and Fluid Mechanics)*
1980   Bryan Edward Richards, BSc, PhD DIC, CEng, FRAES, AFAIAA *(Aeronautics and Fluid Mechanics)*

English Language
A Lectureship was endowed by the Carnegie Trust in 1907. The chair was founded in 1947. Patron: the University Court. (Ordinance 236-Glasgow 53).

Lecturer
1907-1947 Ritchie Girvan, MA, LLD

Professors
1947   Ritchie Girvan, MA, LLD: *later Dean of Faculties*
1949   Norman Davis, MBE, MA: *later Merton Professor of English Language and Literature in the University of Oxford*
1959   Michael Louis Samuels, MA
1990   Graham Douglas Caie, MA, PhD, FEA, FRSA

English Language and Literature (Regius Chair)
Founded in 1861. Patron: the Crown. (Ordinance 22).

1862   John Nichol, MA, LLD
1889   Andrew Cecil Bradley, MA, LLD: *later Professor of Poetry in the University of Oxford*
1900   Sir Walter Alexander Raleigh, MA: *later Professor of English Literature in the University of Oxford*
1904   William Macneile Dixon, MA, LLD, LittD
1935-1963 Peter Alexander, CBE, MA, FBA
1965-1986 Peter Herbert Butter, MA
1990   Alexander Thomas Stephen Prickett, MA, PhD, DipEd, FAHA

English Literature (Bradley Chair)
Founded in 1965. Patron: the University Court. (Ordinance 517-Glasgow 142).

1965   John Cameron Bryce, MA
1979   Andrew Dunnett Hook, MA, PhD
1999   Clifford Haynes Siskin, BA, MA, PhD

Environmental Economics
Patron: the University Court. (Resolution pending).

2000   Nicholas D Hanley, BA, PhD

Equine Clinical Studies
Founded in 1956 as the Chair of Animal Husbandry. Title amended to the Chair of
Animal Husbandry and Veterinary Preventative Medicine in 1968 and again amended to
Equine Clinical Studies in 1995. Patron: the University Court. (Ordinance 309-Glasgow
83; amended by Resolutions 29 and 404).

1956   James Singlie Scott Inglis, BSc, MRCVS
1969-1990 Reginald Gordon Hemingway, MSc, PhD
1995   Sandy Love, BVMS, PhD, MRCVS

European Law (Jean Monnet Chair)
Founded in 1972. Patron: the University Court. (Resolution 94).

1973   Gehard Bebr, JUD, LLM, JSD
1974   Theodore W Vogelaar
1990   Noreen Burrows, LLB, PhD

Experimental Medicine (MacFarlane Chair)
Founded in 1962. The funds are provided by the Greater Glasgow Health Board from the
income of benefactions made to the former Board of Management of the Royal Infirmary
and Associated Hospitals by John E Macfarlane and Robert F Macfarlane, biscuit
manufacturers, of Glasgow. The chair is a visiting chair and the Professor holds office for
such period, not normally exceeding one year, as the University Court may determine.
Patron: a Board of Curators consisting of the Principal of the University, the Dean of the
Faculty of Medicine in the University, three members appointed by the Greater Glasgow
Health Board, and two members appointed by the University Court. (Ordinance 378-
Glasgow 122; amended by Resolution 146).

1963   Rupert Allan Willis, MD, DSc, LLD
1965   George Ivanovics: *Professor of Bacteriology in the University of Szeged*
1967   Lewis Libman Engel, BSc, PhD
1969   Floyd Reginald Skelton, MD, PhD: *Professor at the State University, New York*
1970   David Glick: *Professor of Pathology at Stanford University Medical School, California*

1973	Hermann Karl Benno Pinkus, MD, MS: *Professor of Dermatology in Wayne State University, Detroit*
1976	John M Kinney, MD: *College of Physicians and Surgeons of Columbia University*
1979	Robert John Lukes, MD: *Department of Pathology, University of Southern California*
1979	Joset Lissner: *Direktor der Klinik und Poliklinik fur Radiologie, University of Munich*
1980	G Barry Pierce: *Department of Pathology, University of Colorado*
1981	Richard W Gray: *Clinical Research Center, Medical College of Wisconsin*
1987	Joseph P Kriss, MD: *Stanford University Medical School*

Finance

Patron: the University Court. (Resolution pending).

2000   Robert Watson, BA, PhD

Fine Art (Richmond Chair)

The Richmond Chair was founded in 1965 with an endowment from the Trustees of Sir John Ritchie Richmond KBE, LLD, (1869-1963) senior deputy chairman of the Glasgow engineering firm G and J Weir Ltd and an important collector of nineteenth and twentieth century French paintings. His collection of paintings was gifted to Glasgow Museums and the National Gallery of Scotland. Patron: the University Court. (Ordinance 495-Glasgow 137).

1965   Andrew Mclaren Young, MA
1977   Ronald Pickvance, BA
1984   Alan Andrew Anderson Hutton Tait, MA, PhD

Forensic Medicine (Regius Chair)

Founded in 1839 by Queen Victoria. Patron: the Crown.

1839   Robert Cowan, MD
1841   Harry Rainy, MD
1872   Pierce Adolphus Simpson, MA, MD
1898   John Glaister, Snr, MD, DPH, LLD
1931-1962 John Glaister, Jnr, JP, MD, DSc: *Barrister*
1964   Gilbert Forbes, BSc, MD
1974   William Arthur Harland, MD, PhD
1985   Alan Albert Watson, JP, MA, MB, BS
1993   Peter Vanezis, MD, PhD, FRCPath, DMJ

French Language and Literature (Marshall Chair)

A Lectureship was instituted in 1895. The Marshall Chair of Modern Romantic Languages, with special reference to the Language and Literature of France, was founded in 1917 and endowed by the gift of Robert Marshall, James Clason-Harvie and others. In 1966 the title was amended to the Marshall Chair of French Language and Literature. Patron: the University Court. (Ordinances 56 and 542-Glasgow 17 and 160).

Lecturers

1895	Alfred Mercier, MA
1898	Charles Aristide Martin, MA, DTheol

Professors

1919	Charles Aristide Martin, MA, DTheol
1937	Alan Martin Boase, MA, PhD
1966	Austin Gill, CBE, MA, L-ès-L
1971	Henry Thomas Barnwell, MA, D-de-l'U
1980	Colin Smethurst, MA, BLitt, DipEd, Officier dans l'Ordre des Palmes Académiques: *later Dean of Faculties*
1998	Noel A Peacock, MA

French Language and Literature (Stevenson Chair)

Founded in 1966. Patron: the University Court. (Ordinance 542-Glasgow 160).

1968-1990 Ernest Kenneth Charles Varty, BA, PhD, DLitt, FSA, Chevalier dans l'Ordre des Palmes Académiques
1998-2000 Angus Kennedy, MA, PhD, Officier dans l'Ordre des Palmes Académiques

General Practice (Norie-Miller Chair)

Founded in 1974 with funds from an endowment by the General Accident Fire and Life Assurance Corporation Limited in memory of their late chairman and managing director and subsequently governor, Sir Stanley Norie-Miller. Authority for a chair had originally been given by Resolution 111 but this was set aside in favour of the Norie-Miller Chair. Patron: the University Court. (Resolution 124).

1974	James Hill Barber, MD
1994	Graham CM Watt, BMedBiol, GP, MD, FRCP, MRCGP, MFPHM, FMedSci

Genetics

A Lectureship was instituted in 1945. The Chair was founded in 1955. Patron: the University Court. (Ordinance 304-Glasgow 77).

Lecturer

1945-1955 Guido Pontecorvo, DrAgr, PhD, FRS: *Reader 1952-1955*

Professors

1955-1968 Guido Pontecorvo, DrAgr, PhD, FRS: *later Visiting Professor of Botany and Microbiology in University College, London*
1970   John Arthur Joseph Pateman, BSc, MA, PhD
1980   David John Sherratt, BSc, PhD
1995   Keith Jack Johnson, BSc, PhD, MB ChB

Geography

A Lectureship was instituted in 1908 by the University Court. The chair was founded in 1947 Patron: the University Court. (Ordinance 237-Glasgow 54).

Lecturers

1909   Sir Henry G Lyons, FRS: *later Director of the Science Museum, London*
1911   John Downie Falconer, MA, DSc: *later Director of the Geographical Survey of Nigeria*
1918   Alexander Stevens, MA, BSc, LLD

Professors

1947   Alexander Stevens, MA, BSc, LLD
1953   Ronald Miller, MA, PhD
1976   Ian Bentley Thompson, MA, PhD

Geography

Founded in 1966. Patron: the University Court. (Ordinance 545-Glasgow 163)

1998   Paul M Bishop, BA, DipEd, PhD

Geography

Founded in 1995. Patron: the University Court. (Resolution 408).

1995   Christopher Philo, BA, PhD

Geology
Founded in 1903 and endowed by the gift of the Carnegie Trust, the Bellahouston Trust and other donors and by the attachment of the Honeyman Gillespie Lectureship, previously attached to the Chair of Natural History. Patron: the University Court. (Ordinance 8-Glasgow 3).

1904   John Walker Gregory, DSc, FRS
1929   Sir Edward Battersby Bailey, MC, MA, DSc, FRS: *later Director of HM Geological Survey*
1937   Sir Arthur Trueman, KBE, DSc, LLD, FRS: *later Dean of Faculties, and subsequently Chairman of the University Grants Committee*
1947   Thomas Neville George, DSc, PhD, ScD, D-ès-Sc, LLD, FRS
1974-1997 Bernard Elgey Leake, PhD, DSc, FRSE

Geophysics (Britoil Chair)
Founded in 1987. Patron: the University Court. (Resolution 294).

1988-1998 David Kenneth Smythe, BSc, PhD

Geriatric Medicine (David Cargill Chair)
Founded in 1964 and endowed by the trustees of the late David Traill Cargill. *Patron: the University Court.* (Ordinance 467-Glasgow 132).

1965   Sir William Ferguson Anderson, OBE, MD
1979   Francis Irvine Caird, MA, DM
1994   David J Stott, MD, MRCP

German Language and Literature
This additional chair of German Language and Literature was founded in 1973. Patron: the University Court. (Resolution 108).

1974   Ronald George Finch, MA, PhD
1995-1998 Roger H Stephenson, BA, PhD, FSH: *later William Jacks Professor of Modern Languages*

Greek

Under the *Nova Erectio* the teaching of Greek was in the hands of the regents, and from 1581 onwards one of their number is sometimes given the title of Professor of Greek. In accordance with the recommendation of the Commission of Visitation of 1695 a separate Professorship was instituted in 1704. Patron: the University Court.

1704	Alexander Dunlop, MA, LLD: *previously regent*
1746	James Moore, MA, LLD
1774	John Young, MA
1821	Sir Daniel Keyte Sandford, MA, DCL, MP
1838	Edmund Law Lushington, MA, LLD: *later Rector*
1875	Sir Richard Claverhouse Jebb, MA, LLD, LittD, FBA: *later Regius Professor of Greek in the University of Cambridge*
1889	George Gilbert Aimé Murray, MA, FBA: *later Regius Professor of Greek in the University of Oxford*
1899	John Swinnerton Phillimore, MA, LLD, LittD: *later Professor of Humanity*
1906	Gilbert Austin Davies, MA
1934	William Rennie, CBE, MA, LLD, LittD: *previously Professor of Humanity and later Dean of Faculties*
1946	Arnold Wycombe Gomme, MA, LLD, FBA
1957	Donald James Allan, MA, FBA
1971	Douglas Maurice MacDowell, MA, DLitt, FRSE, FBA

Hannah Chair

Founded in 1970. The person appointed to the Chair is the Director of the Hannah Dairy Research Institute. Patron: the University Court. (Resolution 51).

1971	John Allan Fynes Rook, PhD, DSc *(Animal Nutrition)*
1981	Malcolm Peaker, PhD, DSc, FRSE *(Dairy Science)*

Health Policy and Economic Evaluation (William R Lindsay Chair)

Founded in 1999. Patron: the University Court. (Resolution 472).

2000	Kevin Woods, BSc, PhD

Health Promotion Policy (Health Education Board for Scotland Chair)
Patron: the University Court. (Resolution pending).

2000   Kenneth Franklin Judge, MA, PhD

Hebrew and Semitic Languages
Founded in 1709 by Queen Anne as the Chair of Oriental Languages: the title was changed in 1893. Patron: the University Court, since 1935 acting on the recommendation of a Board consisting of representatives of the University Court and of the General Assembly of the Church of Scotland. (Ordinance 184 of 1934, amended by Ordinance 284 (General 10) of 1952).

1709   Charles Morthland, MA
1745   Alexander Dunlop, MA, LLD: *previously regent*
1751   William Rouet, MA: *later Professor of Ecclesiastical History*
1753   George Muirhead, MA: *later Professor of Humanity*
1755   John Anderson, MA: *later Professor of Natural Philosophy*
1757   James Buchanan, MA
1761   Patrick Cumin, MA, LLD: *later Clerk of Senate*
1761   Robert Trail, MA, DD: *later Professor of Divinity*
1820   Gavin Gibb, MA, LLD: *previously Dean of Faculties*
1831   William Fleming, MA, DD: *later Professor of Moral Philosophy*
1839   George Gray, DD
1850   Duncan Harkness Weir, MA, DD: *later Clerk of Senate*
1877   James Robertson, MA, DD
1907   William Barron Stevenson, MA, DLitt, DD, LLD: *later Dean of Faculties*
1937   Cecil James Mullo Weir, MA, DPhil, DD
1968-1987 John Macdonald, MA, BD, PhD, STM

Hispanic Studies (Stevenson Chair)
Founded in 1924 as the Stevenson Chair of Spanish, and endowed by the gift of Sir Daniel Macaulay Stevenson (1851-1944), philanthropist and later Chancellor of the University, 1934-1944. The conditions of appointment are the same as for the Chair of Italian (Ordinance 131-Glasgow 37). In 1959, the title was amended to Hispanic Studies. (Ordinance 328-Glasgow 95). *(See also Spanish (Ivy McClelland Research Chair).*

1925	William James Entwistle, MA: *later King Alfonso XIII Professor of Spanish Studies in the University of Oxford*
1932	William Christopher Atkinson, MA
1972	Nicholas Grenville Round, MA, DPhil, MITI, Caballero de la Order de Isabel la Católica
1995-2000	D Gareth Walters, BA, PhD

Housing and Urban Studies
Founded in 1988 as the Chair of Urban Studies following the closure of the Department of Town and Regional Planning. The title was changed in 1990 to more accurately reflect the relationship with the Centre for Housing Research. Patron: the University Court. (Resolution 306, amended by 339).

| 1988-1990 | Duncan Maclennan, MA, MPhil, CBE, FRSA: *later Mactaggart Professor of Land Economics and Finance* |
| 1991 | Alan McGregor, MA: *later Professor of Economic Development* |

Housing and Urban Studies
Founded in 1996. Patron: the University Court. (Resolution 422).

| 1996 | Peter Anthony Kemp, MPhil, BSc, PhD |

Human Nutrition (Rank Chair)
Founded in 1988 with funds from the Rank Prize Fund. A sum was also donated to establish the Department of Human Nutrition at the University. Patron: the University Court. (Resolution 310).

| 1988 | Brian Arthur Wharton, MD, FRCP, DCH |
| 1993 | Michael E J Lean, MA, MD, FRCP |

Humanity
Under the *Nova Erectio* the teaching of Latin was in the hands of the regents: the title of Professor of Humanity is occasionally applied to one of their number from 1618 onwards. In accordance with the recommendation of the Commission of Visitation of 1664 a separate Professorship was instituted in 1682: after lapse it was revived in 1706. Patron: the University Court.

| 1682 | James Young, MA: *previously regent* |
| 1706 | Andrew Ross, MA: *previously regent* |

1735   George Ross, MA
1754   George Muirhead, MA: *previously Professor of Oriental Languages*
1773   William Richardson, MA
1815   Josiah Walker, MA
1831   William Ramsay, MA
1863   George Gilbert Ramsay, MA, LLD, LittD: *later Dean of Faculties*
1906   John Swinnerton Phillimore, MA, LLD, LittD: *previously Professor of Greek*
1927   William Rennie, CBE, MA, LLD, LittD: *later Professor of Greek and Dean of Faculties*
1934   Christian James Fordyce, MA, LLD: *later Dean of Faculties and Clerk of Senate*
1972-1991 Patrick Gerard Walsh, MA, PhD, DLitt, FRSE
1995   Roger Philip Hywell Green, MA, BLitt

Immunology (Gardiner Chair)

Founded in 1919 as the Chair of Bacteriology and endowed by William Guthrie Gardiner and Sir Frederick Crombie Gardiner, shipowners in Glasgow. The title was amended in 1990. Patron: the University Court. (Ordinance 75-Glasgow 22, amended by Resolution 330).

1919   Carl Hamilton Browning, MD, LLD, FRS
1951   Sir James William Howie, MD: *later Director of the Public Health Laboratory Service*
1963   Robert George White, MA, DM
1980   Delphine Mary Vera Parrott, DSc, PhD, FRCPath, FRSE
1991   Foo Y Liew, BSc, PhD, DSc, FRSE, FMedSci

Industrial Relations

Founded in 1960. Patron: the University Court. (Ordinance 346-Glasgow 101).

1969-1970 Donald James Robertson, MA: *previously Professor of Applied Economics*

Infectious Diseases

Founded in 1959. Patron: the University Court. (Ordinance 329-Glasgow 94).

1959   Thomas Anderson, CBE, MD
1965-1983 Norman Roy Grist, BSc, MB ChB

Italian (Stevenson Chair)

A lectureship was instituted in 1902. The chair was founded in 1924 and endowed by the gift of Sir Daniel Macaulay Stevenson (1851-1944), philanthropist and later Chancellor of the University, 1934-1944. Patron: the University Court, acting on the nomination of a Selection Board consisting of the Principal, the Professor of Humanity and the Professor of English Language and Literature (all *ex officio*), one member of the University Court appointed by the Court, one Assessor of the General Council on the University Court appointed by the General Council, one person appointed by the Corporation of the City of Glasgow, two persons appointed by the Governors of the Glasgow and West of Scotland Commercial College, one person appointed by the Directors of the Glasgow Chamber of Commerce, and one person appointed by the Glasgow Provincial Committee for the Training of Teachers. The Professor is appointed for a term of five years and is eligible for reappointment. (Ordinance 130-Glasgow 36).

Lecturers

1902	Fernando Agnoletti, DLitt
1910	Ernesto Nicola Giuseppe Grillo, MA

Professors

1925	Ernesto Nicola Giuseppe Grillo, MA
1949	Matthew Fontaine Maury Meiklejohn, MA
1975	Peter Melville Brown, BA, DPhil
1995	Eileen A Millar, MA, PhD, Cav Uff Della Repubblica Italiana

Jurisprudence

A lectureship in Public Law (including Jurisprudence and International Law) was instituted in 1878. From 1893, there was a separate lectureship in General and Comparative Jurisprudence. The chair was founded in 1952. Patron: the University Court. (Ordinance 279-Glasgow 73).

Lecturers

1878	William Galbraith Miller, MA, LLB: *advocate*
1904	James Alexander McCallum, MA, LLB
1913	Andrew Acworth Mitchell, MA, LB
1927	Harold McIntosh, MC, MA, LLB

Professors

1954   David Maxwell Walker, CBE, QC, MA, PhD, LLD, FBA, FRSE: *advocate and barrister, later Regius Professor of Law*

1959-1973 Alexander Elder Anton, MA, LLB, FBA

1978-1990 Thomas Douglas Campbell, MA, PhD, FRSE

Land Economics and Finance (Mactaggart Chair)

Founded in 1990 with a grant from the Ian Mactaggart Trust. Patron: the University Court. (Resolution 338).

1990   Duncan Maclennan, MA, MPhil, CBE, FRSA, FRSE: *previously Professor of Urban Studies*

Law (John Millar Chair)

Founded in 1985. Patron: the University Court. (Resolution 263).

1985   Thomas StJohn Neville Bates, LLB, MA

1988   Martin Loughlin, LLM

1992   J Anthony Prosser, LLB

Law (Regius Chair)

Instituted in 1712 and endowed in 1713 by Queen Anne. Patron the Crown.

1714   William Forbes, MA: *advocate*

1746   William Cross: *advocate*

1750   Hercules Lindsay, LLD

1761   John Millar: advocate

1801   Robert Davidson, LLD: *advocate*

1842   Allan Alexander Wellwood Maconochie, LLD: *advocate*

1855   George Skene: *advocate*

1867   Robert Berry, MA, LLD: *advocate and later Dean of Faculties*

1887   Alexander Moody Stuart, LLD: *advocate*

1905   William Murray Gloag, KC, BA, LLD: *advocate*

1934   Andrew Dewar Gibb, MBE, QC, MA, LLD: *advocate and barrister*

1958   David Maxwell Walker, CBE, QC, MA, PhD, LLD, FBA, FRSE: *advocate and barrister and previously Professor of Jurisprudence*

1991   Joseph M Thomson, LLB, FRSE

Law and Ethics in Medicine (International Bar Association Chair)
Founded in 1990 with sponsorship from the International Bar Association. Patron: the University Court. (Resolution 332).

1990   Sheila A M McLean, LLB, MLitt, PhD, FRSE

Learning Disabilities
Patron: the University Court. (Resolution pending).

1999   Sally Ann Cooper, BSc, MB, BS, MD, MRCPsych

Logic and Rhetoric
Under the *Nova Erectio* the teaching of Moral Philosophy, Logic and Natural Philosophy was shared among the regents. In 1727, separate chairs were instituted and the three Philosophy regents became the first incumbents. Patron: the University Court.

1727   John Loudon, MA
1751   Adam Smith, MA, LLD: *later Professor of Moral Philosophy and Rector*
1752   James Clow, MA
1774   George Jardine, MA
1827   Robert Buchanan, MA, LLD
1864   John Veitch, MA, LLD
1895   Robert Adamson, MA, LLD
1902   Robert Latta, MA, DPhil, LLD
1925   Archibald Allan Bowman, MA, LittD: *later Professor of Moral Philosophy*
1927   Herbert James Paton, MA, DLitt: *later Professor of Moral Philosophy in the University of Oxford*
1938   Charles Arthur Campbell, MA, DLitt: *later Dean of Faculties*
1961-1981 Rodney Julian Hirst, MA: *later Vice-Principal*
1995   Alexander Broadie, MA, PhD, DLitt, FRSE

Management Studies
Founded in 1970. Patron: the University Court. (Resolution 56).

1972-1992 Myles Muir Dryden, BSc, MBA, PhD

Marketing
Patron: the University Court. (Resolution pending).

1996   Luiz A Moutinho, BA, MA, PhD, FCIM

Materia Medica (Regius Chair)
A Lectureship was instituted in 1766. The chair was founded in 1831 by King William IV. In 1989, the chair merged with the Regius Chair of Medicine and Therapeutics. Patron: the Crown.

Lecturers
1766   William Irvine, MD
1787   Thomas Charles Hope, MD, FRS: *previously Lecturer in Chemistry and later Professor of Practice of Medicine in the University and Professor of Chemistry in the University of Edinburgh*
1788   Robert Cleghorn, MD
1791   Richard Millar, MD

Professors
1831   Richard Millar, MD
1833   John Couper, MD
1855   John Alexander Easton, MD
1865   John Black Cowan, MD
1880   Matthew Charteris, MD
1897   Ralph Stockman, MD, LLD
1937   Noah Morris, MD, DSc
1948   Stanley Alstead, CBE, MD
1970   Sir Abraham Goldberg, KBE, MD, DSc, FRCP, FRSE
1978-1989 John Low Reid, BA, DM, FRSE, FMedSci: *later Regius Professor of Medicine and Therapeutics*

Mathematics
Under the *Nova Erectio* the teaching of Mathematics was in the hands of the regents. In accordance with the recommendation of the Commission of Visitation of 1664 the chair was instituted in 1691, when one of the regents was appointed to it. Patron: the University Court.

1691-1696 George Sinclair, MA: *previously regent*
1699   Robert Sinclair, MA, MD
1711   Robert Simpson, MA, MD: *later Clerk of Senate*
1761   James Williamson, MA, DD
1796   James Millar, MA
1832   James Thomson, MA, LLD
1849   Hugh Blackburn, MA
1879   William Jack, MA, LLD
1909   George Alexander Gibson, MA, LLD
1927   Thomas Murray MacRobert, MA, DSc, LLD: *later Dean of Faculties*
1954-1982 Robert Alexander Rankin, MA, PhD, ScD, FRSE: *later Clerk of Senate and Dean of Faculties*
1989   Robert Winston Keith Odoni, BSc, PhD, FRSE

Mathematics (Thomas Muir Chair)
Founded in 1966 as an additional Chair of Mathematics, the name was changed in 1973. The title commemorates the mathematician and educational administrator Sir Thomas Muir (1844-1934), MA 1870, LLD 1884. Patron: the University Court. (Ordinance 544-Glasgow 162, amended by Resolution 121).

1973-1996 Walter Douglas Munn, MA, PhD, DSc, FRSE

Mathematics (Simson Chair)
Founded in 1955. The title commemorates the mathematician Robert Simson (1687-1768), who held the Chair of Mathematics in the University, 1711-1761. Patron: the University Court. (Ordinance 306-Glasgow 78).

1956-1985 Ian Naismith Sneddon, OBE, MA, DSc, FRS, FRSE
1992   Brian Straughan, MSc, PhD, FRSE
2001   Nicholas A Hill, BSc, ARCS, MSc, PhD, DIC (from October)

Mathematics (George Sinclair Chair)
Founded in 1984 and named after George Sinclair, the first Professor of Mathematics at the University, 1691-1696. Patron: the University Court. (Resolution 252).

1984   Raymond William Ogden, MA, PhD, DSc, FRSE

Mechanical Engineering
Patron: the University Court. (Resolution pending).

1998   Kenneth James Hunt, BSc, PhD, CEng

Mechanical Engineering (Rankine Chair)
Founded in 1957 and named after William John Macquorn Rankine (1820-1872), LLD, FRS, Regius Professor of Civil Engineering in the University 1855-1873. Patron: the University Court. (Ordinance 313-Glasgow 86).

1959   George Douglas Stephen MacLellan, MA, PhD: *later Professor of Engineering in the University of Leicester*
1965-1982 John Doughty Robson, MA, PhD

Mechanical Engineering (James Watt Chair)
Founded in 1921 as the James Watt Chair of Theory and Practice of Heat Engines by the Institution of Engineers and Shipbuilders in Scotland in commemoration of the centenary of the death of James Watt (1736-1819), inventor and scientific instrument maker to the University of Glasgow 1756-1773. The name was altered to the James Watt Chair of Mechanical Engineering in 1951. Patron: the University Court. (Ordinances 103 and 280-Glasgow 27 and 71).

1921   William John Goudie, DSc
1938   James Small, DSc, PhD, MIMechE
1966   Robert Simpson Silver, CBE, MA, PhD, DSc
1980-2000 Brian Frederick Scott, BSc, PhD

Mechanical Engineering (Wylie Chair)
Founded in 1987 using income from the Wylie Fund. Patron: the University Court. (Resolution 286).

1987   Peter John Gawthrop, MA, PhD

Medieval History (Edwards Chair)
Founded in 1955 as the Chair of Medieval History. The name was changed in 1989 to commemorate the Glasgow scholar and antiquarian John Edwards (1846-1937). Patron: the University Court. (Ordinance 307-Glasgow 81).

1956   Edward Lionel Gregory Stones, MA, PhD
1978   Alfred Lawson Brown, MA, DPhil, FRHistS: *later Vice-Principal*
1994   David R Bates, MA, PhD

Medical Cardiology (Walton Chair)

Founded in 1966. Patron: the University Court. (Resolution 1).

1966   Thomas Davidson Veitch Lawrie, BSc, MD
1985   Stuart Malcolm Cobbe, MA, MD

Medical Genetics

Founded in 1973. In 1987, the Court agreed to use the Burton Chair of Medicine funds in the appointment of a successor to Professor Ferguson-Smith. Patron: the University Court. (Resolution 109).

1973-1987 Malcolm Andrew Ferguson-Smith, MB ChB, FRS, FRSE, FRCPath

Medical Oncology (Cancer Research Campaign Chair)

Founded as the Cancer Research Campaign Chair of Oncology with funds from the Cancer Research Campaign. The name of the chair was changed in 1985 to take into account the foundation of the Chair of Radiation Oncology. For legal reasons the chair had to be abolished and reconstituted in 1993. Patron: the University Court. (Resolution 130, amended by 272, abolished by 372, re-established by 373).

1974   Kenneth Charles Calman, BSc, MD, PhD, FMedSci: *later Professor of Postgraduate Medical Education in the University, Chief Medical Officer of the Department of Health and Vice-Chancellor of the University of Durham*
1985-2000 Stanley Bernard Kaye, BSc, MD, BS, FRCP, FRCR

Medicine (Burton Chair)

Founded in 1987 applying part of the income from the T M and H G Burton Fund. On the occasion of each appointment to the Chair, the University Court shall determine the branch of medicine being at that time at the forefront of medical research, for which the Professor shall be responsible. During such tenure the professorship shall be designated by the name of that branch. Patron: the University Court. (Resolution 285).

1987   James Michael Connor, MD, DSc, FRCP: *Medical Genetics*
1987   Peter Graham Edward Kennedy, MLitt, MPhil, MD, PhD, DSc, FRCPath, FRCP, FRSE, FMedSci: *Neurology*

Medicine (Muirhead Chair)

Founded in 1911 and endowed by the trustees of Henry Muirhead, MD, LLD (d.1890), of Bothwell. Patron: a Board of eleven Curators, seven appointed by the University Court, two by the managers of the Royal Infirmary or their successors and two by the Muirhead Trustees. (Ordinance 34-Glasgow 10, amended by Resolution 149).

1911	Walter King Hunter, MD, DSc
1934	Archibald Wilson Harrington, MD
1945	Leslie John Davis, MD
1961	Edward McCombie McGirr, CBE, BSc, MD: *later Professor of Administrative Medicine*
1978	Arthur Colville Kennedy, MD
1989	James Hugh McKillop, BSc, MB ChB, PhD, FMedSci

Medicine and Therapeutics (Regius Chair)

Instituted in 1637 as Practice of Medicine; after lapse revived in 1712 and endowed in 1713 by Queen Anne. The title was changed in 1989. Patron: the Crown. (Amended by Resolution 315).

1637-1646	Robert Mayne, MA: previously regent
1714	John Johnstoun, MD
1751	William Cullen, MD: *previously lecturer in Chemistry in the University and later successively Professor of Chemistry and Professor of Medicine in the University of Edinburgh*
1756	Robert Hamilton, MD
1757	Joseph Black, MD: *previously lecturer in Chemistry, Regius Professor of Anatomy and Clerk of Senate in the University and later Professor of Chemistry in the University of Edinburgh*
1766	Alexander Stevenson, MD
1789	Thomas Charles Hope, MD, FRS: *previously Lecturer in Materia Medica, Lecturer in Chemistry and Professor of Practice of Medicine in the University and Professor of Chemistry in the University of Edinburgh*
1796	Robert Freer, MA, MD
1827	Charles Badham, MA, MD, FRS
1841	William Thomson, MD
1852	John MacFarlane, MD
1862	Sir William Tennant Gairdner, KCB, MD, LLD, FRS
1900	Sir Thomas McCall Anderson, MD: *previously Professor of Clinical Medicine*
1908	Samson Gemmell, MD: *previously Professor of Clinical Medicine*

1913	Thomas Kirkpatrick Monro, MA, MD, LLD
1936	Sir John William McNee, DSO, MD, DSc, LLD
1953	Sir Edward Johnson Wayne, MSc, MD, PhD
1967	Graham Malcolm Wilson, MD, DSc
1978	Sir Abraham Goldberg, KBE, MD, DSc, FRCP, FRSE
1989	John Low Reid, BA, DM, FRCP, FRSE, FMedSci: *previously Regius Professor of Material Medica*

Mercantile Law

A lectureship was instituted in 1894. The chair was founded in 1919 and endowed partly by the bequest of John Maclachlan of Glasgow, partly by grants from the Carnegie Trust, and from the Robert and James Dick of Greenhead Fund. Patron: the University Court. (Ordinance 73-Glasgow 20).

Lecturers

1894	James Mackenzie
1900	William Shaw
1907	Thomas Grieve Wright, LLB

Professors

1920	Thomas Grieve Wright, LLB
1930-1940	Sir John James Craik Henderson, BL
1946-1957	Sir John Boyd, MA, LLD
1963	James Bennett Miller, CBE, TD, MA, LLB
1978-1993	Robert Barr Jack, CBE, MA, LLB

Metaphysical Philosophy

Founded in 1995. Patron: the University Court. (Resolution 402).

1995	Robert L V Hale, BA, BPhil, FRSE

Microbiology

Founded in 1964. Patron: the University Court. (Ordinance 435-Glasgow 127).

1966	Iwo Robert Waclaw Lominski, MD, DSc
1970	Alastair Connell Wardlaw, PhD, DSc
1995	Timothy J Mitchell, BSc, PhD

Mining (James S Dixon Chair)

A lectureship was instituted in 1902 and endowed by the gift of James S Dixon, LLD, of Bothwell, coalmaster. The chair was founded as a Chair in Mining in 1907 and endowed by the same donor. The appointments in 1932 and 1947 were jointly made with the Royal Technical College. This agreement was cancelled in 1967 with the formation of the University of Strathclyde. The founding Ordinance was repealed in 1980 when teaching ceased. Patron: a Board of Electors consisting of the members of the University Court, the President of the Mining Institute of Scotland, HM Inspectors of Mines for the Western and Eastern Districts of Scotland and the President of the Lanarkshire Coalmasters' Association. (Ordinance 19-Glasgow 10, repealed by Resolution 210). *(See also James S Dixon Chair of Applied Geology.)*

Lecturer
1902-1907 Charles Latham

Professors
1907-1917 Charles Latham
1923   Robert William Dron, MA
1932-1940 Sir Andrew Meikle Bryan, BSc: *later HM Chief Inspector of Mines*
1947-1967 George Hibberd, PhD

Modern French Studies

Patron: the University Court. (Resolution pending).

2000   William J Marshall, BA, M-es-L, DPhil, MA
2000   Keith Anthony Reader, MA, BPhil, DPhil

Modern History

Founded in 1893 as the Chair of History. In 1956, by minute of the University Court, and subsequently by ordinance the title was altered to Modern History. Patron: the University Court. (Ordinances 28 and 381-Glasgow 112).

1894   Sir Richard Lodge, MA: *later Professor of History in the University of Edinburgh*
1899   Dudley Julius Medley, MA, LLD
1931   Andrew Browning, MA, DLitt, FBA
1957   Esmond Wright, MA
1967   William Ranulf Brock, MA, PhD

1981   Keith Gilbert Robbins, MA, DPhil, DLitt: *previously Professor of Modern History (1979 Chair) and later Senior Vice-Chancellor of the University of Wales*

1992 - 2001 Hew F A Strachan, MA, PhD: *later Chichele Professor of History of War in the University of Oxford*

Modern History

This additional chair was founded in 1979. Patron: the University Court. (Resolution 197).

1980-1981 Keith Gilbert Robbins, MA, DPhil, DLitt: *later Professor of Modern History (1893 chair) and later Senior Vice-Chancellor of the University of Wales*

Modern Languages (William Jacks Chair)

A part-time lectureship was instituted in 1887. It became a full-time appointment in 1899. The William Jacks Chair of Modern Languages was founded in 1919 and endowed by the gift of William Jacks, James Clason-Harvie and others. Patron the University Court (Ordinance 59-Glasgow 18).

Lecturers

1887   Ernst Elster, PhD: *later Professor of German Literature in the Universities of Leipzig and Marburg*

1889   Hermann Georg Fiedler, PhD: *later Professor of German in the University of Oxford*

1890   Alexander Tille, PhD

1900   George Parker Thistlethwaite, BA, PhD

1907   Herbert Smith, MA, PhD

Professors

1919   Herbert Smith, MA, PhD

1951   James Midgley Clark, MA, PhD

1954   William Walker Chambers, MBE, MA, PhD, L-es-L: *later Vice-Principal and Dean of Faculties*

1979-1990 Ronald George Finch, MA, PhD

1998   Roger H Stephenson, BA, PhD: *previously Professor of German Language and Literature*

Molecular Medicine
Founded in 1994. Patron: the University Court. (Resolution 384).

1994   Janet Marjorie Allen, BSc, MBBS, MD, MRCP, FRSE

Moral Philosophy
Under the *Nova Erectio* the teaching of Moral Philosophy, Logic, and Natural Philosophy was shared among the regents. In 1727 separate chairs were instituted and the three Philosophy regents became the first incumbents. Patron: the University Court.

1727   Gerschom Carmichael, MA: *previously regent*
1730   Francis Hutcheson, MA, LLD
1746   Thomas Craigie, MA
1752   Adam Smith, MA, LLD: *previously Professor of Logic and Rhetoric and later Rector*
1764   Thomas Reid, MA, DD
1796   Archibald Arthur, MA: *also University Chaplain*
1797   James Mylne, MA: *later Clerk of Senate and University Chaplain*
1839   William Fleming, MA, DD: *previously Professor of Oriental Languages*
1866   Edward Caird, MA, DCL, LLD: *later Master of Balliol College, Oxford*
1894   Sir Henry Jones, CH, MA, LLD, LittD, FBA: *later Dean of Faculties*
1922   Alexander Dunlop Lindsay CBE, MA: *later Master of Balliol College, Oxford*
1924   Sir Hector James Wright Hetherington, GBE, DL, MA, LLD, DLitt, D-es-L: *later Principal of the University of Liverpool and Principal*
1927   Archibald Allan Bowman, MA, LittD: *previously Professor of Logic and Rhetoric*
1936   Sir Oliver Shewell Franks, GCMG, KCB, CBE, MA, LLD: *later Provost of the Queen's College and Worcester College, Oxford*
1946   William Gauld Maclagan, MA, PhD
1969-2000 Robert Silcock Downie, MA, BPhil, FRSE, FRSA

Music (Gardiner Chair)
Founded in 1928 and endowed by the gift of William Guthrie Gardiner and Sir Frederick Crombie Gardiner, shipowners in Glasgow. The chair and the directorship of the Scottish National Academy of Music were joint appointments from 1929 until 1952. Patron: the University Court. (Ordinances 159 and 290-Glasgow 40 and 74).

1930   William Gillies Whittaker, MA, DMus
1941-1952 Sir Ernest Bullock, CVO, DMus, LLD: *later Director of the Royal College of Music*

1956	Robert Kemsley (Robin) Orr, MA, MusD: *later Professor of Music in the University of Cambridge*
1966	Frederick William Rimmer, CBE, MA, BMus
1980	Hugh John Macdonald, MA, PhD
1990	Graham Barry Hair, MMus, PhD
2001	John Butt, MA, PhD, ARCO, CHM, FRCO, ADCM (from October)

Natural Philosophy

Under the *Nova Erectio* the teaching of Moral Philosophy, Logic, and Natural Philosophy was shared among the regents. In 1727 separate chairs were instituted and the three Philosophy regents became the first incumbents. The Professor is Director of the Physical Laboratories. Patron: the University Court.

1727	Robert Dick, Snr, MA, MD: *previously regent*
1751	Robert Dick, Jnr, MA, MD
1757	John Anderson, MA: *previously Professor of Oriental Languages*
1796	James Brown, MA, MD
1803	William Meikleham, MA, LLD: *previously Professor of Astronomy and later Clerk of Senate*
1846	William Thomson, (Baron Kelvin of Largs), GCVO, MA, DCL, LLD, FRS: *later Dean of Faculties and Chancellor*
1899	Andrew Gray, MA, LLD, FRS
1924	Harold Albert Wilson, MA, DSc, FRS: *later Professor of Physics in the Rice Institute, Houston, Texas*
1926	Edward Taylor Jones, DSc, LLD
1943	Philip Ivor Dee, CBE, MA, FRS
1973	Robert Patton Ferrier, MA, BSc, PhD, FRSE

Natural Philosophy (Cargill Chair)

Founded in 1920 as the Cargill Chair of Applied Physics and endowed by the gift of Sir John Traill Cargill, (1867-1956), director of the Burmah Oil Company. In 1945, the chair became the Cargill Chair of Natural Philosophy. Patron: the University Court. (Ordinances 88 and 212-Glasgow 25 and 48).

1920	James Gordon Gray, DSc
1935	Thomas Alty, DSc, PhD, LLD: *later Vice-Chancellor of Rhodes University*
1949-1982	Sir John Currie Gunn, CBE, MA, DSc, DUniv, FRSE, FInstP, FIMA: *later Vice-Principal and Dean of Faculties*
2000	Günther Rosner, Dipl-Phys, Dr rer nat habil

Natural Philosophy (Kelvin Chair)
Founded in 1961. Patron: the University Court. (Ordinance 369-Glasgow 119).

1964	George Robert Bishop, MA, DPhil
1990	David Harold Saxon, MA, DPhil, DSc, FRSE

Naval Architecture and Ocean Engineering (John Elder Chair)
Founded in 1883 and endowed by Isabella Elder, (1828-1905) in memory of her husband, John Elder, marine engineer, (1824-1869). Patron: the University Court.

1883	Francis Elgar, LLD
1886	Philip Jenkins
1891	Sir John Harvard Biles, DSc, LLD
1921-1942	Percy Archibald Hillhouse, DSc
1944	Andrew McCance Robb, DSc, LLD
1957	John Farquhar Christie Conn, DSc
1973	Douglas Faulkner, BSc, PhD, RCNC, FEng
1995	Nigel D P Barltrop, BSc, CEng, SICE, MRINA

Neurology
Founded in 1964. In 1987, the Court agreed to use the Burton Chair of Medicine funds in the appointment of a successor to Professor Simpson. Patron: the University Court. (Ordinance 467-Glasgow 132).

1965-1987 John Alexander Simpson, MD, FRSE

Neurosurgery
Founded in 1967. Patron: the University Court. (Resolution 17).

1968-1991	William Bryan Jennett, MD
1994	Graham Michael Teasdale, MB, BS, FRCS, FRCP, FMedSci

New Testament Language and Literature
Founded in 1934 in consequence of the union of the United Free Church with the Church of Scotland. Patron: the University Court acting on the nomination of the General Assembly of the Church of Scotland. Suppressed in 1947 by Ordinance. (Ordinance 184 and 230-Glasgow 45 and 51).

1935-1946 William Dickie Niven, MA, DD, LLD: *later Professor of Ecclesiastical History*

Nursing Studies
Founded in 1988. Patron: the University Court. (Resolution 308).

1990   Lorraine Smith, BScN, MEd, PhD, RN, RMN

Obstetrics and Gynaecology (Muirhead Chair)
Founded in 1911 and endowed by the trustees of Henry Muirhead, MD, LLD (d.1890), of Bothwell. Patron: a Board of eleven Curators, seven appointed by the University Court, two by the Managers of the Royal Infirmary or their successors and two by the Muirhead Trustees. (Ordinance 34-Glasgow 10, amended by Resolution 149).

1911   John Martin Munro Kerr, MD, LLD: *later Professor of Midwifery*
1927-1943 James Hendry, MA, MB, BSc: *later Professor of Midwifery*
1946   David Fyfe Anderson, MD
1970   Sir Malcolm Campbell MacNaughton, MD, LLD
1992-2000 Ian A Greer, MD, MRCP, FRCP, MRCOG, MFFP: *later Regius Professor of Obstetrics and Gynaecology*

Obstetrics and Gynaecology (Regius Chair)
Founded in 1815 by King George III. From 1790 to 1815, the subject was taught by a lecturer on the Waltonian Foundation. The chair was originally founded as the Chair of Midwifery, the name being changed by amendment in 1992. Patron: the Crown. (Amended by Resolution 361).

Waltonian Lecturer
1790-1815 James Towers, CM

Professors
1815   James Towers, CM
1820   John Towers, MA, CM
1833   Robert Lee, MD, FRS
1834   William Cumin, MA, MD
1840   John Macmichan Pagan, MD
1868   William Leishman, MD
1894   Murdoch Cameron, MD
1927   John Martin Munro Kerr, MD, LLD: *previously Muirhead Professor of Obstetrics and Gynaecology*
1934   Samuel James Cameron, MB, LLD
1943   James Hendry, MA, MB, BSc: *previously Muirhead Professor of Obstetrics and Gynaecology*

1945   Robert Aim Lennie, MD, LLD
1946   Ian Donald, CBE, BA, MD
1976   Charles Richard Whitefield, MD
1993   Iain T Cameron, BSc, MD, MA
2001   Ian A Greer, MD, MRCP, FRCP, MRCOG, MFFP: *previously Muirhead Professor of Obstetrics and Gynaecology*

Old Testament Language and Literature

Founded in 1934 in consequence of the union of the United Free Church with the Church of Scotland. Patron: the University Court acting on the nomination of the General Assembly of the Church of Scotland. (Ordinance 184 -Glasgow 45; amended by Ordinance 284-General 10 and Continuation Resolution 259 of 1984).

1935   John Mauchline, MA, DD
1972-1991 Robert Davidson, DD, MA, BD, FRSE

Ophthalmology (Tennent Chair)

A Lectureship was instituted in 1828. The chair was founded in 1917 and endowed by the bequest of Gavin Patterson Tennent, MD 1870. Patron: a Board of seven Curators, four appointed by the University Court and three by the managers of the Western Infirmary or their successors. (Ordinance 52-Glasgow 15, amended by Resolution 149).

Lecturers
1828   William MacKenzie, MD
1868   George Rainy, MA, MD
1869   Thomas Reid, MD, LLD
1911   Andrew Maitland Ramsay, MD
1920   Arthur James Ballantyne, MD

Professors
1935   Arthur James Ballantyne, MD
1941   William John Brownlow Riddell, MD
1964   Wallace Stewart Foulds, CBE, MD, ChM
1991   Colin M Kirkness, BMedBiol, MB ChB, FRCS, FRCOPhth

Oral Medicine
Founded in 1966. Patron: the University Court. (Resolution 11).

1967   David Kean Mason, CBE, BDS, MD, FDS, FRCS
1993   David Wray, BDS, MD, FDS

Oral Surgery
Founded in 1951 as the Chair of Dental Surgery with the title being amended in 1977.
Patron: the University Court. (Ordinance 273- Glasgow 67, amended by Resolution 186).

1951   James Aitchison, BSc, DDSc
1964   John Campbell MacDougall, BSc, FDS
1977-1999 David Alexander McGowan, MDS, PhD, FDS

Organisational Behaviour
Founded in 1974. Patron: the University Court. (Resolution 127).

1975   David Thomas Henderson Weir, BA
1991   Roderick Martin, MA, DPhil
2000   Fiona Margaret Wilson, BA, MA, PhD

Orthodontics
Founded in 1951. Patron: the University Court (Ordinance 274-Glasgow 68).

1961   Thomas Cyril White, BSc, FDS
1976   John Kingsley Luffingham, BDS, PhD, FDS
1993   William J S Kerr, DOrth, FDS, FFD

Orthopaedics
The Lectureship in Orthopaedics was established in 1942 and endowed by Fred H Young,
Glasgow. The Lectureship was replaced by the Chair of Orthopaedics which was founded
in 1959. Patron: the University Court. (Ordinance 327-Glasgow 93).

Lecturer
1943   Roland Barnes, CBE, BSc, MB ChB

Professors
1959   Roland Barnes, CBE, BSc, MB ChB
1972-1999 David Lawrence Hamblen, MB, BS, PhD

Palliative Medicine (Macmillan Professor in the Dr Olav Kerr Chair)
Founded in 1994 as the Dr Olav Kerr Chair of Palliative Medicine. The title was amended in 1997. Patron: the University Court. (Resolution 386, amended by 440).

1995   John Welsh, BSc, MB ChB, MRCP

Pathological Biochemistry
Founded in 1964. Patron: the University Court. (Ordinance 458-Glasgow 129).

1965   Henry Gemmell Morgan, BSc, MB ChB
1988   James Shepherd, BSc, MB ChB, PhD, FRCPath, FRCP, FRSE, FMedSci

Pathology
Founded in 1893. Patron: a Board of seven Curators, four appointed by the University Court and three by the managers of the Western Infirmary or their successors. The incumbent is a Pathologist to the Western Infirmary. (Ordinance 29 Glasgow 5, amended by Resolution 149).

1894   Joseph Coats, MD
1899   Sir Robert Muir, MA, MD, ScD, LLD, DCL, FRS: *later Dean of Faculties*
1936   John Shaw Dunn, MA, MD, MSc: *previously St Mungo-Notman Professor of Pathology*
1945   Daniel Fowler Cappell, CBE, MD, LLD: *later Dean of Faculties*
1967   John Russell Anderson, CBE, BSc, MD, LLD
1984   Sir Roderick Norman McIver MacSween, BSc, MD, FRCP, FIBiol, FRSE, FMedSci
2000   Barry Austin Gusterson, BSc, PhD, FRCPath

Pathology (St Mungo-Notman Chair)
Founded in 1911 and endowed by the Governors of St Mungo's College Glasgow. Patron: a Board of eleven Curators, seven appointed by the University Court and four by the Managers of the Royal Infirmary and Associated Hospitals or their successors. The Professor was a Pathologist to the Royal Infirmary. (Ordinance 34-Glasgow 10, amended by Resolution 149).

1911	John Hammond Teacher, MA, MD
1931	John Shaw Dunn, MA, MD, MSc: *later Professor of Pathology*
1937	John William Stewart Blacklock, MD: *later Professor of Pathology in St Batholomew's Hospital, London*
1948	George Lightbody Montgomery, MD, PhD: *later Professor of Pathology in the University of Edinburgh*
1954	Sir Thomas Symington, BSc, MD: *later Professor of Pathology in the British Postgraduate Medical Federation, London*
1970-1987	Robert Barclay Goudie, MD, FRSE

Pharmacology
Founded in 1964. Patron: the University Court. (Ordinance 460-Glasgow 130; amended by Resolution 2).

1968-1992 John Spence Gillespie, MB ChB, PhD, FRSE: *later Vice-Principal and Dean of Faculties*

Pharmacology
This additional Chair of Pharmacology was founded in 1988. Patron: the University Court. (Resolution 301).

1989   Trevor William Stone, BPharm, PhD, DSc

Physiology (Buchanan Chair)
Founded in 1965 and named after Andrew Buchanan (1798-1882), the first Professor of Physiology in the University, 1839-1876. Patron: the University Court. (Ordinance 523-Glasgow 151).

1966-1987 Ian Alexander Boyd, MD, PhD, DSc

Physiology (Regius Chair)
Founded in 1839 by Queen Victoria under the title Theory of Physic or Institutes of Medicine. The title was changed in 1893. Patron: the Crown.

1839	Andrew Buchanan, MD
1876	John Gray McKendrick, MD, LLD, FRS
1906	Diarmid Noel Paton, MD, BSc, LLD, FRS

1928   Edward Provan Cathcart, CBE, MD, DSc, LLD, FRS: *previously Professor of Physiological Chemistry*
1947   Robert Campbell Garry, MB ChB, DSc
1970   Otto Fred Hutter, BSc, PhD
1991   John C McGrath, BSc, PhD

Political Economy (Bonar-Macfie Chair)

Founded in 1962 as the James Bonar Chair of Economics. The title was changed to the Bonar-Macfie Chair of Political Economy in 1990. Patron: the University Court. (Ordinance 388-Glasgow 123, amended by Resolution 336).

1963-1982 Alexander Nove, BSc, DrAgr, FBA
1991   John F Ermisch, BS, MA, PhD
1995   Ian Wooton, MA, MPhil, PhD

Political Economy (Daniel Jack Chair)

Founded in 1985. Patron: the University Court. (Resolution 267).

1985   Andrew Stewart Skinner, MA, BLitt, FRSE, FBA: *later Adam Smith Professor of Political Economy, Clerk of Senate and Vice-Principal*
1994   V Anton Muscatelli, MA, PhD, FRSA

Political Economy (Adam Smith Chair)

A Lectureship was instituted in 1892. The chair was founded in 1896 and endowed by the gift of Andrew Stewart (1832-1901), iron and tube manufacturer in Glasgow. Patron: the University Court acting conjointly with one representative elected by the Merchant's House in Glasgow, one elected by the Trades House of Glasgow, and one elected by the Chamber of Commerce of Glasgow (Ordinance 149).

Lecturer
1892   William Smart, MA, DPhil

Professors
1896   William Smart, MA, DPhil
1915   William Robert Scott, MA, DPhil, LLD, LittD, DLitt, FRBA
1945   Alec Lawrence Macfie, MA, DLitt, LLD: *later Dean of Faculties*

1958   Thomas Wilson, OBE, MA, PhD, FBA

1985   David Anthony Vines, MA, PhD

1994   Andrew Stewart Skinner, MA, BLitt, FRSE, FBA: *previously Daniel Jack Professor of Political Economy and later Vice-Principal*

2000   Gary Koop, MA, PhD

Politics (James Bryce Chair)

Founded in 1965 as a Chair of Government, the designation was changed in 1970 to Politics. Patron: the University Court. (Ordinance 504-Glasgow 139, amended by Resolution 53).

1966   William James Millar Mackenzie, CBE, MA, LLD, DLitt, FBA: *later Edward Caird Professor of Politics*

1970-1984 Allan Meyers Potter, MA, PhD: *later Vice-Principal*

Politics (Edward Caird Chair)

In 1909, a Lectureship in Political Philosophy was founded and endowed from funds raised to commemorate the services of Edward Caird (1835-1908), Professor of Moral Philosophy in the University, 1866-1893. In 1960, the Lectureship was replaced by a Chair in Political and Social Theory. The title was changed to Political and Social Philosophy in 1965 and in 1970 to Politics. Patron: the University Court. (Ordinance 336-Glasgow 92; amended by Ordinance 504-Glasgow 139 and Resolution 52).

Lecturers

1909   Robert Alexander Duff, MA, DPhil

1926   Alexander Knox White, MA

1949   James Howard Warrender, MA

Professors

1960   David Daiches Raphael, MA, DPhil: *later Director and Professor of Philosophy in Imperial College of Science and Technology, London*

1970   William James Millar MacKenzie, CBE, MA, LLD, DLitt, FBA: *previously James Bryce Professor of Politics*

1974   Geraint Burton Parry, BSc, PhD

1985   William Lockley Miller, MA, PhD, FBA, FRSA, FRSE

Postgraduate Medical Education
Founded in 1971. Patron: the University Court. (Resolution 63).

1972	Eric Kennedy Cruickshank, OBE, MD
1980	Gerald Charles Timbury, OBE, MB ChB
1984	Kenneth Charles Calman, BSc, MD, PhD: *previously Professor of Medical Oncology in the University and later Chief Medical Officer of the Department of Health and Vice Chancellor of the University of Durham*
1989	Norman MacKay, MD, FRCP

Professional Legal Practice
Founded in 1984. Patron: the University Court. (Resolution 260).

1984-1993 James Alistair MacFarlane Inglis, CBE, MA, LLB: *simultaneously Professor of Conveyancing*

Protein Crystallography (Joseph Black Chair)
Founded in 1988. Patron: the University Court. (Resolution 300).

1989   Neil William Isaacs, BSc, PhD, FRSE

Protein Science
Patron: the University Court. (Resolution pending).

2000   Nicholas C Price, BA, MA, DPhil

Psychiatry
Founded with funds provided by the Khan Educational Fund for Psychiatric Medicine. Patron: the University Court. (Resolution pending).

1999   Janine Lynda Scott, MBBS, MD

Psychological Medicine
Founded in 1948. Patron: the University Court. (Ordinance 244-Glasgow 59).

1948   Thomas Ferguson Rodger, CBE, BSc, MB ChB
1973-2000 Sir Michael Richard Bond, MD, PhD, FRCS, FRCPsych, FRCP, DPM, FRSE: *later Vice-Principal*

Psychology
Founded in 1947. Patron: the University Court. (Ordinance 238-Glasgow 55).

1955	Ralph William Pickford, MA, PhD, DLitt
1973	Derek Wallace John Corcoran, BSc, PhD
1982	Anthony John Sanford, BSc, PhD, FBPSS

Psychology
This additional chair was founded in 1978. Patron: the University Court. (Resolution 192).

1979	Robert Maclaughlin Farr, MA, PhD
1986	Keith Oatley, BA, PhD
2000	Stefan Robert Schweinberger, DiplPsych, Dr rer soc

Psychology
Founded in 1994. Patron: the University Court. (Resolution 395).

1994	A Michael Burton, BSc, PhD, CPsychol

Public Health (Henry MEchan Chair)
Founded in 1923 and endowed by the gift of Sir Henry Mechan, DL, LLD, (1856-1943), engineer in Glasgow. Patron: the University Court (Ordinance 113-Glasgow 29, amended by Resolution 234).

1923	John Ronald Currie, MA, MD: *later Clerk of Senate*
1940	James MacAlister MacKintosh, MA, MD
1944	Thomas Ferguson, CBE, MD, DSc
1964	Thomas Anderson, CBE, MD
1972	Gordon Thallon Stewart, BSc, MD
1984	Anthony Johnson Hedley, MD, MRCP
1989	James McEwen, MB ChB, FFCM, MFOM, DIH, FMedSci
2000	David Goldberg, BSc, MB ChB, FRCP, MFPMH, FFPHM

Public Law
Founded in 1965. Patron: the University Court. (Ordinance 486-Glasgow 105).

1973-1986 Gordon Strachan Cowie, MA, LLB: *Advocate*

Radiation Oncology
Founded in 1985. Patron: the University Court. (Resolution 273).

1986   Ann Barrett, MD, FRCR, FRCP, FMedSci

Rheumatology (McLeod/Arthritis and Rheumatism Council Chair)
Founded in 1990 with a benefaction from the Arthritis and Rheumatism Council and private individuals. The Chair title recognises one of these individuals, Allan McLeod. Patron: the University Court. (Resolution 331).

1990   Roger Davidson Sturrock, MD, FRCP

Roman Law (Douglas Chair)
Founded originally in 1948 as the Douglas Chair of Civil Law, and endowed by the bequest of John Brown Douglas, solicitor, Glasgow. The title is to be changed to Roman Law in 2001. Patron: the University Court. (Ordinance 243-Glasgow 58, Resolution pending).

1957   Joseph Anthony Charles Thomas, MA, LLB: *Barrister*
1965   William Alexander Jardine Watson, MA, LLB, DPhil: *later Professor of Civil Law in the University of Edinburgh*
1969-1999 William Morrison Gordon, MA, LLB, PhD, FRSE
2001   Olivia F Robinson, MA, PhD (from August)

Russian and East European Studies (Alexander Nove Chair)
The Institute of Soviet and East European Studies was founded in 1960 and changed its name in 1994 to the Centre for Russian and East European Studies and in 1999 again, to the Department of Central and East European Studies. In 1996, the Alexander Nove Chair was established in memory of Professor Alexander Nove (1915-1994), the distinguished scholar of Russian, who held the James Bonar Chair of Economics, 1963-1982. Patron the University Court (Resolution 426).

1997   Johan H L Löwenhardt, MA, PhD

Scottish History and Literature
Founded in 1913 and endowed by a grant from the receipts of the Glasgow Exhibition of 1911 and by contributions from the Merchants House of Glasgow and other donors. The Departments of Scottish History and Literature became administratively separate in 1971 but the Chair remains as Scottish History and Literature. Patron: the University Court. (Ordinance 40-Glasgow 13).

1913 Sir Robert Sangster Rait, MA, LLD: *later Historiographer Royal for Scotland and Principal of the University*

1930 John Duncan Mackie, CBE, MC, MA, LLD: *later Dean of Faculties; and Historiographer Royal for Scotland*

1957 George Smith Pryde, MA, PhD

1962 Archibald Alexander McBeth Duncan, MA, FBA, FRHistS, FRSE: *later Clerk of Senate and Dean of Faculties*

1994 Edward James Cowan, MA

Scottish Literature

Patron: the University Court. (Resolution pending).

1995 Thomas Douglas Gifford, MA, PhD, FRSE

Slavonic Languages and Literature

A lectureship in Russian was founded in 1917 and endowed by Sir William Weir, later Lord Weir of Eastwood (1877-1959), engineer, and other donors. The Chair of Slavonic Languages and Literature was founded in 1974. Patron: the University Court. (Resolution 125).

Lecturers

1917 Hugh George Brennan, MA, L-es-L, BSc

1943 George Arthur Birkett, MA

1949-1974 Victor Edward Joseph Holttum, BA

Professors

1975 Peter Henry, MA

1993 James Michael Kirkwood, MA, DipSocSt

1999 Robert Charles Porter, BA, PhD

Small Animal Clinical Studies

Founded in 1951 as the Chair of Veterinary Surgery. Patron: the University Court. (Ordinance 275-Glasgow 69, amended by Resolution 24).

1951 Sir William Lee Weipers, BSc, DUniv, FRCVS, DVSM: *later Dean of Faculties*

1974 Donald Douglas Lawson, BSc, MRCVS

1987 Neil Thomson Gorman, BVSc, PhD, FRCVS

1996 David Bennett, BSc, BVetMed, PhD, DSAO, MRCVS

Social Policy (Strathclyde Region Chair)
Founded in 1997. Patron: the University Court. (Resolution 443).

1997   Sheila I Riddell, BA, PhD

Social Policy and Social Work
A School of Social Study and Training was founded in 1912, under the auspices of the University, to meet the demand for social workers, connected chiefly with Queen Margaret College Settlement. In October 1943 the School of Social Study and Training became a department of the University. The Chair was founded in 1971. Patron: the University Court. (Resolution 58).

Director of Studies
1912   John Harry Jones, MA, LLD
1920   James Cunnison, OBE, MA, LLD

Director of School
1944   James Cunnison, OBE, MA, LLD
1946   Idris Wynn Phillips, MA
1960-1971 John Anderson Mack, MA

Professors
1972   Frederick Morris Martin, BA, PhD
1987   Rex Carroll Taylor, BA, PhD: *also Director of the Crichton Campus from 1997*

Social Work
Patron: the University Court. (Resolution pending).

2000   Joan E Orme, BA

Sociology
Founded in 1965. Patron: the University Court. (Ordinance 505-Glasgow 140).

1972   John Eric Thomas Eldridge, MA, BSc

Spanish (Ivy McClelland Research Chair)
Founded in 1995. Patron: the University Court. (Resolution 407). (See also Hispanic Studies (Stevenson Chair).

1995   Ann L Mackenzie, MA

Statistics
Founded in 1965. Patron: the University Court. (Ordinance 524-Glasgow 152).

1966   Samuel David Silvey, MA, PhD
1988   Donald Michael Titterington, BSc, PhD, FRSE

Strategic Management
Patron: the University Court. (Resolution pending).

1999   James Hand Taggart, BSc, MA, MBA, PhD

Study of The Child (St Kentigern Chair)
Founded in 1992 and endowed by the Archdiocese of Glasgow. Patron: the University Court. (Resolution 356).

1992   Stewart Asquith, MA, PhD: *later Professor of Social Work*
1999   Malcolm Hill, MA, PhD, DipAppSocSt: *previously Professor of Social Work*

Surgery (Regius Chair)
Founded in 1815 by King George III. Patron: the Crown.

1815   John Burns, MD, FRS
1850   James Adair Lawrie, MA, MD
1860   Joseph Lister, MB, FRS: *later Baron Lister of Lyme Regis*
1869   Sir George Husband Baird Macleod, MD, LLD
1892   Sir William Macewen, MD, LLD, FRS
1924   Archibald Young, BSc, MB, CM
1939   Sir Charles Frederick William Illingworth, CBE, MD, ChM, DSc, LLD: *later Dean of Faculties*
1964-1981 Sir Andrew Watt Kay, MD, ChM, DSc
1999   William David George, MB, MS, FRCS

Surgery (St Mungo Chair)
Founded in 1911 and endowed by the trustees of Henry Muirhead, MD, LLD (d.1890), of Bothwell. Patron: a Board of eleven Curators, seven appointed by the University Court and four by the Managers of the Royal Infirmary. (Ordinance 34-Glasgow 10).

1911	Robert Kennedy, MA, MD, DSc
1924	Peter Paterson, MB, CM
1935	John Adam Gib Burton, MB, LLD
1953	William Arthur Mackey, TD, MB ChB
1972	Leslie Harold Blumgart, BDS, MD
1979	David Craig Carter, MD
1989	Timothy Gordon Cooke, MD, FRCS

Surgery
Founded in 1980. Patron: the University Court. (Resolution 218).

1980-1999 William David George, MB, MS, FRCS: *later Regius Professor of Surgery*

Systematic Theology
Founded in 1934 in consequence of the union of the United Free Church with the Church of Scotland. Patron: the University Court, acting on the nomination of the General Assembly of the Church of Scotland. (Ordinance 184-Glasgow 45, amended by Ordinance 284-General 10, abolished by Ordinance Glasgow 168 of 24 March 1970).

1935-1947 John Gervase Riddell, MA, DD: *later Professor of Divinity*
1948-1969 Ian Henderson, MA, DD

Town and Regional Planning
Founded in 1965. Patron: the University Court. (Ordinance 525-Glasgow 153).

1965   Sir Robert Grieve, MA
1974   Gordon Campbell Cameron, BA
1980-1991 David Vernon Donnison, BA, DLitt, LLD

Transfusion Medicine
Founded in 1995. Patron: the University Court. (Resolution 413).

1996   Ian M Franklin, BSc, MB ChB, PhD

Urban Economic Development
Founded in 1996. Patron: the University Court. (Resolution 424).

1996   Ivan N Turok, MSc, PhD

Veterinary Anatomy
Founded in 1975. Patron: the University Court. (Resolution 144).

1975-2000 Norman Gray Wright, BVMS, PhD, DVM, MRCVS, FRCPath, FRSE, FIBiol

Veterinary Informatics and Epidemiology
Founded in 1997 and joint-funded with the University of Strathclyde. Patron: the University
Courts of the Universities of Glasgow and Strathclyde. (Resolution 439).

1997   Stuart W J Reid, BVMS, PhD, MRCVS

Veterinary Medicine
Founded in 1960. Patron: the University Court. (Ordinance 351-Glasgow 103, amended
by Resolution 24).

1961   William Ian Mackay McIntyre, PhD, MRCVS
1985   Maxwell Murray, BVMS, PhD, DVM, FRCPath, FRSE, MRCVS

Veterinary Parasitology
Founded in 1978. Patron: the University Court. (Resolution 195).

1979   George Macdonald Urquhart, PhD, MRCVS
1991   Andrew Tait, BSc, PhD, FRSE

Veterinary Pathology
Founded in 1951. Patron: the University Court. (Ordinance 276-Glasgow 70, amended by Resolution 24).

1951   John William Emslie, BSc, MRCVS
1968   William Fleming Hoggan Jarrett, PhD, MRCVS
1990   David E Onions, BVSc, PhD, FRSE

Veterinary Physiology
Founded in 1962. Patron: the University Court. (Ordinance 372-Glasgow 121, amended by Resolution 24).

1963   William Mulligan, MSc, PhD: *later Vice-Principal*
1995   Peter H Holmes, BVMS, PhD, MRCVS, FRSE: *later Vice-Principal*

Virology
Founded in 1958. Patron: the University Court. (Ordinance 319-Glasgow 91).

1958   Michael George Parke Stoker, MD, MA: *later Visiting Professor of Zoology and Comparative Anatomy in University College, London*
1968   John Herbert Subak-Sharpe, CBE, BSc, PhD, FIBiol, FRSE
1995   John B Clements, BSc, PhD, FRSA, FRSE

World Religions for Peace
Founded in 1999 with an endowment from the Weisfeld Foundation. Patron: the University Court. (Resolution 458).

2000   Perry Horst Schmidt-Leukel, DipTheol, MA, DTheol, Drhabil

Zoology (John Graham Kerr Chair)
Founded in 1965. Patron: the University Court. (Ordinance 520-Glasgow 148).

1979-1983 Keith Vickerman, PhD, DSc, FRSE, FRS
1985-2000 David William Thomasson Crompton, MA, PhD, ScD, FBiol, FRSE

Zoology (Regius Chair)

Founded in 1807 by King George III under the title of Natural History. In 1903, when the Chair of Geology was founded, the title was changed to Zoology. Patron: the Crown.

1807	Lockhart Muirhead, MA, LLD
1829	William Couper, MA, MD
1857	Henry Darwin Rogers, MA, LLD
1866	John Young, MD: *also Keeper of the Hunterian Museum*
1902	Sir John Graham Kerr, MA, LLD, FRS: *later Member of Parliament for the Scottish Universities*
1935	Edward Hindle, MA, ScD, PhD, FRS: *later Scientific Director of the Zoological Gardens, London*
1944	Charles Maurice Yonge, CBE, PhD, DSc, FRS
1965	David Richmond Newth, BSc, PhD
1984-1998	Keith Vickerman, PhD, DSc, FRSE, FRS: *previously John Graham Kerr Professor of Zoology*

Personal Professorships 1995-2001

On 15 February 1995, the Court agreed that from 1 October 1995 titular professors should be called Professors and should hold personal professorships. As their name suggests, these are personal to their holders and cease to exist if the holder leaves the University or transfers to another post in the University such as an established chair. At that time the Court desired to remove distinctions between appointed professors and personal professors, and (inter alia) agreed that personal professors should be ex-officio members of Senate.

Roger L P Adams, MA, DPhil, FRSE, *Nucleic Acid Biochemistry*	1996
J Stewart Aitchison, BSc, PhD, CPhys, MInstP, MIEEE, *Photonics*	1999
Arthur C Allison, BSc, DipNumMath, PhD, FBCS, *Computing Science and later Vice-Principal*	1995-2001
Anne H Anderson, MA, PhD, *Psychology*	1997
John M Arnold, BEng, PhD, *Applied Electromagnetics*	1995
Asen Mihailou Asenov, MSc, PhD, MIEEE, *Device Modelling*	2000
Stewart Asquith, MA, PhD: *Social Work*	1996
Jeremy Bagg, BDS, PhD, FDSRCSEd, MCRPath, FDS RCPS, FRCPath, *Clinical Microbiology*	1999
John M G Barclay, MA, PhD, *New Testament and Christian Origins*	2000

John R Barker, BSc, MSc, PhD, FBIS, FRSE, *Electronics* 1995
A John Barlow, BSc, PhD, DIC, ACGI, MIEE, CEng, *Electronics* 1995-1999
Lawrence D Barron, BSc, DPhil, MInstP, FRSE, *Physical Chemistry* 1995
J David Barry, BSc, PhD, *Molecular Parasitology* 1996
Philip B Beaumont, MEc, PhD, *Employee Relations* 1995
Steven P Beaumont, MA, PhD, CEng, MIEE, *Nanoelectronics* 1995
Peter O Behan, MD, FACP, FRCP, *Neurology* 1995-1999
Wilhelmina M H Behan, MB ChB, MD, FRCP, FRCPath, *Muscle Pathology* 2000
Christopher J Berry, BA, PhD, *Political Theory* 1995
Paul C Bishop, BA, DPhil, *to be decided (from August)* 2001
Brian J Bluck, DSc, PhD, FRSE, FgS, *Sedimentation and Tectonics* 1995
J Drummond Bone, MA, *English Literature and later Vice-Principal* 1995-2000
Adrian W Bowman, BSc, DipMathStat, PhD, *Statistics* 1995
John S Boyd, BVMS, PhD, MRCVS, *Veterinary Clinical Anatomy* 1995
John A Briggs, BA, PhD, MH, *Geography* 1996
Kenneth A Brown, MSc, PhD, *Mathematics* 1995
Robert Brown, BSc, PhD, *Cancer Therapeutics* 1999
S Moira Brown, BSc, PhD, FRCPath, FRSE, *Neurovirology* 1996
G G Browning, MD, FRCS: *Otorhinolaryngology* 1995-1998
G Kenneth S Browning, BSc, PhD, *Computer Publishing* 1995-2000
Muffy Calder, BSc, PhD, *Formal Methods* 1999
Ailsa M Campbell, BSc, PhD, *Biochemical Immunology* 1998
Maria Saveria Campo, BSc, PhD, *Viral Oncology* 2000
Stuart Carmichael, BVMS, MVM, DSAO, *Veterinary Clinical Studies* 1999
Robert P Carroll, *Hebrew and Semitic Studies* 1995-2000
Susan Castillo, BA, MPhil, PhD, *John Nichol Professor of American Literature* 2001
John M Caughie, MA, *Film and Television Studies* 1995
John N Chapman, MA, PhD, MInstP, FRSE, *Physics* 1995
John R Coggins, MA, PhD, FRSE, *Molecular Enzymology* 1995
Samuel K Cohn, MA, PhD, *Medieval History* 1995
John MC Connell, MD, FRCP, *Endocrinology* 1995
Joseph D Connolly, DSc, PhD, CChem, FRSE, FRSC, *Organic Chemistry* 1995
Graham H Coombs, BSc, PhD, *Biochemical Parasitology* 1995
Alan Cooper, BSc, PhD, CPhys, FInstP, CChem, FRSC, *Biophysical Chemistry* 1998
Johnathan Mark Cooper, BSc, MSc, PhD, *Bioelectronics and Bioengineering* 1998
Christine A Corrin, BA, DPhil, *Feminist Politics* 2000
Michael John Cowling, BEng, PhD, CEng, MIM, *Marine Technology* 1995
Alan J Craven, MA, PhD, *Physics* 1998

Richard Cronin, BA, BLitt, *English Literature*		2000
Margaret Anne Crowther, BA, DPhil, FRHS, *Social History*		1995
Alan Crozier, BSc, PhD, *Plant Biochemistry and Human Nutrition*		2000
Purnendu Kumar Das, BE, ME, PhD, CEng, *Marine Structures*		2001
Christine T H Davies, BA, MA, PhD, *Physics*		1999
John H Davies, BA, MA, PhD, *Physical Electronics*		2000
Richard M De La Rue, BSc, MASc, PhD, CEng, MIEE, FRSE, *Optoelectronics*		1995
Eileen Devaney, BSc, PhD, *to be decided (from August)*		2001
James H Dickson, BSc, MA, PhD, FLS, FRSE, *Archaeobotany and Plant Systematics*		1997
Anna F Dominiczak, MD, MRCPath, FRCP, *Cardio Vascular Medicine*		1997
Julian A T Dow, MA, PhD, *Molecular and Integrative Physiology*		1999
James L Duncan, BVMS, PhD, MRCVS, *Clinical Veterinary Parasitology*		1995
Richard M Elliott, BSc, DPhil, *Molecular Virology*		1995
D Alan Ervine, BSc, PhD, *Water Engineering*		1997
Anthony E Fallick, BSc, PhD, FRSE, *Isotope Geosciences*		1996
Lindsay A Farmer, LLB, MPhil, PhD, *Law*		1999
Michael J G Farthing, BSc, MD, FRCP, *Medicine*		2000
David R Fearn, BSc, PhD, *Applied Mathematics*		1995
Gordon S Fell, BSc, PhD, FDS, RCS, RCPS, *Pathological Biochemistry*		1995-1998
Harvie Ferguson, MA, PhD, DSc, *Sociology (from August)*		2001
Charles A Fewson, BSc, PhD, FIBiol, CBiol, FRSE, *Microbial Biochemistry*		1995
W Fitch, BSc, MB ChB, PhD, FCAnaesth, RCOG: *Anaesthesia*		1995-1998
Julie Lydia Fitzpatrick, BVMS, PhD, *Farm Animal Medicine*		1999
Peter Flynn, MA, *Latin American Studies*		1995
Ian Ford, BSc, PhD, FRSE, Statistics: *later Professor of Biostatistics*		1995-1998
Margaret C Frame, BSc, PhD, *Molecular Cell Biology*		2000
J H Freer, MSc, PhD, *Bacterial Toxinology*		1995-2000
David P Frisby, BSc, PhD, DSSc, *Sociology*		1995
Andrew Furlong, BSc, PhD, *Sociology*		2000
Robert W Furness, BSc, PhD, *Seabird and Fishing Interactions*		1998
Simon C Garrod, MA, PhD, *Cognitive Psychology*		1995
Alexander F Garvie, MA, FRSE, *Classics*		1998-1999
Curtis G Gemmell, BSc, PhD, *Bacterial Infection and Epidemiology*		2000
Johanna M Geyer-Kordesch, MA, PhD, MedHabil, FRHistS, *History of European Medicine*		2000
David A F Gillespie, BSc, PhD, *Transcription and Cell Cycle Control*		2000
Christopher J Gilmore, BSc, PhD, CChem, FRSC, *Crystallography*		1998
Brian Girvin, BA, MA, PhD, *Comparative Politics*		2000
Robina Goodlad, MA, MPhil, *Housing and Urban Studies*		1998

Gwyn W Gould, BSc, PhD, *Membrane Biology* — 1997

David I Graham, MB ChB, PhD, FRCP, FRCPath, FRSE, *Neuropathology* — 1995

John Paxton Grant, BA, LLB, PhD, *Public International Law* — 1995-1999

David R Green, BSc, PhD, MSc, CEng, FIStructE, *Structural Engineering and later Vice-Principal* — 1995

Ian Griffiths, BVMS, PhD, FRCVS, *Comparative Neurology* — 1995

Paul Hagan, BSc, PhD, *Parasitology* — 2000

John W Hancock, BSc, PhD, *Mechanical Engineering* — 1995

Philip W Hanlon, BSc, MD, MPH, *Public Health* — 1999

William S Hanson, BA, PhD, *Roman Archaeology* — 2000

Malcolm Hill, MA, PhD, DipAppSocSt: *later St Kentigern Professor of the Study of the Child* — 1996-1999

Edith M Hillan, PhD, MSc, PhD, DipLSc, RGN, RSCN, RM, *Midwifery* — 1998

W Stewart Hillis, MB ChB, FRCP, *Cardiovascular and Exercise Medicine* — 1997

David Hole, MSc, MFPHM, *Epidemiology and Biostatistics* — 2001

James Hough, BSc, PhD, FRSE, FRAS, *Physics* — 1995

David C Houston, BSc, DPhil, *to be decided (from August)* — 2001

Joseph Houston, MA, BD, DPhil, *Philosophical Theology* — 2000

Felicity A Huntingford, BA, DPhil, FRSE, *Functional Ecology* — 1995

Charles N Ironside, BSc, PhD, *Quantum Electronics* — 1999

Howard Jacobs, BSc, PhD, *Molecular Genetics* — 2000

Sergei Merkulov, MSc, PhD, *Pure Mathematics* — 2000

James Oswald Jarrett, BVMS, PhD, MRCVS, FRSE, *Comparative Virology* — 1995

David Jasper, MA, BD, PhD, *Literature and Theology* — 1998

Gareth I Jenkins, BSc, PhD, *Plant Cell and Molecular Biology* — 2000

Christopher Wiliam Johnson, MSc, MA, DPhil, *Computing Science* — 1997

Barry T Jones, BSc, PhD, *Psychology* — 1997

Kim Kaiser, BSc, PhD, *Neurogenetics* — 1998

Christian J Kay, MA, DipGenLing, *English Language* — 1996

Adrian Joseph Kearns, BA, *Urban Studies* — 2000

James G Kellas, MA, PhD, FRHistS, FSA, *Politics* — 1995

Malcolm W Kennedy, BSc, PhD, *Infection Biology* — 1996

Lawrence J Keppie, MA, DPhil, *Roman History and Archaeology* — 1999

Denis F Kinane, BDS, PhD, FDSRCS, FDSRCPS, *Periodontology and Oral Immunology* — 1995

James Kirk, MA, PhD, DLitt, *Scottish History* — 1999

A Bernard Knapp, MA, PhD, *Mediterranean Archaeology* — 1999

Walter Kolch, MD, *Molecular Cell Biology* — 2000

John R Kusel, BA, PhD, *Cellular Biochemistry* 1996
Peter Langhorne, MD, PhD, FRCP, *to be decided (from August)* 2001
Peter J R Laybourn, MA, PhD, *Electronic Engineering* 1995
Robin E Leake, MA, DPhil, *Endocrine Oncology* 1998
Kenneth DW Ledingham, PhD, DSc, FInstP, *to be decided (from August)* 2001
Kennedy R Lees, BSc, MD, FRCP, *Cerebrovascular Medicine* 1999
William R Lees, MD, FRCPath, FRSE: Ophthalmic Pathology 1995-1998
William F Lever, MA, DPhil, *Urban Studies* 1995
John G Lindsay, BSc, PhD, *Medical Biochemistry* 1995
Andrew R Long, MA, PhD, CPhys, MInstP, *to be decided (from August)* 2001
Gordon D O Lowe, MD, FRCP, *Vascular Medicine* 1995
Douglas K Macbeth, MSc, CEng, MIEE, MBIN, MInstPS, *Supply Chain Management* 1995
Kenneth E L McColl, MD, FRCP, *Gastroenterology* 1995
James McCulloch, BSc, PhD, *Neuroscience* 1995
D Gordon MacDonald, BDS, PhD, FRCPath, FDSRCPS, *Oral Pathology* 1995
P W MacFarlane, BSc, PhD, FBCS, CEng, FRSE, *Electrocardiology* 1995
T Wallace MacFarlane, DDS, DSc, FRCPath, FDSRCPS, *Oral Microbiology* 1995
Bartholomew J McGettrick, BSc, MEd, *Education* 1999
Alan McGregor, MA, *Economic Development* 1995
Colin R McInnes, BSc, PhD, *Space Systems Engineering* 1999
James R B McIntosh, MA, PhD, *Social Policy* 2000
Neil P McKeganey, BA, MSc, PhD, *Drug Misuse Research* 1997
Qunitin A McKellar, *Veterinary Pharmacology* 1996-1997
Margaret R MacLean, BSc, PhD, *Pulmonary Pharmacology* 2000
Malcolm D McLeod, MA, BLitt, FRSE, *African Studies and later Vice-Principal* 1995
Michael K C MacMahon, BA, PhD, DipLing, *Phonetics* 1997
John McMurray, BSc, MD, ChB, FRCP, FESC, *Medical Cardiology* 1999
Willy T Maley, BA, PhD, *Renaissance Studies* 1999
James Malley, BA, MPhil, PhD, *Economics* 1999
John H Marsh, BA, MEng, PhD, CEng, MIEE, *Optoelectronic Systems* 1996
William Martin, BSc, PhD, *Cardiovascular Pharmacology* 1995
Ian M Maudlin, MSc, PhD, *Molecular Entomology* 1997-2000
Evan Mawdsley, MA, PhD, FRHistS, *International History* 1999
Thomas Melham, BSc, PhD, *Computing Science* 1998
Neil Metcalfe, BSc, PhD, *to be decided (from August)* 2001
Robert F Miles, BSc, PhD, *Sociology* 1995
Keith Millar, BA, PhD, CPsychol, FBPSS, *Behavioural Science* 1995
T J E Miller, BSc, PhD, CEng, MIEE, SenMemIEEE, *Electrical Engineering* 1995

Graeme Milligan, BSc, PhD, *Molecular Pharmacology* 1995
Elizabeth A Moignard, MA, DPhil, *Classical Art and Archaeology* 2000
Ilya Molchanov, Dr rer nat habil, PhD, *Applied Probability* 1998
Patricia Monaghan, BSc, PhD, *Animal Ecology* 1997
Hywel Morgan, BSc, PhD, CPhys, MInstP, *to be decided (from August)* 2001
Brian Morris, BSc, PhD, *to be decided (from August)* 2001
Jillian M Morrison, MB ChB, MSc, PhD, DRCOG, DCH, FRCGP, *to be decided*
   (from August) 2001
Michael S Moss, MA, *Archival Studies* 1997
Jeremy C Mottram, BSc, PhD, *Molecular and Cellular Parasitology* 2000
Allan M Mowat, BSc, MB ChB, PhD, FRCPath, *Mucosal Immunology* 2000
James L Murdoch, LLM, *Public Law* 1998
Gordon Douglas Murray, *Medical Statistics* 1996-1996
T Stuart Murray, MD, PhD, FRCP, FRCGP, DRCOG, *General Practice* 1995
David J Murray-Smith, MSc, PhD, CEng, FIEE, MInstMC, *Engineering Systems*
   and Control 1995
Nanette Mutrie, MEd, PhD, DPE, DipEd, *Physical Activity and Health Science* 2000
Andrew S Nash, BVMS, PhD, CBiol, FIBiol, MRCVS, *Small Animal Medicine* 1995
James C Neil, BSc, PhD, *Virology and Molecular Oncology* 1995
James A R Nicoll, BSc, MD, FRCPath, *to be decided (from August)* 2001
Hugh G Nimmo, MA, PhD, FRSA, *Plant Biochemistry* 1995
Andrea Nolan, MVB, PhD, DVA, *Veterinary Pharmacology* 1998
John O'Reilly, PhD, DSc, CEng, FIMA, MIEE, MIEEE, *Control Engineering* 1996
Patrick J O'Dwyer, MB BCh, BAO, MCh, FRCS, *Gastrointestinal Surgery* 1998
A Esin Örücü, BA, LLB, PhD, *Comparative Law* 1995
Peter J O'Shaughnessy, BSc, PhD, *Reproductive Biology* 1997
Robert O Owens, MA, DPhil, *Physics* 1995
Christopher J Packard, BSc, PhD, MCCPath, DSc, FRCPath:
   Pathological Biochemistry 1995-1997
Ronan Paddison, BA, PhD, *Geography* 1997
Miles J Padgett, MSc, PhD, *Physics* 1999
James J Parkins, BSc, PhD, CBiol, FIBiol, *Animal Health* 1995
John B Parr, BSc, MA, PhD, *Regional and Urban Economics* 1995
Anthony P Payne, BSc, PhD, *Anatomy* 1995
Iain W Percy-Robb, MB ChB, PhD, FRCP, FRCPath, *Pathological Biochemistry* 1995
John C Peterson, BSc, MA, PhD, *Politics* 1999
R Stephen Phillips, BSc, PhD, CBiol, FIBiol, *Parasitology* 1995
Gregory Philo, BSc, PhD, *to be decided (from August)* 2001

Stephen J Pride, BSc, PhD, FRSE, *Mathematics* 1995
Roy Rampling, BSc, PhD, MSc, MBBS, *Neuro-Oncology* 2000
Jacqueline Reid, BVMS, PhD, MRCVS, DVA, *Veterinary Anaesthesia* 1998
Mark Roberts, BSc, PhD, *Molecular Bacteriology* 1999
Norna A Robertson, BSc, PhD, *Experimental Physics* 1999
David J Robins, PhD, DSc, FRSC, CChem, *Bio-organic Chemistry* 1995
Jay R Rosenberg, BA, PhD, *Neurophysiology* 1995
W P Saunders, BDS, PhD, FDSRCS: Endodontology 1995-1999
Larry Schaaf, *Research Professor in the Faculty of Arts* 1999
Philippe G Schyns, PhD,*Visual Cognition* 1998
E Marian Scott, BSc, PhD, *Environmental Statistics* 2000
R D Scott, BSc, PhD, CPhys, FInstP, FRSE, *Nuclear Science* 1995-1998
Maria Slowey, BComm, DipSocSc, MLitt, *Adult and Continuing Education* 1996
Alan G R Smith, MA, PhD, FRHistS, FRSE, *Early Modern History* 1995
Godfrey L Smith, BSc, PhD, *Cardiovascular Physiology* 1998
Hamilton Smith, BSc, PhD, CChem, FRSC, FRCPath, FRSE, *Forensic Medicine* 1995-1999
Jeremy J Smith, BA, MPhil, PhD, *English Philology* 2000
Kenway M Smith, BSc, PhD, FRSE, *Physics* 1995
Patrick F Smith, MA, MSc, PhD, *Mathematics* 1995
S E Solomon, BSc, PhD, WPSA, WOSMG, *Poultry Science* 1995
Neil C Spurway, MA, PhD, *Exercise Physiology* 1996
Richard F Stalley, MA, Bphil, *Ancient Philosophy* 1997
C R Stanley, BEng, PhD, CEng, MIEE, MIEE, CPhys, MInstP,
    Semiconductor Materials 1995
Michael J Stear, BSc, PhD, *Immunogenetics* 1999
Kenneth W Stephen, BDS, DDSc, HDD, RCPS, FDSRCS, *Dental Public Health* 1995
Duncan E S Stewart-Tull, MA, PhD, *Microbial Immunology* 1995-2000
Raymond Stokes, MA, Phd, *to be decided (from August)* 2001
David H Stone, BSc, MD, FRCP, FFPHM, FRCPCH, *Paediatric Epidemiology* 2000
Martin Sullivan, BVMS, PhD, DVR, MRCVS, DipECVDI, *Veterinary Surgery
    and Diagnostic Imaging* 2000
David J Taylor, MA, VetMB, PhD, *Veterinary Bacteriology and Public Health* 1999
Neil Campbell Thomson, MD, ChB, FRCP, *Respiratory Medicine* 2001
Nigel R Thorp, BA, MA, PhD, *History of Art* 2000
Hillel H Ticktin, BA, BSc, *Marxist Studies* 2000
Andrew J Todd, BSc, MB, BS, PhD, *Neuroscience (from August)* 2001
Janet Todd, *English Literature* 2000
Richard H Trainor, MA, DPhil, FRHistS, *Social History and later Vice-Principal* 1995-2000

Mark G Ward, BA, *German Language and Literature* 1997
Susan A Ward, BSc, MA, DPhil, *Exercise Science and Medicine* 1998
David A Watt, BSc, PhD, DipCompSc, MBCS, *Computing Science* 1995
Jonathan MR Weaver, MA, DPhil, *to be decided (from August)* 2001
Richard Y Weaver, MBA, *Entrepreneurship* 1999
Geoffrey Webb, PhD, DSc, CChem, FRSC, FRSE, *Catalytic Science* 1995
Jeffrey R L Webb, BSc, DPhil, FRSE, *Mathematics* 1995
Raymond C Welland, BSc, MSc, MBCS, *Software Engineering* 2000
Robert J White, BSc, PhD, *Gene Transcription* 2000
Stephen L White, MA, PhD, DPhil, *Government* 1995
Rex R Whitehead, DSc, PhD, FRSE, *Theoretical Physics* 1995
Brian Whiting, MD, FRCP, FFPM, *Clinical Pharmacology* 1995
J Eric Wilkinson, BSc, MEd, PhD, CPsychol, *Education* 1998
John M Winfield, BSc, PhD, ARCS, CChem, FRSC, *Inorganic Chemistry* 1995
Duncan Wu, MA, DPhil, *English Literature* 1999-2000
Daniel Greer Young, MB ChB, FRCS, FRCPH, DTM&H, *Surgical Paediatrics* 1995-1998

Endowed Lectureships, Assistantships and Demonstratorships

Arnott and Thomson Demonstratorship in Experimental Physics

Founded in 1875 and endowed by Sir William Thomson, Professor of Natural Philosophy in the University, and Mrs Arnott, widow of Dr Neil Arnott, founder of the Arnott Prizes, for the encouragement of the study of Experimental Physics. The Demonstratorship was attached to the Physical Laboratory of the University. The holder was appointed annually by the Professor of Natural Philosophy, subject to the approval of the University Court. His duties were to perform, and direct the performances of, experimental research in the Physical Laboratory under the direction of the Professor, to give practical laboratory courses suitable for Medical and Engineering students and to take part in the teaching of the Natural Philosophy Class if required by the Professor, and in such a way and at such times as the Senatus may appoint.

1875	James Thomson Bottomley, MA, DSc, FRS
1899	Sir James Wallace Peck, MA: *later Secretary of the Scottish Education Department*
1903	James Muir, MA, DSc: *later Professor of Natural Philosophy in the Royal Technical College*
1906	James Gordon Gray, BSc: *later Professor of Applied Physics*
1908-1940	George Edwin Allan, DSc

*Barclay Lectureship in Surgery and Orthopaedics
in Relation to Infancy and Childhood*

Founded in 1919 by Robert Francis Barclay, LLB 1892, LLD 1935, writer in Glasgow. In 1956 a separate Lectureship in Orthopaedics was instituted. Patron: a Committee of representatives of the Senatus, the University Court, and the Royal Hospital for Sick Children, Glasgow.

1919	Alexander Maclennan, MB
1938	Matthew White, MA, MB
1954	Wallace Milne Dennison, MD
1956	Wallace Milne Dennison, MD *(Surgery)*
1956	Noel Jackson Blockey, MB, MChOrth *(Orthopaedics)*
1987	Michael GH Smith, MB ChB
1996	Robert Carachi, MD, PhD, FRCS

William Baxter Demonstratorship in Geology

Founded in 1888 and endowed by the bequest of William Baxter. Patron: the Senate. The regulations for the award of the Demonstratorship were approved by the University Court on 16 December 1940.

1921	John Weir, MA
1923	W J MacCallien, BSc
1926	Duncan Leitch, BSc
1929	James H M McNaughton
1931	Samuel Elder, BSc
1936	Cyril G Dixon, BSc
1938	Eric O Lundholm, BSc
1946	Alexander Simpson, BSc
1947	Gordon Y Craig, BSc
1949-1951	Alexander M Honeyman, MA, BSc
1957	Ian B Paterson
1968	Elizabeth M Graham, BSc
1972	Ian R Vann, BSc
1976-1978	David R Atkins, BSc
1985-1986	Paul G Nicholson, BSc

Lectureships in Pathological Biochemistry

Endowed by an anonymous donor, who in 1925 established a Medical Research Fund for the provision, in one or more of the Glasgow Hospitals connected with the University, of professorships or lectureships designed for the advancement of medical knowledge by means of biochemical or other special methods of scientific study and research. Three lectureships have been established.

Western Infirmary

1925	Stephen Veitch Telfer, BSc, MB ChB
1951	Edward Bruce Hendry, BSc, PhD, MB ChB
1974	Adam Fleck, BSc, MB ChB, PhD

Royal Infirmary

1926	Sir David Paton Cuthbertson, BSc, MB ChB
1934	Alan Bruce Anderson, BSc, PhD, MRCS, LRCP
1944-1966	James Caithness Eaton, BSc, MB ChB

Royal Hospital For Sick Children
1928   Noah Morris, BSc, MB, PhD
1938-1965 Harry Ellis Charter Wilson, MB, DSc
1967-1998 Robert W Logan, MB ChB, BSc

Maurice Bloch Lectureship

Founded in 1956 and endowed from a trust established by Sir Maurice Bloch (d. 1964), distiller in Glasgow. Patron: the University Court. The endowment originally provided for an annual lecture on the general subject 'Medicine in relation to the Community'. The funds in 2001 were used for PhD studentships.

1957   Lord Cohen of Birkenhead
1958   John Cruickshank, CBE, MD, LLD: *Emeritus Professor of Bacteriology in the University of Aberdeen*
1959   Sir James Learmonth, KCVO, CBE, MD, ChM, DSc, LLD: *sometime Professor of Surgery in the University of Edinburgh*
1960   Sir Russell Brain, Bt, DM, LLD, DCL: *previously President of the Royal College of Physicians*
1961   Sir Aubrey Lewis, MD: *Professor of Psychiatry in the British Postgraduate School of the University of London*
1963   Alastair Goold MacGregor, BSc, MD: *Regius Professor of Materia Medica and Therapeutics in the University of Aberdeen*
1965   David Waldron Smithers, MD: *Director of the Radiotherapy Department at the Royal Marsden Hospital, London*
1966   Sir Theodore Fox, MA, MD, LLD: *Director of the Family Planning Association*
1967   Kenneth Robinson, MP: *Minister of Health*
1969   Sir Solly Zuckerman, OM, KCB, MA, MD, DSc, FRS: *Chief Scientific Advisor to HM Government*
1970   Brian Gilmore Maegraith, CMG, MA, MB, BSc, DPhil: *Dean of the Liverpool School of Tropical Medicine*
1971   Sir Derrick Dunlop, BA, MD: *Emeritus Professor of Therapeutics and Clinical Medicine in the University of Edinburgh*
1972   Sir Charles Stuart-Harris, CBE, MD: *Professor of Medicine in the University of Sheffield*
1972   Richard Howard Stafford Crossman, PC, OBE, MA: *Member of Parliament*
1975   Sir Dugald Baird, BSc, MD, LLD: *previously Regius Professor of Midwifery in the University of Aberdeen*

1975   Sir George E Godber, GCB: *previously Chief Medical Officer, Department of Health and Social Security*

1976   David Martin Scott Steel, MA, LLB, MP: *Member of Parliament for Roxburgh, Selkirk and Peebles*

1977   Sir Hugh Robson: *Principal and Vice-Chancellor of the University of Edinburgh*

1978   John P Mackintosh: *Member of Parliament*

1979   Sir Douglas Andrew Kilgour Black, MD, *President of the Royal College of Physicians*

1981   Sir Alexander Walter Morrison, BSc, PhD, DL, LLD, DSc, FRS, FRSA, *Chairman of the Committee of Vice-Chancellors and Vice-Chancellor of the University of Bristol*

1982   Renee Short: *Member of Parliament*

1983   Sir Henry Yellowlees: *Chief Medical Officer for Health*

1984   Roy Deans Weir, OBE, MD, DPh, FRCP

1985   Alwin Smith

1986   Stephen Penford Lock, MA, MB, FRCP: *British Medical Journal*

Bronte-Stewart Memorial Lectureship

Founded in 1967 and endowed by private subscription. The endowment provides for an annual lecture as a memorial to the late Brian Bronte-Stewart, Director of the Medical Research Council Atheroma Research Unit in the Western Infirmary, and Honorary Clinical Lecturer in the University.

1968   Sir George W Pickering, MD, FRS: *Regius Professor of Medicine in the University of Oxford*

1969   Richard S Ross, MD: *Clayton Professor of Cardiovascular Disease in the Johns Hopkins University Medical School, Maryland*

1970   Velva Schrire, MD, MSc, PhD: *Associate Professor of Medicine in the University of Cape Town*

1972   Michael Francis Oliver, MD: *Senior Lecturer in Medicine in the University of Edinburgh*

1972   Gordon Cumming, BSc, MB ChB, PhD: *Reader in Medicine in the University of Birmingham*

1974   Donald Nixon Ross, BSc, MB ChB: *Thoracic Surgeon in Guy's Hospital, London*

1975   Jeremy N Morris, MA, DSc, FRCP, MRCS: *Professor in the Department of Community Health, London School of Hygiene and Tropical Medicine*

1977   Richard H Lovell, MD, MSc: *Professor in the Royal Melbourne Hospital*

1977   J R A Mitchell, MA, BSc, DPhil, FRCP: *Professor in the Department of Medicine, University of London*

1977	A G Shaper, MB ChB, FRCP, FFCM, MRCPath: *Department of Clinical Epidemiology and Social Medicine, Royal Free Hospital, London*
1978	Jane Kathleen Lloyd, MD: *Department of Child Health, St George's Hospital Medical School, University of London*
1998	John C Burnett, Jnr, MD: *Director of the Cardiorenal Research Laboratory at the Mayo Clinic, Rochester, USA*
1999	Donald D Heistad, MD: *Professor of Internal Medicine and Pharmacology in the University of Iowa, USA*
2000	M J (Geil) Janse: *Editor-in-Chief of the Journal of European Society of Cardiology, Cardiovascular Resarch Institute, Amsterdam*
2001	Michael Davies: *British Heart Foundation, London*

W A Cargill Memorial Lectureship

Founded in 1964 and endowed by an anonymous donor. Patron: the University Court. The foundation originally provided for a public lecture in the University biennially or as funds permit, on a subject related to Fine Art. The lecturer then, at the discretion of the Professor of Fine Art, conducted a discussion with a class or classes in Fine Art on the day following the lecture. Since 2000, the endowment has funded a Lectureship within the Department of History of Art in partnership with Glasgow Museums.

1967	Tom John Honeyman, JP, MB ChB, LLD
1969	Kenneth Mackenzie, Lord Clark of Saltwood, CH, KCB, LLD, DLitt, FBA
1971	Rudolf Wittkower, FBA: *Emeritus Professor of Fine Arts in the University of Columbia and Slade Professor of Fine Art in the University of Cambridge*
1973	Ellis Kirkham Waterhouse, CBE, MA, AM, DLitt: *previously Barber Professor of Fine Arts in the University of Birmingham*
1975	Sir John Summerson, CBE, FBA: *Curator of Sir John Soane's Museum, London*
1977	John Golding BA, PhD: *History of Art, Courtauld Institute of Art, London*
1979	Colin Thompson MA: *Director of the National Gallery of Scotland*
1982	John Rewald, D-es-L: *New York*
1983	Peter J Parish: *University of London*
1984	Peter Kidson, MA, PhD: *London*
1987	Christopher Brown: *National Gallery*
1992	Jean Clair: *Director of the Picasso Museum, Paris*
1995	Sir Eduardo Paolozzi: *Her Majesty's Sculptor-in-Ordinary in Scotland*
2000	Elizabeth Hancock, BA, AMA

Colquhoun Lectureship in Business History

Founded in 1959 from funds raised through an appeal sponsored by the Glasgow Chamber and Junior Chamber of Commerce. The title commemorates Patrick Colquhoun of Kelvingrove, LLD 1797, Provost of Glasgow, who in 1783 was a founder member and first president of the Chamber of Commerce. The Lectureship is attached to the Department of Economic History and the main theme of the lectures is the History of Business in Glasgow and the West of Scotland.

1959	Peter Lester Payne, BA, PhD: *later Professor of Economic History in the University of Aberdeen*
1969	Anthony Slaven, MA, BLitt: *later Professor of Business History in the University*
1988-1994	Alan Mackinlay, BA, DPhil: *later Professor of Management in the University of St Andrews*

Cramb Music Lectureship

Founded in 1911 by Susan Cramb of Helensburgh. In 1947 provision was made for a visiting lecturer to give an annual Cramb Lecture. Patron: the Cramb Trustees.

1923	Percy Carter Buck, MA, DMus
1924	Sir Henry Walford Davies, MusD, LLD: *Professor of Music in the University of Wales*
1925	Donald Francis Tovey, BA, DMus: *Professor of Music in the University of Edinburgh*
1926	Gustav Holst: *composer*
1927	Henry Cope Colles, MA, BMus
1928	George Dyson, DMus: *Master of Music in Winchester College*
1931	William Gillies Whittaker, MA, DMus: *Professor of Music in the University*
1933	Henry George Farmer, MA, PhD
1934	Michel D Calvocoressi
1935	Sir Donald Francis Tovey, BA, DMus: *Professor of Music in the University of Edinburgh*
1937	Edmund Horace Fellowes, MA, MusDoc: *Canon of St George's, Windsor*
1939	Sir Hugh Percy Allen, GCVO, MA, DMus, DLitt: *Professor of Music in the University of Oxford*
1946	Charles Henry Phillip, DMus
1947	Ronald Ernest Woodham, BA, DMus
1951	Frederick William Rimmer, MA, BMus: *late Professor of Music*
1947	Frank Howes, MA: *Music Critic of "The Times"*

1948	Thomas Armstrong, MA, MusD: *Organist of Christ Church Cathedral, Oxford*
1949	Sir George Dyson, MA, DMus, LLD: *Director of the Royal College of Music, London*
1950	Sir Steuart Wilson, MA: *Director of Music of the BBC*
1951	Ivor Benjamin Hugh James, FRCM, HonRAM: *Professor in the Royal College of Music, London*
1952	Frank Howes, MA: *Music Critic of "The Times"*
1953	Herbert Wiseman, DMus: *Former Director of Scottish Music, BBC*
1954	Herbert Kennedy Andrews, MA, DMus: *Fellow and Organist of New College, Oxford*
1955	Gordon Jacob, DMus, FRCM, HonRAM: *Royal College of Music*
1956	Sydney Newman, MA, DMus: *Reid Professor of Music in the University of Edinburgh*
1957	Erik Chisholm, DMus, FRCO: *Professor of Music in the University of Capetown*
1958	Alan Douglas, MIRE, MAIEE
1959	Thurston Dart, MA: *Lecturer in Music in the University of Cambridge*
1960	Anthony Lewis, MA, MusB: *Professor of Music in the University of Birmingham*
1961	Peter Pears, CBE
1962	Aaron Copland, MusD
1963	Henry McLeod Havergal, MA, DMus: *Principal of the Royal Scottish Academy of Music*
1964	Keith Falkner, FRCM: *Director of the Royal College of Music*
1965	William Mann, BA, MusB: *Music Critic of "The Times"*
1966	Wilfrid Mellers, MA, DMus: *Professor of Music in the University of York*
1967	Hugh Tracey, HonDMus: *Director of the International Library of African Music*
1968	Sir Jack Westrup, MA, HonDMus: *Heather Professor of Music in the University of Oxford*
1969	Peter Angus Evans, MA, DMus, FRCO: *Professor of Music in the University of Southampton*
1970	Cedric Thorpe Davie, OBE, LLD, FRACM: *Reader in Music in the University of St Andrews*
1971	Iain Ellis Hamilton, DMus: *Professor of Music in Duke University*
1972	Witold Lutoslawski: *Composer*
1973	Denis Matthews, FRAM: *Professor of Music in the University of Newcastle upon Tyne*
1975	Ivor Keys, MA, DMus, FRCO: *Professor of Music in the University of Birmingham*
1976	Luciano Berio: *composer*
1977	Thomas Jeffrey Hemsley, MA: *opera and concert singer*
1977	Thea Musgrave, MusD: *composer*
1979	Howard Chandler Robbins Landon, BMus: *author and music historian*

1985	Wilfred Howard Mellers, OBE, MA, DMus, DPhil: *Professor of Music in the University of York*
1986	Alena Nemcova: *Music Information Centre of the Czech Music Fund*
1987	Peter Branscombe, MA, PhD: *author*
1987	Neil Fl Sorrell, MA, PhD: *senior lecturer in the University of York and co-founder of the English Gamelan Orchestra*
1988	Hans Tischler: *Emeritus Professor of Musicology, University of Indiana*
1988	Peter Maxwell Davies, CBE, BMus: composer and conductor
1989	David Charlton, BA, PhD: *lecturer in Royal Holloway College, University of London*
1989	Yury Kholopov: *Moscow Conservatoire*
1990	Joan Rimmer: *musician*
1997	Jane Glover: *conductor*
2000	Richard Taruskin: *Professor in the University of California, Berkeley*

Dalrymple Lectureship in Archaeology

Established in the years 1907-1912 by the annual covenant of James D G Dalrymple of Woodhead, formerly James Dalrymple Duncan, writer, of Glasgow, secretary of the Glasgow Archaeological Society, and subsequently endowed by his bequest. In 1935, it was decided to appoint a permanent lecturer and, in alternate years, a special lecturer for that year only. Patron: a Board of Curators, four appointed by the University Court, and three by the Council of the Glasgow Archaeological Society. In 1939, the lectureship was associated with duties in the Hunterian Museum and in 1944 provision was made for a visiting lecturer to give a Dalrymple lecture in alternate years.

1907	Robert Carr Bosanquet, MA: *Professor of Classical Archaeology in the University of Liverpool*
1908	Sir George Macdonald, MA, LLD: *Assistant Secretary of the Scottish Education Department*
1910	Robert Munro, MA, MD, LLD
1911	Robert Alexander Stewart Macalister MA: *Professor of Celtic Archaeology in University College, Dublin*
1937	Robert Eric Mortimer Wheeler, MC, MA, DLitt: *Keeper of the London Museum*
1938	Reginald Allender Smith, BA: *Keeper of British and Mediaeval Antiquities in the British Museum*
1938	Ian Alexander Richmond, MA: *Lecturer in Archaeology in the University of Durham*
1939	Anne Strachan Robertson, MA, DLitt: *Hunterian Museum*
1945	Gerhardt Bersu: *Curator of the Manx Museum*

1947-1948 Charles Francis Christopher Hawkes, MA: *Professor of European Archaeology in the University of Oxford*

1950 Victor Eric Nash-Williams, MA, DLitt: *Lecturer in Archaeology in University College of South Wales*

1952-1953 William Douglas Simpson, DLitt: *Librarian of the University of Aberdeen*

1955 John Grahame Douglas Clark, MA, PhD, ScD, FBA: *Disney Professor of Archaeology in the University of Cambridge*

1956 Ian Alexander Richmond, MA, DLitt, LLD, FBA: *Professor of Archaeology of the Roman Empire in the University of Oxford*

1958 Courtenay Arthur Ralegh Radford, MA, DLitt, FBA

1960-1961 Rupert Leo Scott Bruce-Mitford, BA: *Keeper of British and Mediaeval Antiquities in the British Museum*

1964 Jocelyn Mary Catherine Toynbee, MA, DPhil, FBA: *Lawrence Professor Emerita of Classical Archaeology in the University of Cambridge*

1966 Stuart Piggott, DLitt, FBA: *Abercromby Professor of Prehistoric Archaeology in the University of Edinburgh*

1968 Kathleen Mary Kenyon, CBE, MA, DLitt, FBA: *Principal of St Hugh's College, Oxford*

1970 David Mackenzie Wilson, MA: *Reader in Scandinavian Studies in University College, London*

1972 Geoffrey William Dimbleby, BSc, MA, DPhil: *Professor of Human Environment in the University of London*

1972 Eric Birley, MBA, MA, FBA: *previously Professor of Roman British History and Archaeology in the University of Durham*

1975 A Colin Renfrew, MA, PhD: *Professor of Archaeology in the University of Southampton*

1977 Robert Barron Kerr Stevenson, MA, FSA, FMA: *Keeper of the National Museum of Antiquities of Scotland*

1979 Michael Joseph O'Kelly, MA, DLitt: *Department of Archaeology, University College, Cork*

1981 Maurice Willmore Barley, MA: *previously University of Nottingham*

1983 Piers Roland Giot: *University of Rennes*

1984 Peter S Wells: *Harvard University*

1985 Kristian Kristiansen: *Denmark*

1986 Jaroslav Sasel: *Slovenian Academy of Sciences*

1988 Martin Biddle, MA, FBA

1989 Alexander Fenton, MA: *Keeper of the National Museum of Antiquities of Scotland*

1993 Vassos Karageorghis: *Nicosia, Cyprus*

1994 Rosemary Cramp: *Emeritus Professor of Archaeology, University of Durham*

1995	Emmanuel Anati: *Director, Centro Camuni di Studi Preistorici and Professor of Palaeo-Ethnology, University of Lecce, Italy*
1996	George Bass: *Professor in the Institute of Nautical Archaeology, Texas A and M University*
1997	John Robert Hume, BSc, ARCST, FSA: *Chief Inspector, Historic Scotland*
1999	Lord Renfrew of Kaimsthorn, FBA: *Director of the McDonald Institute for Archaeological Research, Cambridge*

Philip Ivor Dee Memorial Lecture

Founded in memory of Philip Ivor Dee CBE, FRS, (1904 - 1983), Professor of Natural Philosophy in the University, 1943-1972.

1986	William Ernest Burcham, CBE, FRS: *Oliver Lodge Professor of Physics, University of Birmingham*
1989	Rendel Sebastian Pease, FRS: *Director of the Culham Laboratory, UKAEA*
1995	Sir Arnold Whittaker Wolfendale, PhD, DSc, FRS, FInstP, FRAS: *Professor of Physics in the University of Durham*
1996	G C Morrison: *School of Physics and Space Research, University of Birmingham*
1999	Ian Halliday: *Chief Executive, Particle Physics and Astronomy Research Council*
2001	Jelto Smits: *Honorary Professor, Department of Physics and Astronomy and Vice-President for Corporate Strategy, Philips International BV*

Dundas and Wilson Lecturer in Commercial Law

Founded in 1997 and endowed by Dundas and Wilson, the University solicitors, to provide a Lectureship in Commercial Law. Patron: the University Court.

1997	Laura MacGregor, LLM, DipLP

Edwards Lectureship in Palaeography and Diplomatic

By the bequest of John Edwards, LLD 1919, an endowment was provided in 1943 for a Lectureship in Palaeography and Diplomatic. Until 1957, the endowment was applied to provide instruction in these branches of study by a lecturer in each of the departments of Humanity, History and Scottish History. It is now applied to provide instruction by a lecturer in the department of History in any year in which the students offer themselves, and to make provision for a periodic lecture in which new palaeographical material is used.

1959	Neil Ripley Ker, MA, BLitt, FBA: *Reader in Palaeography in the University of Oxford*
1964	Christopher Robert Cheney, MA, FBA: *Professor of Mediaeval History in the University of Cambridge*
1972	The Right Reverend Monsignor David McRoberts, STL, DLitt
1976	Thomas Julian Brown MA, FSA: *Professor in the Department of Palaeography, Kings College, London*
1977	Pierre Theophile Victorien Marie Chaplais, MA, PhD, FBA: *Wadham College, Oxford*
1984	Geoffrey Wallis Steuart Barrow, DLitt, FBA, FRSE: *Professor of Scottish History in the University of St Andrews*
1985	John Durkan, MA, PhD, DLitt: *author and historian*
1986	Nicholas Peter Brooks, MA, DPhil, FRHistS, FSAScot
1993	Thomas Zotz: *Historisches Seminar, Albert-Ludwigs Universitat, Freiburg*
1996	H Mayr-Harting: *St Peter's College, University of Oxford*
1997	RB Dobson: *University of Cambridge*
1998	Barbara Harvey: *Somerville College, Oxford*
1999	Diana Greenway: *Institute of Historical Research, University of London*
2000	Andrew Murray: *University College, Oxford*
2001	Anne Elizabeth Curry: *University of Reading*

Frazer Lectureship in Social Anthropology

Founded by subscription in 1920, with similar lectureships in the Universities of Oxford, Cambridge and Liverpool, in commemoration of the services contributed to learning by Sir James George Frazer, MA 1874, LLD 1895, Fellow of Trinity College, Cambridge. The lecturer, who is appointed every fourth year, is required to deliver a lecture on some subject connected with Social Anthropology. Patron: the University Court.

1924	William James Perry, MA, DSc: *Reader in Cultural Anthropology in the University of London*
1928	Edward Alexander Westermarck, PhD, LLD: *Professor of Sociology in the University of London*
1932	Sir Arthur Keith, MD, LLD, FRS
1936	Warren Royal Dawson, FRSE
1940	William Reginald Halliday, MA, LLD: *Principal of King's College, London*
1944	Morris Ginsberg, MA, DLitt: *Martin White Professor of Sociology in the University of London*
1948	Alexander Macbeath, MA: *Professor of Logic and Metaphysics in the Queen's University of Belfast*

1952	Herman Max Gluckman, MA, DPhil: *Professor of Social Anthropology in the University of Manchester*
1956	Meyer Fortes, MA, PhD: *Professor of Social Anthropology in the University of Cambridge*
1960	John Peristiany, MA, DPhil: *Lecturer in Social Anthropology in the University of Oxford*
1967	Ian George Cunnison, MA, DPhil: *Professor of Social Anthropology in the University of Hull*
1969	Eric Robertson Dodds, MA, DLitt, FBA: *Emeritus Professor of Greek in the University of Oxford*
1977	Ernst Andre Gellner, MA, PhD, FBA: *Department of Sociology, London School of Economics*
1981	Peter Maurice Worsley, BA, MA, PhD: *University of Manchester*
1985	Gilbert Lewis, BM, BCh, PhD, MA, MRCP: *Cambridge*
1990	Peter Ucko: *University of Southampton*
1993	Alexander Fenton, CBE, MA, DLitt, FRSE, FSA, FRSGS, FSAScot: *Director of the School of Scottish Studies, University of Edinburgh*
1997	Paul Henley: *Director, Granada Centre for Visual Anthropology, University of Manchester*

Gardiner Lectureship in the Pathology of Diseases of Infancy and Childhood

Founded in 1928 and endowed by Sir Frederick Crombie Gardiner and William Guthrie Gardiner, shipowners in Glasgow. The lecturer is appointed annually by the University Court. He is also a Pathologist to the Royal Hospital for Sick Children.

1928	John William Stewart Blacklock, MD: *later St Mungo-Notman Professor of Pathology*
1937	George Lightbody Montgomery, MD, PhD: *later St Mungo-Notman Professor of Pathology*
1949	Alistair Mitchell MacDonald, MD

Gibson Lectureship in the History of Mathematics

Founded in 1928 and endowed from funds raised by friends of George Alexander Gibson, Professor of Mathematics in the University, 1909-1927. The foundation provides for the periodic delivery of lectures on the History of Mathematics, either Pure or Applied. The appointment of the lecturer and arrangements for the lectures are made by a Committee consisting of the Principal, the Professors of Mathematics, Natural Philosophy, and Astronomy, and the Principal of Strathclyde University.

1933	Albert Einstein, DSc, LLD: *previously Professor of Physics in the University of Berlin*
1937	John Dougall, MA, DSc
1945	Alexander Craig Aitken, MA, DSc, FRS: *Reader in Actuarial Science in the University of Edinburgh*
1949	Herbert Westren Turnbull, MA, FRS: *Professor of Mathematics in the University of St Andrews*
1953	Charles Alfred Coulson, MA, PhD, DSc, FRS: *Rouse Ball Professor of Mathematics in the University of Oxford*
1957	Joseph Needham, MA, PhD, ScD, FRS: *Sir William Dunn Reader in Biochemistry in the University of Cambridge*
1961	Edward Foyle Collingwood, CBE, MA, PhD, ScD, DSc: *previously Fellow of Trinity College, Cambridge*
1965	Clifford Truesdell, PhD: *Professor of Rational Mechanics in Johns Hopkins University*
1969	Derek T Whiteside, BA, PhD: *Assistant Director of Research, Whipple Science Museum, Cambridge*
1973	Robert Schlapp, MA, PhD: *previously senior lecturer in Mathematical Physics in the University of Edinburgh*
1977	Gerald J Whitrow, MA, DPhil: *History and Applications of Mathematics, Imperial College of Science and Technology, London*

Gifford Lectureship in Natural Theology

Founded in 1887, with similar lectureships in the other three ancient Scottish Universities, by the bequest of Adam Gifford, one of the Senators of the College of Justice, for promoting, advancing and diffusing the study of Natural Theology in the widest sense of that term - in other words, 'the Knowledge of God, the Infinite, the All, the First and Only Cause, the One and the Sole Substance, the Sole Being, the Sole Reality, and the Sole Existence, the Knowledge of His Nature and Attributes, the Knowledge of the Relations which men and the whole universe bear to Him, the Knowledge of the Nature and Foundation of Ethics or Morals, and of all the Obligations and Duties thence arising". In 1986, a series of Gifford Research Fellowships tenable in alternate years by more junior scholars interested in research in Natural Theology and Philosophy, was introduced. The Fellow is expected to engage in full-time research and to give occasional lectures, which are open to the general public. Patron: the Senatus. The lecturer is appointed for a period of two years, but the same person may be reappointed for other two periods of two years each, provided that no person shall hold the office of lecturer in this University for more than six years in all. The lecturer is subjected to no test, and the founder expressed the wish that the subject should be treated as a strictly natural science. The lectures are open to the public.

1888   Friedrich Max Müller, PhD, LLD: *Professor of Comparative Philology in the University of Oxford*

1892   John Caird, MA, DD, LLD: *Principal*

1893   William Wallace, MA: *Professor of Moral Philosophy in the University of Oxford*

1895   John Caird, MA, DD, LLD: *Principal*

1896   Alexander Balmain Bruce, MA, DD: *Professor of Exegesis, in the Free Church College, Glasgow*

1900   Edward Caird MA, DCL, LLD: *Master of Balliol College, Oxford*

1903   Emile Boutroux: *Professor of Philosophy in the University of Paris*

1906   Andrew Cecil Bradley, MA, LLD: *Professor of Poetry in the University of Oxford*

1910   John Watson, MA, LLD: *Professor of Moral Philosophy in Queen's University, Kingston*

1913   Arthur James Balfour: *Member of Parliament*

1916   Samuel Alexander, MA, LLD, FBA: *Professor of Philosophy in the University of Manchester*

1921   Sir Henry Jones, CH, MA, LLD, FBA: *Professor of Moral Philosophy*

1922   Arthur James Balfour: *Member of Parliament*

1923   William Paterson Paterson, MA, DD: *Professor of Divinity in the University of Edinburgh*

1926   John Scott Haldane, MA, LLD, FRS: *Fellow of New College, Oxford*

1928   John Alexander Smith, MA, LLD: *Wayneflete Professor of Mental Philosophy in the University of Oxford*

1930   William Temple, MA, DD, DLitt: *Archbishop of York*

1934   William Macneile Dixon, MA, LittD, LLD: *Emeritus Professor of English Language and Literature*

1937   William Ernest Hocking, PhD, DD, LLD: *Professor of Natural Religion, Moral Philosophy and Civil Polity in Harvard University*

1939   John Laird, MA, LLD, FBA: *Professor of Moral Philosophy in the University of Aberdeen*

1947   Ralph Barton Perry, MA, PhD, LLD: *Professor of Philosophy in Harvard University*

1949   Herbert Henry Farmer, MA, DD: *Professor of Systematic Theology and Apologetics in Westminster College, Cambridge*

1952   John Macmurray, MC, MA: *Professor of Moral Philosophy in the University of Edinburgh*

1956   Leonard Hodgson, DD, DCL: *Regius Professor of Divinity in the University of Oxford*

1959   Carl Friedrich Von Weizsäcker: *Professor of Philosophy in the University of Hamburg*

1961	Charles William Hendel, PhD: *Professor of Moral Philosophy in Yale University*
1965	Sir Herbert Butterfield, MA, LLD, DLitt: *Master of Peterhouse, Cambridge*
1971	Sir Richard William Southern, MA, DLitt, FBA: *President of St John's College, Oxford*
1974	Basil G Mitchell, MA: *Nolloth Professor of the Philosophy of the Christian Religion in the University of Oxford*
1978	Sydney Bremner, DPhil, FRS: *MRC Laboratory of Molecular Biology, Cambridge*
1982	Stephen Richard Lyster Clark, MA, DPhil: *Department of Moral Philosophy*
1982	Christina Jessy Larner, MA, PhD: *Department of Sociology*
1983	Kenneth Philip Arthur Drew, MA: *Department of English*
1983	Anthony John Sanford, BSc, PhD: *Department of Psychology*
1984	Allan Douglas Galloway, MA, BD, PhD, STM: *Professor of Divinity*
1985	Carl E Sagan: *Cornell University*
1986	Donald MacCrimmon MacKay, BSc, PhD, FInstP: *Emeritus Professor of Communication in the University of Keele*
1987	Euan Thomson
1988	John David Barrow, BSc, DPhil: *Astronomy Centre, University of Sussex*
	John Stapylton Habgood, MA, PhD: *Archbishop of York*
	Clinton Richard Dawkins, MA, DPhil: *New College, Oxford*
	Don Cupitt: *Dean of Emmanuel College, Cambridge*
	John Morris Roberts, MA, DPhil: *Warden, Merton College, Oxford*
	Anthony John Patrick Kenny, MA, DPhil, DLitt, FBA: *Master of Balliol College, Oxford*
1990	George Steiner: *Professor of English and Comparative Literature, University of Geneva*
1992	Mary Warnock: *Mistress of Girton College, Cambridge*
1993	J S K Ward: *Regius Professor of Divinity, Christ Church, Oxford*
1995	Geoffrey N Cantor: *University of Leeds*
	John H Brooks, *University of Lancaster*
1997	RJ Berry: *University College, London*
1999	Ralph McInerny: *Michael Grace Professor of Mediaeval Studies and Director of the Jacques Maritain Center, University of Notre Dame, Indiana*
2001	Brian Hebbltethwaite: *Queen's College, Cambridge,*
	Lynne Baker: *University of Massachusetts*
	George Lakoff: *University of California at Berkeley*
	Philip Johnson-Laird: *Princeton University*
	Michael Ruse: *Florida State University*

Leonard Gow Lectureship on the Medical Diseases
of Infancy and Childhood

Founded in 1919 by Leonard Gow, shipowner in Glasgow. Patron: a Committee consisting of representatives of the University Court, the Senatus and the Royal Hospital for Sick Children. The lecturer is attached to the professorial unit in the Royal Hospital for Sick Children.

1919	Leonard Findlay, MD, DSc: *later Professor of Medical Paediatrics*
1924	Geoffrey Balmanno Fleming, MBE, BA, MD: *later Samson Gemmell Chair of Child Health*
1930	Stanley Galbraith Graham, MD: *later Samson Gemmell Chair of Child Health*
1947	James Holmes Hutchison, OBE, MD: *later Samson Gemmell Chair of Child Health*
1962	Gavin Cranston Arneil, MD, PhD
1989	Eric Norman Coleman, MD
1992	Thomas L Turner, MB ChB, FRCP, FRCPCH

Grieve Lectureship in Physiological Chemistry

Founded in 1905 and endowed by the bequest of John Grieve, MA 1846, MD 1850. The lecturer was originally attached to the Department of Biochemistry and is now in the Division of Biochemistry and Molecular Biology of the Faculty of Biomedical and Life Sciences. His or her duties are defined by regulations approved by the University Court on the 9 February 1905.

1905	Edward Provan Cathcart, MD, DSc, FRS: *later Professor of Physiology*
1919	David Burns, MA, DSc: *later Professor of Physiology in the University of Durham*
1921	George Macfeat Wishart, BSc, MD: *later Professor of Physiological Chemistry*
1934	Sir David Paton Cuthbertson, DSc, MD: *later Director of the Rowett Research Institute*
1946	Hamish Nisbet Munro, BSc, PhD
1957	George Thomas Mills, BSc, PhD, MD
1959	Robert Martin Stuart Smellie, DSc, PhD: *later Cathcart Professor of Biochemistry*
1964	George Leaf, MSc, PhD
1987	W Harry Holms, BSc, PhD
1992	Robert Y Thomson, BSc, PhD
1994	David P Leader, MA, DPhil

Bernard Hague Memorial Lectureship

Founded in 1961 by Sheila T Mackay in memory of her father, Bernard Hague, PhD, DSc, Professor of Electrical Engineering in the University, 1946-1960. The foundation provides for a public lecture to be delivered in the University once every four years or as funds permit, on a subject in, or relative to, the field of Electrical Engineering. The visiting lecturer is to be chosen on each occasion by the Professor or Professors of Electrical Engineering and the Dean of the Faculty. Where a Professor of Electrical Engineering is also the Dean of the Faculty, the visiting lecturer will be chosen by the Professor or Professors of Electrical Engineering with the approval of the Faculty.

1963	Leszek Filipczynski, DrEng: *Professor in the Polish Academy of Sciences*
1964	Warren Perry Mason, BS, AM, PhD: *Head of Mechanics Research Group, Bell Telephone Laboratories, New Jersey, USA*
1971	Harold Everard Monteagle Barlow, BSc, PhD, FRS: *Emeritus Professor of Electrical Engineering in University College, London*
1972	Martin Chodorow, MA, PhD: *Professor of Applied Physics and Electrical Engineering and Director of the Microwave Acoustics Laboratory in Stanford University*
1974	Wiliam Shen Chie Chang, MSEe, PhD: *Professor of Electrical Engineering in Washington University, St Louis*
1987	Cyril Hilsum, PhD, FRS, FEng, FInstP, FIEE
1988	Yuri Gulyaev: *Director of the Institute of Radioengineering and Electronics at the Russian Academy of Sciences*

Hastie Lectureship

Founded in 1905 by subscription in memory of William Hastie, Professor of Divinity, 1895 - 1903, for the encouragement of the study of Theology among the ministers of the Church of Scotland. The fund is administered by six trustees, three official and three elected. The official trustees are the Principal, the Dean of the Faculty of Divinity, and the Professor of Divinity. Should the Professor of Divinity also be Dean, then the third official Trustee is a Professor in the Faculty of Divinity, nominated by the Faculty. The other Trustees were elected by the subscribers from their own number; in certain contingencies vacancies in the number of the elected Trustees are filled alternately by the Senatus and by the Presbytery of Glasgow. The lecturer is appointed by the Trustees and holds office for three years; and he or she must deliver not fewer than four, nor more than six, lectures in the University elsewhere as the Trustees may determine. The lectures are open to the public.

1906   Donald McMillan, DD: *Minister of Kelvinhaugh*
1909   James Hutton Mackay, MA: *Minister of the English Church, Middelburg and Flushing*
1912   William Seath Provand, MA: *Minister of St Ninian's, Glasgow*
1915   Thomas Wilson, BD: *Minister of Stow*
1918   Duncan Cameron, BD: *Minister of St Paul's, Leith*
1921   Andrew James Campbell, BA: *Minister of St John's, Glasgow*
1924   Thomas Meikle Watt, MA: *Minister of St Modan's, Falkirk*
1927   William McMillan, MA, PhD: *Minister of St Leonard's, Dunfermline*
1930   John Garrow Duncan, BD: *Minister of St Michael's, Kirkmichael*
1934   George Smith Hendry, BD: *Minister of St Andrew's, Bridge of Allan*
1937   Archibald McBride Hunter, BD, PhD: *Professor of New Testament Greek in Mansfield College, Oxford*
1941   George Matthewson Dryburgh, MA: *Minister of Battlefield East, Glasgow*
1950   John Roger Gray, BD: *Minister of St Stephen's Buccleuch, Glasgow*
1953   Allan Douglas Galloway, BD, PhD: *Minister of Auchterhouse, Dundee*
1956   James Neil Stewart Alexander, BD, STM: *Lecturer in Biblical Criticism in the University of Aberdeen*
1959   John Macquarrie, MA, BD, PhD: *Lecturer in Divinity in the University*
1962   Alexander Allan McArthur, MA, BD, PhD: *Minister of Pollockshields-Titwood, Glasgow*
1965   James Waterson Leitch, MA, BD, DrTheol: *Minister of the Reformed Church in Basle*
1971   Duncan Shaw, PhD, ThDr: *Minister of Craigentinny*
1977   David Gentles Hamilton, MA, BD
1988   James Waterson Leitch, MA, BD, DrTheol
1996   Robert Davidson, DD, MA, BD, FRSE: *Emeritus Professor of Old Testament Language and Literature*
1997   Lloyd Ridgeon, MA, MPhil, PhD: *lecturer in Islamic Studies*
1999   Na'im Ateek: *Episcopal Diocese of Jerusalem and the Middle East and Director of the Sabeel Ecumenical Liberation Theology Centre*
2001   Richard V Frederick Holloway, BD: *Bishop of Edinburgh, Primus of the Scottish Episcopal Church*

Honeyman Gillespie Lectureship in Geology

Founded in 1876 by Mrs Elizabeth Honeyman Gillespie of Torbanehill in memory of her husband, William Honeyman Gillespie, undergraduate in Arts, 1826. The Lectureship was originally attached to the Chair of Natural History; when the Chair of Geology was founded in 1904 the Trustees, in virtue of their powers, transferred the Lectureship to be held by the incumbent of that chair. *(See the established Chair of Geology on page 100 for a list of incumbents.)*

W P Ker Lectureship

Founded in 1938 by the bequest of John Brown Douglas, MA 1875, writer in Glasgow, in memory of William Paton Ker, undergraduate in Arts, 1870-1874, LLD 1898, Professor of English Literature in the University of London and Professor of Poetry in the University of Oxford. Patron: the University Court. The foundation originally provided for an annual lecture on some branch of literary or linguistic studies.

1939	Raymond Wilson Chambers, MA, DLitt, FBA: *Professor of English Language and Literature in the University of London*
1940	William Macneile Dixon, MA, LittD, LLD: *Emeritus Professor of English Language and Literature*
1941	Thomas Stearns Eliot, MA, LittD, LLD: *Honorary Fellow of Magdalene College, Cambridge*
1943	Lord David Cecil, MA: *Fellow of New College, Oxford*
1944	Edward Morgan Forster, LLD: *previously Fellow of King's College, Cambridge*
1945	Charles Langbridge Morgan, MA: *author*
1946	Edwin Muir: *author*
1947	Helen Waddell, MA, DLitt, LLD: *scholar and author*
1948	Harold George Nicolson, CMG: *author*
1949	Roger Aubrey Baskerville Mynors, MA, FBA: *Kennedy Professor of Latin in the University of Cambridge*
1950	Sir William Craigie, MA, LLD, DLitt, FBA: *Professor Emeritus of English, University of Chicago*
1951	Geoffrey Langdale Bickersteth, MA: *Professor of English Literature in the University of Aberdeen*
1952	Sydney Castle Roberts, MA: *Master of Pembroke College, Cambridge*
1953	John Ronald Reuel Tolkien, MA: *Merton Professor of English Language and Literature in the University of Oxford*
1954	Sigurdur Nordal: *Minister at Copenhagen*

1955	Benjamin Ifor Evans, MA, DLitt: *Provost of University College, London*
1956	Geoffrey Winthrop Young, MA, DLitt
1957	Wystan Hugh Auden, MA: *Professor of Poetry in the University of Oxford*
1959	Clive Staples Lewis, MA, D-ès-L, DD, FBA: *Professor of Mediaeval and Renaissance English in the University of Cambridge*
1961	James Runcieman Sutherland, MA, BLitt, LLD, FBA: *Lord Northcliffe Professor of Modern English Literature in University College, London*
1965	Cleanth Brooks, BA, BLitt: *Professor of English in Yale University*
1968	Gwyn Jones, CBE, MA: *Professor of English at the University College of South Wales and Monmouthshire*
1970	Eyvind Fjell Halvorsen, DoctPhilos: *Professor of Norse Philology in the University of Oslo*
1972	John Frank Kermode, MA: *Lord Northcliffe Professor of Modern English Literature in University College, London*
1974	Denis Donoghue, MA, PhD: *Professor of Modern English and American Literature in University College, Dublin*
1976	E Peter M Dronke, MA: *University of Cambridge*
1979	Francis Berry, MA: *Department of English at Royal Holloway College, University of London*
1981	Ian Dalrymple Mcfarlane, MBE, MA, DUParis, FBA: *University of Oxford*
1983	William Lobov: *University of Pennsylvania*
1986	George Steiner, MA, DPhil
1995	Lee Paterson: *Yale University*

Kilbrandon Lectureship

The Centre for the Study of the Child in Society, in conjunction with the Scottish Executive, organises a biannual public Kilbrandon lecture to commemorate the establishment of the Scottish Children's Hearing System. It is named after Charles James Dalrymple Shaw, Lord Kilbrandon (1906-1989), widely recognised as the founder of the Children's Hearing System.

1993	Sandford Fox: *Professor of Law in Boston College Law School*
1995	Frederick Hope Stone: *Consultant Psychiatrist, Royal Hospital for Sick Children, Glasgow*
1997	Donald Dewar, MP: *Secretary of State for Scotland*
1999	Anthony Clare: *Broadcaster and Clinical Professor of Psychiatry at Trinity College Dublin*
2001	Neil MacCormick: *Member of the European Parliament and Professor of Public Law in the University of Edinburgh*

Loudon Lectureship in Engineering Production

Founded in 1926 and endowed by George F Loudon, engineer and machine tool maker, of Glasgow, and his wife. The lectureship is attached to the Department of Mechanical Engineering. The lecturer is required to deliver a course of class lectures of not less than forty hours and five public lectures on 'Machine Tool Types, the Art of Cutting Metals, and the Methods of Production.' Patron: the University Court.

1926	Kenneth Moir Sloan
1934	Ian Garvie, BSc
1951	John Loudon
1956	David Lancaster Nicolson, BSc
1958	Walter Millen Adam, TD, BSc, CA
1960	John Henderson Shankland, BSc
1967	James Dobbie Houston
1969	Ronald Shade Hamilton, MSc
1972	Kenneth Neville Davies, BSc, PhD
1975	John Frank Woodward, BSc
1975	L H Peach: *Group Director of Personnel, IBM Europe*
1976	M Fores: *Senior Economic Adviser, the Department of Industry*
1976	Franz Koenigsberger: *Emeritus Professor of Machine Tool Engineering, University of Manchester Institute of Science and Technology*
1976	G Robertson: *Scottish Organiser, the General and Municipal Workers Union and Board Member, Scottish Development Agency*
1977	J A Kelly: *Director of Manpower Intelligence and Planning, Manpower Services Commission*
1977	G L Reid: *Works Manager and Director, General Motors, Scotland, Ltd*

McCall Anderson Lectureship in Dermatology

Founded in 1909, in memory of Sir Thomas McCall Anderson, Professor of Clinical Medicine, 1874-1900 and then Practice of Medicine, 1900-1908, by the Directors of the Glasgow Hospital for Skin Diseases, on the transfer of the work of the Hospital to the Western Infirmary. The Lectureship is attached to the Western Infirmary. Patron: the University Court.

1909	John Wyllie Nicol, MD
1928	Joseph Goodwin-Tomkinson, MD
1934	Allison David McLachlan, MD
1947	James Sommerville, MB ChB

1960   John Alexander Milne, MB ChB
1978-2000 Rona McLeod Mackie, MD, DSc, FRCP, FRCPath, FRSE, FMedSci: *Professor of Dermatology*

McCash Lectureship in the History of Engineering

Founded in 1972 and endowed by James Alexander McCash in memory of his parents William Lithgow McCash and Margaret Martin (or McCash) of Gallowhill Farm, Kirkintilloch. The foundation provides for a lecture to be delivered biennially on a subject connected with the History of Engineering. In alternate years, or if for any reason the lecture is not delivered, the income from the funds shall be made available for the purchase, as and when convenient, of books, drawings, prints or manuscripts on the History of Engineering.

1977   Andrew Meikle Bryan, DSc, LLD
1985   A Ian Bowman, MA
1987   Robert Simpson Silver, CBE, MA, BSc, PhD, DSc, FInstP, FIMechE, FRSE

Sir William Macewen Memorial Lectureship in Surgery

Founded in 1926 and endowed from a fund promoted to commemorate the work of Sir William Macewen, Regius Professor of Surgery in the University, 1892-1924. The foundation provides for a lecture to be delivered biennially on a subject connected with the advancement of surgery. Both members of the University and the general public may attend. After delivery the lecture is to be published as a University of Glasgow Publication. Patron: the University Court, acting on the nomination of a Committee consisting of the Regius Professor of Surgery, the St Mungo Professor of Surgery, and the President of the Royal College of Physicians and Surgeons of Glasgow.

1927   Harvey Williams Cushing, AM, MD, LLD, DSc, FRS: *Professor of Surgery in Harvard University*
1929   Sir Charles Alfred Ballance, KCMG, CB, MVO, MD, FRCS
1934   René Leriche, FRCS: *Professor of Surgery in the University of Strasbourg*
1937   Ferdinand Sauerbruch: *Professor of Surgery in the University of Berlin*
1939   George Grey Turner, MB, DCh, FRCS: *Professor of Surgery in the British Postgraduate Medical School*
1948   Geoffrey Jefferson, FRS: *Professor of Neurology in the University of Manchester*
1952   Matthew John Stewart, CBE, MD, LLD: *Emeritus Professor of Pathology in the University of Leeds*
1954   Reynaldo Dos Santos: *Professor of Surgery in the University of Lisbon*

1955	Sir James Rognvald Learmonth, KCVO, CBE, MD, LLD: *Professor of Surgery and Regius Professor of Clinical Surgery in the University of Edinburgh*
1958	Charles Huggins, SM, MD, ScD: *Professor of Surgery in the University of Chicago*
1961	Sir Russell Brock, FRCS: *Member of Council and former Vice-President of the Royal College of Surgeons*
1963	Francis Daniels Moore, MD: *Professor of Surgery in Harvard University*
1965	Joseph Trueta, MA, MD, DSc, FRCS: *Nuffield Professor of Orthopaedic Surgery in the University of Oxford*
1967	Sir Charles Illingworth, CBE, MD, ChM, DSc, LLD: *Emeritus Professor of Surgery*
1970	John W Kirklin, BA, MD, FACS: *Professor of Surgery in the University of Alabama*
1972	Sir Hedley John Bernard Atkins, KBE, DM, MCh: *previously Professor of Surgery in Guy's Hospital, London and a past President of the Royal College of Surgeons of England*
1975	Sir Michael Woodruff, BEE, MD, MS, FRS: *Professor of Surgery in the University of Edinburgh*
1977	Sir Rodney Smith, KBE, MS, PRCS: *President of the Royal College of Surgeons of England*
1980	Denton A Cooley, MD
1982	Tan Sri Guan Bee Ong, OBE, MD, DSc
1986	Robert Shields, MD, FRCS, FRCSE
1996	John Daly, MD: *Professor in Cornell University, New York, USA*

Sir Fitzroy Maclean Memorial Lecture

Founded in memory of author and statesman Sir Fitzroy Hew Maclean (1911-1996), who was awarded an honorary LLD by the University in 1969.

1996	Vladimir Velebit: *lawyer, historian and former Yugoslav Ambassador to the Court of St James*
1997	Martin Bell: *journalist and Member of Parliament*
1999	Lord Carrington: *former Secretary of State for Defence*
2000	Frederick Forsyth: *author*

Mitchell Lectureship on Methods of Statistics

Founded in 1925 and endowed by the businessman and president of the Glasgow Chamber of Commerce, 1923-1925, Sir George Arthur Mitchell, MA 1880, LLD 1936. The appointments in 1986 and 1988 were full members of the University staff. Patron: the University Court.

1925	George Alexander Carse, MA, DSc: *lecturer in Natural Philosophy in the University of Edinburgh*
1926	William Arthur, MA: *lecturer in Mathematics*
1931	Major Greenwood, DSc, FRS: *Professor of Epidemiology in the University of London*
1932	William Arthur, MA
1944	Richard Alexander Robb, MA, DSc
1966	John Aitchison, MA, DSc, DipMathStat, FRSE
1979	Sir David Roxbee Cox, MA, PhD, FRS: *Professor of Statistics at the Imperial College of Science and Technology*
1980	Friedrich Pukelsheim, PhD: *University of Freiburg*
1981	John Ashworth Nelder, DSc, FRS: *Rothamsted Experimental Station*
1981	John Anthony Anderson, DPhil: U*niversity of Newcastle*
1982	Stephen Elliott Fienberg, BSc, AM, PhD: *Carnegie Mellon University*
1983	Robert Nicholas Cumow, BA, PhD
1983	Murray Alan Aitkin, BSc, PhD: *University of Lancaster*
1983	Vic Barnett, MSc, PhD, DSc, FIS: *University of Sheffield*
1984	Michael John Romer Healy, MBA, MA: *London School of Hygiene and Tropical Medicine*
1984	James M Dickey, PhD: *University of Minnesota*
1985	Robert Nicholas Cumow, BA, PhD: *University of Reading*
1986	Peter Jeffrey Smith, BSc, PhD
1988	John Hope McColl, MA, MSc
1999	Noel Cressie, BSc, MA, PhD: *Ohio State University*
2000	Henry Wynn, MA, PhD: *Warwick University*
2001	Sandy Weisberg: *University of Minnesota*

Muirhead Demonstratorship in Physiology

Founded in 1877 and endowed by Henry Muirhead, MD, LLD (d. 1890), of Bothwell, and attached to the Chair of Institutes of Medicine, now Physiology. The Demonstrator is required to act as an assistant to the Regius Professor of Physiology in teaching and in original investigation. He or she is expected to engage in independent investigation under the direction of the Professor and to devote his or her entire time to the duties of the office. The Demonstrator is appointed annually by the Senatus, subject to the approval of the University Court, on the recommendation of the Professor of Physiology, who must furnish evidence of the suitability of the person recommended.

David Murray Lectureship

Founded in 1929, in memory of David Murray (1842-1928), Glasgow lawyer, antiquary and bibliographer, MA 1863, LLD 1888. The foundation originally provided for the delivery of one or more lectures annually on the History of Learning, especially in relation to History, Archaeology, Law or Bibliography. From 1958, the Lectures have been given biennially.

1931	Montague Rhodes James, MA, DLitt: *Provost of Eton College*
1932	Percy Stafford Allen, MA, DLitt: *President of Corpus Christi College, Oxford*
1933	Sir George Macdonald, KCB, MA, DLitt
1934	Sir Frederick George Kenyon, GBE, KCB, MA, DLitt: *Principal Librarian of the British Museum*
1935	Viscount Dunedin, GCVO, LLD, DCL
1936	Albert Frederick Pollard, MA, DLitt, FBA: *Director of the Institute for Historical Research in the University of London*
1937	Roger Bigelow Merriman, MA, DLitt, FBA: *Professor of History in Harvard University*
1938	Alfred Edward Stamp, CB, MA: *Deputy Keeper of the Records of Scotland*
1939	Francis De Zulueta, MA, DCL: *Regius Professor of Civil Law in the University of Oxford*
1939	Hermann Kantorowicz, DrJurUtr: *Assistant Director of Research in Law in the University of Cambridge*
1943	Denis William Brogan, MA: *Professor of Political Science in the University of Cambridge*
1944	Vivian Hunter Galbraith, MA, FBA: *Professor of History in the University of Edinburgh*
1945	Robert William Chapman, MA, DLitt, LLD: *Fellow of Magdalen College, Oxford*
1946	David Douglas, MA: *Professor of History in the University of Oxford*
1947	Henry William Meikle, CBE, MA, DLitt, LLD: *HM Historiographer in Scotland*
1948	Geoffrey Chevalier Cheshire, MA, DCL: *Professor of English Law in the University of Oxford*
1949	Francois Louis Ganshof, LLD: *Professor of Mediaeval History in the University of Ghent*
1950	Harold Cooke Gutteridge, KC, MA, LLD: *sometime Professor of Comparative Law in the University of Cambridge*
1951	Herbert Butterfield, MA, LLD, DLitt: *Professor of Modern History in the University of Cambridge*
1952	Thomas Mackay Cooper, Lord Cooper, MA, LLD: *Lord Justice-General of Scotland*
1953	George Norman Clark, MA, DLitt, LLD, FBA: *Provost of Oriel College, Oxford*

1954	Archibald Hunter Campbell, MA, BCL, LLM: *Regius Professor of Public Law in the University of Edinburgh*
1955	John Goronwy Edwards, MA, DLitt, FBA: *Director of the Institute for Historical Research in the University of London*
1956	Hector McKechnie, QC, BA, LLB: *Sheriff of Inverness, Moray, Nairn and Ross and Cromarty*
1957	Frank Chalton Francis, MA, FSA: *Keeper in the Department of Printed Books in the British Museum*
1958	Sir Reader Bullard, KCB, KCMG, CLE, MA
1960	Alfred Thompson, Baron Denning of Whitchurch, MA, LLD: *A Lord of Appeal in Ordinary*
1963	Richard William Southern, MA, DLitt, FBA: *Chichele Professor of Modern History in the University of Oxford*
1965	Alan Noel Latimer Munby, MA, LittD: *Fellow and Librarian of King's College, Cambridge*
1967	Robert Feenstra, JUD, Drhc: *Professor of Roman Law in the University of Leyden*
1969	Ernest Campbell Mossner, PhD: *Professor of Philosophy in the University of Texas*
1970	Cecil Herbert Stuart Fifoot, MA, FBA: *Honorary Fellow of Hertford College, Oxford*
1973	John Kenneth Sinclair St Joseph, OBE, MA, MA, PhD, FBA: *Director in Aerial Photography in the University of Cambridge*
1976	William Beattie, CBE, MA, LLD, LittD: *Professor in the Institute for Advanced Studies in the Humanities, University of Oxford*
1979	Willem H Nagel: *University of Leiden*
1982	Denys Hay, MA, FBA, FRSE: *Professor of Medieval History in the University of Edinburgh*
1983	Robin Carfrae Alston, BA, MA, PhD: *British Library*
1987	Peter Gonville Stein: *University of Cambridge*
1990	Lord Briggs of Lewes: *Provost of Worcester College, Oxford*
1991	David Maxwell Walker, CBE, QC, MA, PhD, LLD, FBA, FRSE: *Emeritus Professor of Law in the University*
1992	Lotte Hellinga: *British Library*
1993	Donald Watt: *University of St. Andrews*
1994	Lord Rodger of Earlsferry: *Lord Advocate for Scotland*

Pilcher Memorial Lecture

Founded in memory of Percy Sinclair Pilcher (1866-1899), pioneer of aviation. Pilcher was one of the few British participants in the race to invent the airplane. He was a lecturer at the University in 1891.

1996	Keith McKay: *British Aerospace Defence Ltd*
1997	Robert M McKinley, CBE: *former Chairman of British Aerospace Airbus Ltd*
1998	Peter Wilby: *GKN Westland Helicopters Ltd*
1999	Philip Jarrett: *aviation historian and author*
2001	Dugald Cameron, OBE: *former Director of Glasgow School of Art and Aviation historian* and Roderick Galbraith: *Shoda Professor of Aerospace Systems*

Robert Pollok Lectureship in
Materia Medica and Pharmacology

Founded in 1914 and endowed by Miss Jeanie Pollock and Mrs Janet P Gilchrist in fulfilment of the intention of their brother, Robert Pollock, MB 1876, for research in Materia Medica and Pharmacology.

1914	Walter James Dilling, MB: *later Professor of Pharmacology in the University of Liverpool*
1921	Sir David Campbell, MA, BSc, MD: *later Professor of Materia Medica in the University of Aberdeen*
1931	John Macqueen Johnston, MB ChB
1932	Stanley Alstead, MD: *later Professor of Materia Medica*
1947	Alexander Slessor, MB ChB
1958	John Gordon Macarthur, MC, MB ChB
1979	William Stewart Hillis, MB ChB

A C B Reid Lectureship

The A C B Reid Lectureship was set up in 1988 by a bequest from A C B Reid to establish two prizes and to endow an annual lecture on the subject of Freedom, with particular emphasis on any threats to freedom which may exist. The lectures are administered by the Selection Board of the Stevenson Citizenship Fund Trust - when appropriate, a Stevenson lecture is designated as incorporating the A C B Reid lecture in Freedom.

1996	Helena Kennedy, QC
1998	Partha Mitter: *University of Sussex*

Alexander Robertson Lectureship

Founded in 1901 by the Revd Alexander Robertson for the defence of the Christian Religion. The lecturer is appointed by the University Court on the nomination of a Committee consisting of the Principal and the Professors of the Faculty of Divinity. He or she must give a course of not fewer than five lectures and the course is to be held not oftener than once in every two years. The lectures are open to the public.

1904	John Morrison, MA, DD: *Principal of the Church of Scotland College, Calcutta*
1906	Ernest Findlay Scott, MA, DD: *Minister of the South United Free Church, Prestwick*
1908	Andrew Miller, MA, DD: *Minister of Bluevale*
1910	James Moffat, MA, DLitt, DD: *Minister of the East United Free Church, Broughty Ferry*
1912	Henry Johnstone Wotherspoon, MA, DD: *Minister of St Oswald's, Edinburgh*
1914	John Ebenezer Honeyman Thomson, MA, DD: *missionary of the Free Church in Palestine*
1916	Thomas Hunter Weir, BD: *lecturer in Arabic in the University*
1918	John Alexander Hutton, MA, DD: *Minister of Belhaven United Free Church, Glasgow*
1922	Arthur Clutton-Brock, BA
1924	William Fulton, MA, BSc, DD: *Professor of Systematic Theology in the University of Aberdeen*
1928	Robert Harvey Strachan, MA, DD: *Professor of New Testament Language and Literature in Westminster College, Cambridge*
1930	Charles Earle Raven, MA, DD: *Canon of Liverpool*
1932	Charles Frederick D'Arcy, MA, DD, FBA: *Archbishop of Armagh*
1934	Walter Robert Matthews, MA, DD: *Dean of St Paul's*
1937	Emil Brunner: *Professor of Systematic Theology in the University of Zürich*
1940	John Baillie, DLitt, DD: *Professor of Divinity in the University of Edinburgh*
1948	Emil Brunner: *Professor of Systematic Theology in the University of Zürich*
1949	Joseph Hromadka: *Professor of Theology in the University of Prague*
1952	James Sutherland Thomson, MA, DD, LLD: *Dean of the Faculty of Divinity in McGill University*
1956	Friedrich Gogarten: *Professor of Theology in the University of Göttingen*
1958	Helmut Richard Niebuhr, PhD, DD: *Sterling Professor of Theology and Christian Ethics in Yale University Divinity School*
1964	Alexander Roper Vidler, MA, LittD, DD: *Fellow and Dean of King's College, Cambridge*
1967	Gunther Bornkamm: *Professor of New Testament Theology in the University of Heidelberg*

1982	Alvin Plantinga, AB, MA, PhD
1983	Charles Kingsley Barrett
1984	Jill Raitt
1985	Christopher Francis Evans, MA
1986	Louis Bouyer
1988	William David Davies
1988	Lesslie Newbiggin, CBE, DD: *Bishop of the Church of South India*
1993	Gustav Adolph Benrath, *Professor of Church History in the University of Mainz*
1995	Marion Anne Fraser, Lady Fraser: *Chair of Christian Aid*
1996	Daniel Wambutda: *Dean of the Faculty of Arts, University of Jos, Nigeria*

Donald Robertson Memorial Lectureship in Urban Studies

Founded in 1972 jointly by the University Court and the Board of Management of the journal *Urban Studies* to commemorate Donald James Robertson, Professor of Applied Economics, 1961-1969 and Industrial Relations, 1969-1970, and first Chairman of *Urban Studies* Board of Management.

1972	Lowdon Wingo, AB, PhD: *Director of Regional and Urban Studies, Resources for the Future, Incorporated, Washington, DC*
1974	David Vernon Donnison, BA: *Director, Centre for Environmental Studies, London*
1977	Ruth Glass, MA
1984	Benjamin Chinitz, MA, PhD: *Dean of the College of Management Sciences, University of Lowell, USA*
1986	Leo Klaassen, PhD: *Netherlands Economic Institute*
1988	Gordon C Cameron, MA, FRSA: *Cambridge*
1990	Charles L Leven: *Washington*
1992	Edwin von Boventer: *University of Munich*
1994	G McCrone: *Centre for Housing Research and Urban Studies*
1996	Jim Hughes: *Wales European Centre, Brussels*
1998	Sir Peter Hall: *Bartlett School of Planning, University College, London*
2000	John Hills: *London School of Economics*

Royal Samaritan Lectureship in Gynaecology

Founded in 1926 and endowed by the Governors of the Royal Samaritan Hospital for Women. Patron: the University Court, acting on the recommendation of a Selection Committee consisting of the Chairman, the Deputy Chairman and the Convenor of the Medical Committee of the Hospital, a representative of the University Court, and a representative of the Senatus. The lectureship was attached to the Royal Samaritan

Hospital (closed in 1990), now being attached to the Queen Mother's Hospital, Glasgow. The lecturer must be a Visiting Surgeon of the Hospital with charge of wards in it. At least one course of practical instruction must be given by the lecturer each year.

1926   David Shannon, MB ChB
1933   Donald McIntyre, MD
1955   John Hewitt, MB ChB
1962   William Cunningham Armstrong, MB ChB
1967   Robin Murdoch, TD, MD
1976   Matthew MacMaster Garrey, MB ChB
1979   Alistair William Frank Miller, MB ChB
2000   William R Chatfield, MD, ChB, MRCOG, FRCS, FRCOG

Shoda Memorial Lecture

Founded in 1996 with a gift from family and friends in memory of Paul Taizo Shoda who graduated from the University in 1916 and was awarded a DSc by the University in 1988 for his contribution to engineering in Japan. The endowment was set up with three functions - this annual lecture, a Shoda Prize for an outstanding student in Aerospace Engineering and to provide a fund for the promotion and development of Aerospace Engineering.

1997   Roderick A M Galbraith, BSc, PhD: *Shoda Professor of Aerospace Systems*
1998   John Farley, OBE: *former chief test pilot, Hawker Siddeley*
1999   Williamson Berry: *European Space Agency*
2000   Colin R McInnes, BSc, PhD: *Professor of Space Systems Engineering*
2001   Henry McDonald: *Director of NASA Ames Reseacrh Centre, California*

Stevenson Lectureship in Citizenship

Founded in 1921 by Sir Daniel Macaulay Stevenson (1851-1944), philanthropist and later Chancellor of the University, 1934-1944. Patron: the University Court, acting on the nomination of a Selection Board consisting of the Principal, the Professors of Moral Philosophy and Political Economy, a representative of the University Court, the Lord Provost of the City of Glasgow or a deputy appointed by him, a representative of the Corporation of the City of Glasgow, a representative of the Chamber of Commerce of Glasgow, a representative of the Glasgow Education Authority, and a representative of the Workers' Educational Association (Scottish Branch). In 1980, the appointment of a visiting lecturer to give four lectures was approved. In 1982, the award of a fee to a member of staff in either the Department of Philosophy or of Economics was approved for six lectures as part of an undergraduate course which would be open to the public.

In 1987, a rota was established for the Departments of Philosophy, Politics and Political Economy to take turns on an annual basis to host visiting scholars and arrange public lectures.

1922	Sir William Henry Hadow, CBE, MA, DMus: *Vice-Chancellor of the University of Sheffield*
1923	Herbert Albert Laurens Fisher, MP, MA, LLD, FRS: *President of the Board of Education*
1924	William George Stewart Adams, MA: *Professor of Political Theory and Institutions in the University of Oxford*
1925	Ernest Barker MA, DLitt, LLD: *Principal of King's College, London*
1926	Lawrence Pearsall Jacks, MA, DD, DLitt, LLD: *Principal of Manchester College, Oxford*
1927	Cecil Delisle Burns, MA, DLitt
1937	Arthur David Kemp Owen, BA, MComm
1945	Edwin Bidwell Wilson, AB, PhD: *Emeritus Professor of Vital Statistics in Harvard University*
1946-1963	John Anderson Mack, MA: *later Director of the School of Social Study*
1972	David Daiches Raphael, MA, DPhil: *Professor of Philosophy in the University of Reading*
1979	William Ross, Lord Ross of Marnock, MA, LLD: *previously Secretary of State for Scotland*
1981	Julius Tomin: *University of Oxford*
1982	Joel Fleishman: *Vice-Chancellor Director of the Institute of Policy Sciences and Public Affairs and Professor of Law and Policy Sciences at Duke University, North Carolina*
1982	Raymond Plant, BA, PhD
1986	Robert Silcock Downie , MA, BPhil

1988 **Department of Politics**
Karl Heinz Reif, MA, DipPol, PhD, DSc
Jack Mcleod, BS, MS, MA, PhD: *Wisconsin*
Joseph Eugene Stiglitz, BA, PhD: *Stanford*

1989 **Department of Economics**
W J Baumol: *New York University*
Partha Sarathi Dasgupta: *University of Cambridge*
Frank Horace Hahn: *University of Cambridge*
Edmond Malinvand: *Institut National de la Statistique, Paris*
E Stiglitz: *Princeton University*

1990   Andrei Anikin: *Institute of World Economy and International Relations in Moscow*
       Peter Thal: *Professor of Economics at the University of Halle, East Germany*
       Ian Ross: *Professor of English at the University of British Columbia*
       Angela McRobbie: *Lecturer in Sociology, Ealing College of Further Education*
       Glasgow European City of Culture Series
       Andrew S Skinner, MA, BLitt, FRSE, FBA: *Daniel Jack Professor fo Political Economy*
       Edward McCombie McGirr, CBE, BSc, MD, FRSE: *Emeritus Professor of Administrative Medicine*
       Andrew C Ross: *University of Edinburgh*
       Ronald Mavor: *University of Saskatchewan*
       David Maxwell Walker, CBE, QC, MA, PhD, LLD, FBA, FRSE: *Emeritus Professor of Law*
       Harold Ellis: *University of London*
       Maxwell Murray: *Professor of Veterinary Medicine*
       Rex Whitehead: *Professor of Theoretical Physics*
       John A Carty: *lecturer in the Department of Public, International and European Law*
       Alexander C Cheyne: *University of Edinburgh*
       Martin Loughlin: *John Millar Professor of Law*
1991   **Department of Philosophy**
       Catherine McCall *(four lectures)*
1992   **Department of Politics**
       Roy Hattersley, MP: *Deputy Leader of the Labour Party*
       Lord Armstrong of Ilminster: *former British Cabinet Secretary*
       Fedor Burlatski: *previously member of USSR Supreme Soviet*
       Lord Jenkins of Hillhead: *former UK Home Secretary*
       Elemer Hankiss: *former dissident, President of Hungarian TV*
1993   **Department of Economics**
       A Atkinson: *University of Cambridge*
       Lawrence Summers: *The World Bank*
       Gordon Tullock: *University of Arizona*
       James M Buchanan: *George Mason University*
       Alberto Alesina: *Harvard University*
       Tommaso Padoa-Schioppa: *Banca d'Italia*
1994   **Department of Philosophy**
       Bernard Williams: *University of Oxford*
       Neil MacCormick: *University of Edinburgh*
1995   **Department of Politics: *Inclusive and Exclusive Aspects of Citizenship***
       Vytautas Landsbergis: *Leader of the Opposition in Lithuanian Parliament*

Justice Richard Goldstone: *South African Judge and Chief UN Prosecutor for War Crimes in the former Yugoslavia*
John Hume MP, MEP: *Leader of the Social Democratic and Labour Party*
Lord Raymond Plant of Highfield: *Master of St Catherine's College, Oxford*
Cornelia Schmalz-Jacobsen: *Federal Government Commissioner for Foreigners in Germany*
Allan Macartney: *Member of the European Parliament for North-East Scotland*
George Robertson, MP: *Shadow Secretary of State for Scotland*

1995-1996 **Women's Centenary Series**
Frances Cairncross: *The Economist*
Dame Jennifer Jenkins
Anthea Tinker: *Age Concern Institute of Gerontology, King's College, London*
Lady Howe of Aberavon: *Broadcasting Standards' Council*
Baroness Williams of Crosby, PC
Kirsty Wark: *broadcaster*
Rt Hon Baroness Blackstone: *Master of Birbeck College, London*
Kate Adie: *broadcaster*

1996-1997 **Department of Economics: *The Shrinking World: Globalisation and the Challenge for the Nation State***
Peter Jay
Peter Kenen
Richard Freeman
Otmar Issing
Anne Krueger: *Stanford University, California*
Sir Leon Brittan: *Commissioner Vice-President of European Commission*

1997-1998 **Department of Philosophy: *Contemporary Values***
John Skorupski: *University of St Andrews*
Ian Kennedy: *King's College, London*
Sir Roger Bannister
Andrew Marr: *The Independent*
Charles Kennedy, MP

1998-1999 **Department of Politics: *Ethics in Government***
Baroness Chalker of Wallasey: *Independent Adviser on Africa and Development*
Lord Nolan
Janos Bertok: *Organisation for Economic Cooperation and Development*
Sir Richard Scott
Anita Gradin: *Former EU Commissioner*

1999-2000 **Department of Economics:** *The Prospects for the Welfare State in the New Century.*
Frank Field MP: *Minister for Welfare Reform*
Vito Tanzi: *Fiscal Affairs Department, International Monetary Fund*
Andrew Dilnot: *Director of the Institute for Fiscal Studies, London*
Hans-Werner Sinn: *Centre for Economic Studies, University of Munich*

Alexander Stone Lecture in Bibliophily

Endowed in 1978 by Sir Alexander Stone, (1907-1998), LLD 1986, Glasgow solicitor and bibliophile. In 1982, the Stone Lectureship Committee appointed two Stone fellows in Bibliophily who carried out research in their chosen field, held informal weekly seminars for Honours students, and gave a public lecture at the end of their term in residence. It has otherwise been given as a single lecture.

1980	A R Turnbull: *Secretary to Edinburgh University Press*
1981	Madeleine B Stern and Leona Rostenberg: *antiquarian booksellers, New York*
1982	N J Rogers: *Emmanuel College, Cambridge*
1982	E J W McCann: *lecturer at Queen's University, Belfast*
1983	Jack Baldwin: *Keeper of Special Collections in the University Library*
1984	Elizabeth L Eisenstein: *Alice Freeman Palmer Professor of History, University of Michigan*
1984	Ruari McLean: *typographer and author*
1984	Lady Antonia Fraser: *writer*
1985	Peter M Daly: *Professor in the Department of German, McGill University*
1986	Martin J Weiner: *Professor in the Department of History, Rice University*
1986	Arthur D Boney: *Professor of Botany in the University*
1987	Sir William Rees-Mogg: *Chairman of the Arts Council of Great Britain*
1987	W Gordon Graham: *Chairman of Butterworths Publishers*
1988	Seamus Heaney: *Boylestone Professor of Rhetoric, Harvard University*
1989	Philip D Hobsbaum: *Titular Professor of English Literature*
1989	Derick S Thomson: *Professor of Celtic*
1990	David Daiches: *former Director, Institute of Advanced Studies in the Humanities, University of Edinburgh*
1990	Edwin Morgan: *Emeritus Professor of English*
1991	Kenneth White: *Professor of Twentieth Century Poetics, The Sorbonne, Paris*
1991	Penelope Lively: *prizewinning children's author*
1992	Sir Graham Hills: *former Principal of the University of Strathclyde*
1992	Nigel Barley: *Museum of Mankind, British Museum, London*

1993   Liz Lochhead: *poet and playwright*
1993   Anne Etra: *Children's Book Division, Oxford University Press*
1994   Phyllis Dorothy White James, Baroness James of Holland Park: *author 'P D James'*
1994   Anthony Clare: *broadcaster and Clinical Professor of Psychiatry at Trinity College Dublin*
1995   Arnold Kemp: *former editor of The Herald*
1997   Ronald Stuart Thomas: *minister of religion and poet*
1999   Alison Louise Kennedy: *writer*
2001   Ruth Rendell: *crime novelist*

Alexander Stone Lecture in Rhetoric

Endowed in 1978 by Sir Alexander Stone, (1907-1998), LLD 1986, Glasgow solicitor and bibliophile.

1990   Charles Peter Kennedy, MA: *Member of Parliament*
1991   Laurie Taylor: *Professor in the Department of Sociology in the University of York*
1992   David Craig: *Professor of Creative Writing in the University of Lancaster*
1993   Murdo Ewen Macdonald: *Emeritius of Practical Theology, Trinity College*
1994   David Jenkins: *Bishop of Durham*
1995   Sir Michael Rose: *Adjutant General*
1996   Graham P Durant, BSc, PhD: *Deputy Director of the Hunterian Museum*
1998   Deborah Cameron: *University of Strathclyde*

Taylor Memorial Lectureship

In 1996, an endowment was received from the late Edward Graham Taylor, Senior Lecturer in the French Department 1957-1987, to be used for an annual lecture by an eminent specialist of contemporary French History. The first lecture will be given in 2001.

William C Teacher Lectureship in Bacteriology

Founded in 1928 and endowed by William Curtis Teacher, (d.1929), distiller, of Glasgow. The lecturer is appointed annually by the University Court on the recommendation of a Selection Committee. He or she is also a Bacteriologist to the Royal Infirmary.

1928   Robert Cruickshank, MD
1935-1944   Robert Douglas Stuart, MD
1947   Robert Douglas Stuart, MD
1950   John Charles James Ives, MB ChB
1978   Morag Crichton Timbury, MD, PhD
1992   David J Platt, BSc, PhD

Tumelty Lecture

Founded in 1978 by subscription in memory of James J Tumelty, Assistant, Lecturer and Senior Lecturer in History from 1950 until 1978. The funds are used to provide a prize for the best Honours graduate in Modern History and the lecture series, with any residue used to purchase History books for the Library. It is administered by a Committee appointed by the University Court.

1982	Geoffrey Best, MA, PhD, FRHistS: *Professor of History in the University of Sussex*
1983	John Prest: *Balliol College Oxford*
1984	Peter J Parish: *Professor of American History at the University of London*
1985	Fred Parsons: *lecturer in History*
1986	David Dilks: *Professor of International History in the University of Leeds*
1987	J Taylor: *Newcastle upon Tyne*
1988	Maurice J M Larkin, MA, PhD: *Professor of Modern European History in the University of Edinburgh*
1989	G B A M Finlayson: *senior lecturer in Modern History*
1990	Zara Steiner: *lecturer and Fellow in Cambridge*
1991	Martin Pugh: *Professor of Modern History in the University of Newcastle Upon Tyne*
1993	P D G Thomas: *Professor in History in the University of Wales, Aberystwyth*
1995	David Gillard
1997	James McMillan: *Professor in the University of Strathclyde*
1999	Jill Stephenson: *lecturer in the University of Edinburgh*
2001	Fiona Montgomery: *Edge Hill University College*

Waltonian Medical Lectureship

Founded in 1788 and endowed by William Walton, MA, MD 1763, Rector of Upton in the County of Huntingdon. The lecturer is required to take for his subject that branch of Medicine or Science connected with Medicine assigned to him by the governing body of the University. Patron: the University Court. In 1926, the Court decided to use the Waltonian funds for the endowment of a Lectureship in Materia Medica at the Royal Infirmary.

1792	James Towers, CM *(Midwifery)*
1816	Richard Millar, MD *(Materia Medica)*
1831-1868	William Mckenzie, MD *(Ophthalmology)*
1871-1900	Thomas Reid MD, LLD *(Ophthalmology)*
1909-1919	Thomas Stewart Patterson, PhD, DSc *(Organic Chemistry)*
1926-1942	John Clark Middleton, MA, BSc, MB *(Materia Medica)*
2000	Martin McIntyre, BSc, MB ChB, PhD, MRCP *(Medicine and Therapeutics)*

Sir William Weipers Memorial Lecture

Originally named the Sir William Weipers Commemorative Lecture, the lectureship, sponsored by Pedigree Petfoods Ltd, takes place annually to commemorate the contribution that Professor Sir William Weipers (1904-1990) made to Veterinary Medicine and to the University. After his death the title was changed to the Memorial Lecture. The lecture has been given biennially since 1994.

1976	A Gwynn Benyon, CB, MRCVS, DVSM: *President of the Royal College of Veterinary Surgeons*
1977	Roger Valentine Short, BVSc, MSc, PhD, ScD, FRS: *Director of the MRC Unit of Reproductive Biology, Edinburgh*
1978	Sir James Whyte Black, MB ChB, FRS: *Director of Therapeutic Research, Wellcome Foundation Ltd*
1979	Sir Kenneth Lyon Blaxter, BSc, PhD, DSc, FRS: *Director of the Rowett Research Institute*
1980	John Morton Boyd, BSc, PhD, DSc, FRSE: *Director in Scotland of the Nature Conservancy Council*
1981	Lord Michael Meredith Swann, MA, PhD, FRSE: *Provost of Oriel College, Oxford*
1982	Leo K Bustad, BS, DVM, PhD: *Dean of the College of Veterinary Medicine, Washington State University*
1983	H J Bendixen, DrMedVet: *Head of the Division of Legislation relating to Veterinary matters and Zootechnics, European Commission*
1984	Sir William Henderson: *Chairman of the Horserace Betting Levy Board Advisory Committee*
1985	A R W Porter, CBE: *Secretary and Registrar, Royal College of Veterinary Surgeons*
1986	Benjamin L Hart, DVM, PhD: *School of Veterinary Medicine, University of California*
1987	Ronald S Anderson, BVMS, PhD: *Professor of Animal Husbandry, University of Liverpool*
1988	William Fleming Hoggan Jarrett, PhD, MRCVS: *Professor of Veterinary Pathology in the University*
1989	F J Bourne, BVetMed, PhD: *Director of the AFRC Institute for Animal Health*
1990	A R Mitchell, BVetMed, BSc, PhD: *Department of Veterinary Medicine, Royal Veterinary College, London*
1991	Maxwell Murray, BVMS, PhD, DVM, FRCPath, FRSE, MRCVS: *Professor of Veterinary Medicine in the University*
1994	Kenneth C Calman, MD, PhD, FRCS, FRCP, FRCGP, FRCR, MFCM, FRSE: *Chief Medical Officer, Department of Health, London*

1996	George Gettinby, BSc, DPhil: *Department of Statistics and Modelling Science, University of Strathclyde*
1998	Ian McConnell, FRSE: *University of Cambridge*
2001	Sir William Stewart, PhD, DSc, FRS, FRSE: *President of the Royal Society of Edinburgh*

William Weir Assistantship in Materia Medica

Founded in 1914 and endowed by the bequest of William Weir of Kildonan and Adamton, Ayrshire, ironmaster.

1914	George Herbert Clark, MD
1924	John Macqueen Johnston, MB
1925	Gavin McCallum, MB
1930	William Whitelaw Snedden, MA, BSc
1933	Andrew Wilson, PhD
1938	John Brown MacDonald, MB
1939	Alexander Slessor, MB
1947-1953	Francis John Hebbert, MB
1996	E M El-Omar, MD

James Wood Lecture

The lecture is funded from the James Wood Bequest Fund which was created under the will of James Wood of Wallhouse, Torphichen, coal merchant, from the residue of his estate. The first donations were made in 1935. This lecture was proposed by the Trustees in 1986 as a special five year annual donation to the University of Glasgow Stair Building Appeal. The lectureship has been given annually since 1987 and is organised by the Faculty of Law and Financial Studies at the University.

1987	Lord Fraser of Tullybelton: *Lord of Appeal in Ordinary*
1988	Lord Hunter: *former Senator of the College of Justice in Scotland*
1989	Eric M Clive: *Scots Law Commission*
1990	David Maxwell Walker, CBE, QC, MA, PhD, LLD, FBA, FRSE: *Emeritus Professor of Law in the University*
1991	Francis David Jacobs, QC: *Advocate General for the European Court of Justice*
1992	William Adam Wilson: *Lord President Reid Professor of Law in the University of Edinburgh*
1993	Lord Clyde: *Senator of the College of Justice in Scotland and Chairman of the Orkney Enquiry*

1994   J Anthony Weir: *Trinity College, Cambridge*

1995   Sir William Kerr Fraser: *Principal*

1996   Matthew Clarke, QC

1997   Lord Dervaird: *Dickson Minto Professor of Company Law in the University of Edinburgh*

1998   Lord Hope of Craighead: *Lord President of the Court of Session*

1999   David Johnston: *Regius Professor of Civil Law in the University of Cambridge*

2000   Kenneth Miller: *Professor of Law in the University of Strathclyde*

2001   Lord Gill: *Senator of the College of Justice and Chairman of the Scottish Law Commission*

Arthur Young Lectureship in Accountancy

The Lectureship was established with financial assistance from Arthur Young, accountants, to provide a public lecture by eminent academics and practitioners.

1978   Robert Ian Tricker, MA, FCA, FCMA: *Director, Oxford Centre for Management Studies*

1979   George J Benston: *University of Rochester, New York*

1980   David Solomons, DSc: Wharton School, *University of Pennsylvania*

1981   Bryan Carsberg, MA, MSc, FCA: *London School of Economics and Political Science*

1982   Athol Sprott Carrington, PhD

1983   H Thomas Johnson, PhD

1985   Alan Harold Williams, BComm

1985   David A Wilson, MBA: *Institute of Chartered Accountants, Ontario*

1987   John Rankin Small, CBE: *Professor in the Department of Accountancy and Finance at Heriot-Watt University*

Graham Young Lectureship

A lectureship in Metallurgical Chemistry was instituted in 1899 and endowed in 1908 by the Trustees of Thomas Graham Young. Patron: the University Court. The University Court decided in June 1959 and January 1964 to apply the income of the endowment to the foundation of a visiting lectureship to be offered annually to a person of distinction in the field of Chemistry or Engineering or Physics.

1899   William Carrick Anderson, MA, DSc

1905   Charles Edward Fawsitt, PhD, DSc: *later Professor of Chemistry in the University of Sydney*

1908   Cecil Henry Desch, DSc, PhD: *later Superintendent of the Department of Metallurgy, National Physical Laboratory*

1919   William Carlaw Gray, ARTC

1920   Robert Hay, BSc, PhD, LLD

1960   Robert Burns Woodward, PhD, ScD, DSc: *Morris Loeb Professor of Chemistry in Harvard University*

1961   Max Ferdinand Perutz, PhD, FRS: *Director of the Medical Research Council Unit for Molecular Biology and Reader at the Davy-Faraday Laboratory at the Royal Institution*

1962   Vladimir Prelog, DrIng: *Professor of Organic Chemistry in the Technische Hochschule of Zurich*

1963   Francis Harry Compton Crick, BSc, PhD: *Nobel Laureate*

1964   Denys Haigh Wilkinson, FRS: *Professor of Nuclear Physics in the University of Oxford*

1965   Melvin Calvin, DSc: *Nobel Laureate, Professor of Chemistry in the University of California*

1967   Sir Alfred Pugsley, OBE, DSc, FRS: *Professor of Civil Engineering in the University of Bristol*

1969   Sir Edward Bullard, MA, PhD, ScD, FRS: *Professor of Geophysics in the University of Cambridge*

1970   Sir Derek Harold Richard Barton, DSc, PhD, FRS: *Nobel Laureate, Professor of Organic Chemistry in the Imperial College of Science and Technology, London*

1972   Alexander Thom, PhD, DSc, MA, LLD: *previously lecturer in Engineering and Emeritus Professor of Engineering Science in the University of Oxford*

1974   Alfred Brian Pippard, MA, PhD, ScD, FRS: *Cavendish Professor of Physics in the University of Cambridge*

1975   Sir William Hawthorne, CBE, FRS: *Churchill College, Cambridge*

1976   Manfred Eigen: *Professor in the Max-Planck Institut für Biophysikalische Chemie, Göttingen*

1978   Walter Charles Marshall, CBE, FRS: *UK Atomic Energy Authority*

1979   Charles Alan Maynard May, FEng, FIEE, FBCS: *Director of Research, Post Office Research Centre*

1980   William Nunn Lipscomb, BS, PhD: *Nobel Laureate, University of Harvard*

1984   Martin John Rees, MA, PhD, FRS: *Cambridge*

Graduation

Regulations

The University has the power to confer degrees on graduands by authority of the founding Papal Bull of 1451. Regulations governing the content and type of degrees awarded are set by Resolutions of the University Court under powers granted by the Universities (Scotland) Act of 1966. The current regulations for entitlement to graduate can be found in the latest edition of University Calendar.

Ceremonial Procedure

Graduation ceremonies follow tradition that has developed over the centuries. Roughly translated as 'taking a step', graduation symbolises the move of the former student (now called graduand) into wider society as a graduate, there to use the talents developed as a member of this society and which the University acknowledges by the conferment of a degree.

The University confers four types of degree:
- Doctorates awarded as Honorary Degrees in recognition of work of great distinction (for example, LLD, DLitt, DSc, DUniv)
- Doctorates for research presented in a thesis - the PhD is the only degree awarded in all Faculties
- Masters' for advanced study taken by graduates (for example, MPhil, MSc)
- First degrees, such as the Bachelors' in Science, Engineering and some Arts subjects; the principal first degree in Arts and Social Sciences is the Master of Arts.

At graduation, students are presented for degrees by the Dean of the Faculty in which they studied. The order of presentation is that of the 'seniority' of the Faculties and of degree, with 'higher' degrees coming before first degrees. For example, three Deans in succession may present graduands for PhDs, then two may present Masters' and then all the Deans in sequence present their first degrees.

The Procession

The Procession enters the Bute Hall to the strains of the organ playing *Gaudeamus Igitur*. The playing, and often the singing, of this medieval academic anthem is traditional on such occasions:

Gaudeamus Igitur

Gaudeamus Igitur, juvenes dum sumus,	*Vivat Academis, vivant Professores*
Gaudeamus Igitur, juvenes dum sumus,	*Vivat Academis, vivant Professores,*
Post jucundem juventutem,	*Vivat membrum quodilbet,*
post molestam senectutem	*vivant membra quaelibet,*
Nos habebit humus, nos habebit humus.	*Semper sint in flore, semper sint in flore!*

At the head of the procession comes the Mace, symbol of the University's authority, carried by the Bedellus.

Behind him comes the person conferring the degrees; by right it is the Chancellor but he may delegate his powers to the Vice-Chancellor (the Principal). In their absence degrees may be conferred by a senior professor, usually the Dean of Faculties or Clerk of Senate.

Next come the Professor of Divinity, the Clerk of Senate and the Dean of Faculties, followed by the Deans of the Faculties, members of Senate and other teaching staff.

The Ceremony

After the Mace has been placed on the table in front of the platform party, and before anyone sits, the Professor of Divinity opens the proceedings in Latin with a prayer written by the Dutch scholar, Erasmus (c.1466-1536):

Prayer of Thanksgiving

Aeterne Deus et Clementissime Pater, gratias tibi quam maximas agimus quod nos a fera et agresti vita ad artes ingenuas et scientarum cognitionem deduxeris, quod domum nostram perpetua largitate et misericordia usque ad hunc diem prosecutus sis quod viam nobis et veritatem et vitam in Filio tuo indicaveris.

A te, Pater, petimus ut servi tui graduandi, ab his profecti intitiis, ad metam perfectionis adspirent, et nobis nostraeque reipublicae laudi et ornamento esse possint. Tibi, Pater, Filio, et Spiritui Sancto sit laus, honor et gloria in saecula saeculorum. Amen

The first Dean presents the graduands for their degrees. Each graduand is called, moves forward and kneels to be touched lightly on the head or 'capped' with a flat velvet cap by the presiding official, who pronounces Latin words of conferment.

The precise words said vary according to the degree. For the PhD these will be *'Te Philosophiae Doctorum creamus'*, which translated is, *'we create you a Doctor of Philosophy'*. The words are repeated for each graduand in turn. With Masters and First degrees, the full wording - for example - *'Te Medicinae Baccalaureum et Chirurgiae Baccalauream creamus'* which translated is, *'we create you Bachelor of Medicine and Bachelor of Surgery'* is used only for the first graduand, and it is usual to say *'Te quoque'* (and you also) for those who follow.

The Bedellus then puts the graduate's hood in place, the Head of the Registry hands over the diploma and the graduate leaves the platform.

Hoods are different colours according to the degree conferred with many of the colours being taken from the native flora of Scotland. *(See also section on Academic Dress on page 188).*

Medical Graduates' Oath

Every candidate for the degrees of Bachelor of Medicine, Bachelor of Surgery and Bachelor of Dental Surgery must at graduation subscribe to the following declaration:

I do solemnly and sincerely declare that, as a Graduate in Medicine of the University of Glasgow, I will exercise the several parts of my profession, to the best of my knowledge and abilities, for the good, safety, and welfare of all persons committing themselves or committed to my care and direction; and that I will not knowingly or intentionally do anything or administer anything to them to their hurt or prejudice for any consideration or from any motive whatever. And I further declare that I will keep silence as to anything I have seen or heard while visiting the sick which it would be improper to divulge.

And I make this solemn declaration in virtue of the Provisions of the Promissary Oaths Act, 1868, substituting a Declaration for Oaths in certain cases.

This declaration takes the place of the Latin oath which until 1868 was required of all graduates in medicine. The terms of this oath were:

Testor Deum omnipotentem me hoc iusiurandum pro virili servaturum; victus rationem aegris commodam et salutarem pro virili servaturum; nullius intercessione nec sponte noxium pharmacum cuiquam propinaturum; sed sancte et caste vitam artemque meam instituturum; in quascunque domos intravero ad aegrotantium duntaxat salutem ingressurum et ab omni iniuria inferenda procul futurum: quaecunque inter curandum videro audiverove siquidem ea efferre non expediat silentio suppressurum.

The Charge

When the last graduate has been capped, the presiding official makes a speech giving a charge to the graduates to remember their responsibilities to the University and its reputation. There may also be a comment on some aspect of the University affairs or wider issues affecting the University.

Everyone then rises, the Professor of Divinity gives the Benediction.

Benediction

Gratia Domini nostri Iesu Christ et caritas Dei et communicatio Spiritus Sancti sint cum omnibus vobis.

The Academic Procession, followed by the graduates, leaves the Hall, bringing the graduation ceremony to a close.

Academic Dress

All members of the University taking part in University ceremonies wear their proper academic dress with dark clothes, and white bow-tie for men. Caps are worn or carried.

Gowns

Undergraduates: Scarlet material, with full sleeves half the length of the gown. A difference indicating the Faculty may be worn, in the form of a narrow band of silk on the breast of each side of the gown, of the colour of the hood-lining proper to the lowest degree in the Faculty.

Bachelors: Black material, with open pointed sleeves reaching to the foot of the gown. Bachelors who are Masters of Arts wear a master's gown with the hood proper to their bachelor's degree.

Masters: Black silk or material, with cord and button on the yoke and closed sleeves (with horizontal arm-slit) reaching to the foot of the gown and ending in a crescent shaped cut (the points of the crescent facing back).

Higher Doctorates: *Undress:* Black silk or material, with a collar falling over the yoke and full sleeves half the length of the gown. *Full dress:* Scarlet material, faced with silk of the colour of the hood-lining proper to the degree, with cord and button on the yoke and open pointed sleeves reaching to the foot of the gown.

Doctors of Philosophy: *Undress:* Black silk or material, with a collar falling over the yoke and full sleeves half the length of the gown. *Full dress:* The same, with the addition of facings of crimson silk.

Doctorates of Medicine, Dental Surgery and Practitioner Doctorates *Undress:* Black silk or material, with a collar falling over the yoke and full sleeves half the length of the gown. *Full dress:* The same, with the addition of facings of silk the colour of the hood-lining proper to the degree.

Chancellor: Black watered silk, with long closed sleeves and square collar, trimmed with gold lace and gold frogs.

Rector: Black material, with square collar and full-length cape-like sleeves; five gold bands on each sleeve.

Vice-Chancellor: Black watered silk, with long closed sleeves and square collar, trimmed with silver lace and silver frogs.

Depute Vice-Chancellor: Black watered silk, with long closed sleeves, with sleeve cuts trimmed with half inch oakleaf lace and facings, and square collar trimmed with one inch silver oakleaf lace.

Principal: Purple silk, with open sleeves, facings of black silk and a border of purple velvet.

Dean of Faculties: Black silk, with square velvet collar, full-length cape-like sleeves and velvet frogs.

Members of the University Court: The Secretary of Court and past and present members of the University Court may be distinguished by the wearing of frogs on the sleeves of their gowns.

Students' Representative Council President and Senior Vice-President: Purple silk or material, faced with crimson silk, with golden cord and button on the yoke, full sleeves half the length of the gown and badges.

Students' Representative Council Past President: Purple silk or material, faced with crimson silk, with silver cord and button on the yoke, full sleeves half the length of the gown and badges.

Members of the Students' Representative Council Executive: Purple silk or material, faced with a narrow band of black silk or material, with silver cord and button on the yoke, full sleeves half the length of the gown and badges.

Students' Representative Council Court Assessor: Dark red silk or material, with a golden cord and button on the yoke, with full sleeves, half the length of the gown.

Hoods

All hoods are of the 'full' shape. *Note.* Bachelors who are also Masters may wear Bachelors' hoods of silk.

Bachelor of Accountancy (BAcc): Black material, lined with slate grey silk and bordered on the outer edge with scarlet cord.

Bachelor of Animal Health (BAH): Black material, lined with terracotta silk, and trimmed inside the top edge with gold-coloured silk (colour of whin blossom, *Ulex europaeus*) and bordered on the outer edge with scarlet cord.

Bachelor of Arts (BA): Black material, lined and edged with purple silk (colour of bell heather, *Erica cinerea*) and bordered on the outer edge with scarlet cord.

Bachelor of Community Education and Community Development (BCommEdCommDev): Black material, lined with sky blue silk and bordered on the outer edge with scarlet cord.

Bachelor of Dental Surgery (BDS): Black material, lined with emerald green silk and bordered on the outer edge with scarlet cord.

Bachelor of Divinity (BD): Black material, lined with light cherry silk and bordered on the outer edge with scarlet cord.

Bachelor of Education (BEd) in Primary Education: Black material, lined with blue silk (colour of bluebell of Scotland, *Campanula rotundifolia*) and bordered on the outer edge with scarlet cord.

Bachelor of Engineering (BEng): Black material, lined with plum coloured silk and bordered on the outer edge with scarlet cord.

Bachelor of Engineering Studies (BES): Black material, lined with gold coloured silk (colour of whin blossom, *Ulex europaeus*) and bordered on the outer edge with scarlet cord.

Bachelor of Financial and Legal Studies (BFLS): Black material, lined with slate grey silk, and trimmed inside the top edge with venetian red silk and bordered on the outer edge with scarlet cord.

Bachelor of International Business Administration (BIBA): Black material, lined with orange silk (colour of Slender St John's Wort, *Hypericum pulchrum*) and trimmed inside the top edge with purple silk (colour of bell heather, *Erica cinerea*) and bordered on the outer edge with scarlet cord.

Bachelor of Laws (LLB): Black material, lined with venetian red silk and bordered on the outer edge with scarlet cord.

Bachelor of Medical Science (BMedSci): Black material, lined with scarlet silk, and trimmed inside the top edge with emerald green silk and bordered on the outer edge with scarlet cord.

Bachelor of Medicine and Bachelor of Surgery (MB ChB): Black material, lined with scarlet silk and bordered on the outer edge with scarlet cord.

Bachelor of Music (BMus): Black material, lined with azure blue silk and bordered on the outer edge with scarlet cord.

Bachelor of Nursing (BN): Black material, lined with cornflower blue silk and bordered on the outer edge with scarlet cord.

Bachelor of Science (BSc): Black material, lined with gold coloured silk (colour of whin blossom, *Ulex europaeus*) and bordered on the outer edge with scarlet cord.

Bachelor of Technological Education (BTechEd): Black material, lined with plum coloured silk, and trimmed inside the top edge with blue silk (colour of bluebell of Scotland, *Campanula rotundifolia*) and bordered on the outer edge with scarlet cord.

Bachelor of Theology (BTheol): Black material, lined and edged with light cherry silk and trimmed inside the top edge with blue silk (colour of bluebell of Scotland, *Campanula rotundifolia*) and bordered on the outer edge with scarlet cord.

Bachelor of Veterinary Medicine (BVMS): Black material, lined with terracotta silk and bordered on the outer edge with scarlet coloured cord.

Master of Accountancy (MAcc): Black silk or material, lined and edged with slate grey silk.

Master of Arts (MA): Black silk or material, lined and edged with purple silk (colour of bell heather, *Erica cinerea*).

Master of Arts (Social Sciences) (MA SocSci): Black silk or material, lined and edged with purple silk (colour of bell heather, *Erica cinerea*).

Master of Business Administration (MBA): Black silk or material, lined and edged with orange silk (colour of Slender St John's Wort, *Hypericum pulchrum*).

Master of Community Care (MCC): Black silk or material, lined and edged with sky blue silk.

Master of Education (MEd): Black silk or material, lined and edged with blue silk (colour of bluebell of Scotland, *Campanula rotundifolia*).

Master of Engineering (MEng): Black silk or material, lined and edged with gold coloured silk.

Master of Laws (LLM): Black silk or material, lined and edged with venetian red silk.

Master of Letters (MLitt): Black silk or material, lined and edged with white silk.

Master of Midwifery (MM): Black silk or material, lined and edged with cornflower blue silk and edged with white silk.

Master of Music (MMus): Black silk or material, lined and edged with azure blue silk.

Master of Nursing (MN): Black silk or material, lined and edged with cornflower blue silk.

Master of Philosophy (MPhil): Black silk or material, lined and edged with white silk.

Master of Public Health (MPH): Black silk or material, lined and edged with gold coloured silk (colour of whin blossom, *Ulex europaeus*).

Master of Research (MRes): Black silk or material, lined and edged with gold coloured silk (colour of whin blossom, *Ulex europaeus*).

Master in Science (MSci): Black silk or material, lined and edged with gold coloured silk (colour of whin blossom, *Ulex europaeus*) and edged with scarlet silk.

Master of Science (MSc): Black silk or material, lined and edged with gold coloured silk (colour of whin blossom, *Ulex europaeus*).

Master of Science (Adult and Continuing Education): Black silk or material, lined and edged with gold coloured silk (colour of whin blossom, *Ulex europaeus*).

Master of Social Work (MSW): Black silk or material, lined and edged with sky blue silk.

Master of Theology (MTh): Black silk or material, lined and edged with light cherry silk.

Master of Veterinary Medicine (MVM): Black silk or material, lined and edged with terracotta silk.

Doctor of Divinity (DD): Scarlet material, lined with white silk.

Doctor of Laws (LLD): Scarlet material, lined with venetian red silk.

Doctor of Letters (DLitt): Scarlet material, lined with purple silk (colour of bell heather, *Erica cinerea*).

Doctor of Music (DMus): Scarlet material, lined with azure blue silk.

Doctor of Science (DSc), includes DSc in Dentistry, in Engineering and in Medicine: Scarlet material, lined with gold coloured silk (colour of whin blossom, *Ulex europaeus*).

Doctor of Veterinary Medicine and Surgery (DVMS): Scarlet material, lined with terracotta silk.

Doctor of Veterinary Medicine (DVM): Scarlet material, lined with terracotta silk.

Doctor of Veterinary Surgery (DVS): Scarlet material, lined with terracotta silk.

Doctor of Clinical Psychology (DClinPsy): Black silk, lined and edged with gold coloured silk (colour of whin blossom, *Ulex europaeus*).

Doctor of Dental Surgery (DDS): Black silk, lined and edged with emerald green silk.

Doctor of Engineering (DEng): Scarlet material, lined and edged with plum coloured silk.

Doctor of Medicine (MD): Black silk, lined and edged with scarlet silk.

Doctor of Philosophy (PhD): Black silk, lined and edged with crimson silk.

Doctor of the University (DUniv): Scarlet material, lined with black silk with one inch gold ribbon on the outside edge, with cord and button on the yoke, and open pointed sleeves to the foot of the gown.

Degrees awarded in conjunction with Glasgow School of Art
Bachelor of Architecture (BArch): Black material, lined with lime coloured silk (colour of lime flower, *Tilia europaea*) and bordered on the outer edge with scarlet cord.

Bachelor of Arts (BA) in Design and Bachelor of Arts (BA) in Fine Art: Black material, lined on the right with malachite green silk and on the left with swiss white silk and bordered on the outer edge with scarlet cord.

Master of Architecture (MArch): Black silk or material, lined and edged with lime coloured silk *(*colour of lime flower, *Tilia europaea*).

Master of Design (MDes): Black silk or material, lined and edged on the right with malachite green silk and on the left with swiss white silk.

Master of Fine Art (MFA): Black silk or material, lined and edged on the right with malachite green silk and on the left with swiss white silk.

Degrees awarded in conjunction with the Scottish Agricultural College
Bachelor of Science (BSc) in Applied Plant and Animal Science: Black material, lined with gold coloured silk (colour of whin blossom, *Ulex europaeus*) and bordered on the outer edge with scarlet cord.

Bachelor of Technology (BTechnol) - all degrees: Black material, lined on the right with green silk (colour of bottle sedge, *Carex rostrata*) and on the left with blue silk (colour of vipers bugloss, *Echium vulgare*) and bordered on the outer edge with scarlet cord.

Degrees and Qualifications no longer awarded by the University of Glasgow after July 2001
Bachelor of Law (BL): Black material, bordered on the inside with venetian red silk.

Master of Applied Science (MAppSc): Black silk or material, lined and edged with gold-coloured silk.

Master of Dental Surgery (MDS): Black silk or material, lined and edged with emerald green silk.

Master of Science (Dental Science): Black silk or material, lined and edged with gold-coloured silk.

Master of Surgery (ChM): Black silk or material, lined and edged with scarlet silk.

Master of University Administration (MUnivAdmin): Black silk or material, lined and edged with orange silk (colour of slender st john's wort, *Hypericum pulchrum*).

Doctor of Dental Surgery (DDS): Scarlet material, lined with emerald green silk.

Doctor of Dental Science (DDSc): Scarlet material, lined with emerald green silk and edged with yellow silk.

Doctor of Medicine (MD): Scarlet material, lined with scarlet silk.

Licentiate in Theology (LTh): Bachelors gown with a black epitoge edged with light cherry coloured silk worn over the left shoulder.

Degrees formerly awarded in conjunction with the Royal Scottish Academy of Music and Drama, 1983 - 1994
Bachelor of Education (BEd) in Music: Black material, lined blue silk (colour of bluebell of Scotland, *Campanula rotundifolia*) and bordered on the outer edge with scarlet cord.

Bachelor of Arts (BA) in Dramatic Studies: Black material, lined and edged with purple silk (colour of bell heather, *Erica cinerea*) and bordered on the outer edge with scarlet cord.

Bachelor of Arts (BA) in Musical Studies: Black material, lined and edged with purple silk (colour of bell heather, *Erica cinerea*) and bordered on the outer edge with scarlet cord.

Caps

Undergraduates, Bachelors, Masters, Doctors of Philosophy and Practitioner Doctors wear the black trencher cap with tassel. Higher Doctors wear the black velvet 'John Knox' cap. The Chancellor and the Rector wear a black velvet trencher trimmed with gold lace and with a gold tassel, the Vice-Chancellor a black velvet trencher cap trimmed with silver lace and a silver tassel.

Dress for Graduands

At graduation ceremonies, graduands, whether they are already graduates or not, wear the full dress gown, and carry the hood proper to the degree which they are about to receive; no other gown or hood shold be worn.

The dress worn by graduands at graduation ceremonies is: **For men:** Dark trousers and jacket or suit with white shirt, black shoes or boots, unpatterned black tie. **For women:** Dark trousers, skirt or suit with white blouse, or white or dark dress; dark shoes; tie, if worn, to be black. National or military dress may be worn by men and women.

Robemakers to the University

The appointed robemakers are Ede and Ravenscroft, 46 Frederick St, Edinburgh, EH2 1EX.

Honorary and Official Degrees

Regulations

Honorary and official degrees are granted by the Senatus in accordance with the following regulations. (Resolution pending).

1. The following degrees may be conferred honoris causa: **(a)** the Degree of Doctor of Divinity (DD), the Degree of Doctor of Laws (LLD), the Degree of Doctor of Letters (DLitt), the Degree of Doctor of Music (DMus), the Degree of Doctor of Science in Medicine (DSc(Med)), the Degree of Doctor of Engineering (DEng), the Degree of Doctor of Doctor of Veterinary Medicine and Surgery (DVMS), the Degree of Doctor of the University (DUniv). **(b)** the Degree of Master of Arts (MA), the Degree of Master of Science (MSc), the Degree of Master of Science (Science Education), the Degree of Master of Science (Medical Science), Degree of Master of Science (Veterinary Science), and the Degree of Master of Engineering (MEng).

2. The following degrees may be conferred iure officii on any Professor or recognised officer of the University of Glasgow or of a recognised institution who is not already a university graduate: **(a)** Degree of Master of Arts (MA) and the Degree of Bachelor of Science (BSc). **(b)** Master of Science (MSc), the Degree of Master of Science (Science Education), the Degree of Master of Science (Medical Science), and the Degree of Master of Science (Veterinary Science).

3. The Senatus Academicus shall annually appoint a Committee, to be called the Committee on Honorary Doctor's Degrees, consisting of the Principal and other such members of the Senatus as the Senatus shall from time to time determine. It shall be the duty of the Committee to select persons to be recommended to the Senatus for the conferment of the Honorary Degrees listed in Section 1(a) and to present its recommendations to the Senatus.

4. No resolution to confer any honorary Doctor's Degree shall be moved in the Senatus except upon special notice given after a fortnight has elapsed from the date when the recommendation was presented.

5. The Senatus Academicus shall constitute the Senate Business Committee on Honorary Masters' Degrees and on Official Degrees. This Committee may, at any time during the academic year, select persons to be recommended to the Senatus for the conferment of the Honorary and Official Degrees listed in Sections 1(b) and 2 and present its recommendations to the Senatus.

6. A resolution to confer any Honorary Master's Degree or Official Degree may be moved at the same meeting of the Senatus at which the recommendation has been presented.

7. The conferment upon any person of an Honorary or Official Degree shall not in itself qualify that person to become a candidate for any other Degree or Diploma.

8. No application from or on behalf of any person desirous of receiving any Honorary degree or Official Degree shall be entertained.

Honorary and Official Graduates 1978-2001

For lists of honorary degrees conferred 1897-1950, see *University Calendar, 1953-1954*; for degrees conferred 1951-1960, see *University Calendar, 1966-1967*; for degrees conferred 1961-1965, see *University Calendar, 1972-1973*; for honorary degrees conferred 1966-1977, see *University of Glasgow: History and Constitution 1977-1978*; for honorary degrees of MA and BSc conferred 1949-1961, see *University Calendar 1973-1974*. For honorary degrees conferred prior to 1897, consult Archive Services.

The following is a list of honorary degrees awarded up to 31 March 2001.

Doctor of Divinity

Best, Ernest, *Emeritus Professor of Divinity and Biblical Criticism*	1997
Brown, Raymond Edward, *Auburn Professor of Biblical Studies in the Union Theological Seminary, New York*	1978
Browning, Don Spencer, *Alexander Campbell Professor of Religious Ethics and the Social Sciences*	1998
Childs, Brevard Springs, *Professor of Religion at Yale University*	1992
Davidson, The Very Rev Robert, *Emeritus Professor of Old Testament Language and Literature, and Moderator of the General Assembly of the Church of Scotland, 1990-91*	1993
Durkan, John, *Honorary Senior Research Fellow in Scottish History*	1998
Evans, Christopher Francis, *Emeritus Professor of New Testament Studies, King's College, University of London*	1987
Forrester, Duncan Baillie, *Dean of the Faculty of Divinity in the University of Edinburgh*	1999
Grant, Robert McQueen, *Professor of Humanities in the University of Chicago*	*1979*
Herron, Andrew, *Moderator of the General Assembly of the Church of Scotland and previously Clerk to the Presbytery of Glasgow*	1989
Lohse, Eduard, *Bishop of Hanover*	1984

Martin, James, *Minister of the Church of Scotland in the Parish of High
    Carntyne, Glasgow* 1983
McIndoe, The Very Rev John Hedley, *Moderator of the General Assembly
    of the Church of Scotland and previously Minister at St Columba's
    Church of Scotland, London* 2000
Morris, William James, *Minister of Glasgow Cathedral* 1979
Plantinga, Alvin, *Professor of Philosophy at Calvin College, Michigan and
    Notre Dame University, Indiana* 1982
Russell, David Syme, *General Secretary of the Baptist Union of Great Britain
    and Northern Ireland* 1980
Scott, The Rev John Alexander Miller, *Minister of St Andrew's Scots Memorial
    Church, Jerusalem* 1986
Shaw, The Very Rev Douglas William David, *Professor of Divinity and Principal
    of St Mary's College, University of St Andrews* 1991
Taize, Brother Roger of, *founder of the Taize Community, Cluny, France* 1991
Theissen, Gerd, *Professor of New Testament Studies, University of Heidelberg* 1990
Winning, The Most Rev Thomas Joseph, *Roman Catholic Archbishop of Glasgow* 1983

Doctor of Engineering

Ash, Sir Eric Albert, *previously Rector of Imperial College of Science Technology
    and Medicine, University of London* 1994
Astrom, Karl Johan, *Professor of Automatic Control at the Lund Institute
    of Technology, Sweden* 1998
Bennett, George Aitken, *General Manager and Corporate Vice-President
    of Motorola SPS, East Kilbride* 1997
Broers, Alec Nigel, *Professor of Electrical Engineering, University of Cambridge
    and Master of Churchill College, Cambridge* 1996
Garrick, Sir Ronald, *previously Managing Director and Chief Executive of the
    Weir Group PLC* 1998
Grant, Alexander, *Joint Managing Director of Norfrost Ltd, Castletown, Caithness* 2000
Hu, Evelyn Lynn, *Professor of Electrical and Computer Engineering, University
    of California, Santa Barbara* 1995
Kao, Charles Kuen, *Vice Chancellor, Chinese University of Hong Kong* 1992
MacDonald, Allan Anthony, *Director of Regional Marketing, British Aerospace PLC* 1996
MacFarlane, Alistair George James, *Principal and Vice-Chancellor
    of Heriot-Watt University* 1995
McDonald, Henry, *Director of the NASA Ames Research Centre at Mountain
    View, California* 1997

Robinson, Ian, *Chief Executive, Scottish Power PLC* 1999
Scott, Ronald Fraser, *Professor of Civil Engineering, California Institute
of Technology* 1995
Singer, Josef, *L Shirley Tark Emeritus Professor of Aircraft Structures
at Technion, Israel Institute of Technology, Haifa* 1993
Thurlimann, Bruno, *Emeritus Professor of Structural Engineering at the Swiss
Federal Institute of Technology, Zurich* 1997
Vette, Alwyn Gordon, *Air Pilot and Aviation Safety Consultant* 1998
Weir, William Kenneth James, The Right Honorable The Viscount Weir,
Chairman of the Weir Group PLC 1993
Zunz, Sir Gerhard J, *previously Chairman of the Ove Arup Partnership* 1994

Doctor of Laws
Armour, Mary Nicol Neill, *painter and previously teacher at Glasgow School of Art* 1980
Attenborough, David Frederick, *biological scientist and producer and
administrator in television* 1980
Barnes, Sir Harry Jefferson, *Director of Glasgow School of Art* 1980
Bates, Sir David Robert, *Professor of Theoretical Physics in the Queen's
University of Belfast* 1979
Bremner, Sydney, *member of the Medical Research Council, member of the
Scientific Staff of the Laboratory of Molecular Biology, Cambridge, and Fellow
of King's College, Cambridge* 1981
Brennan, William Joseph, *Associate Justice of the Supreme Court of the
United States of America* 1989
Bruce, Andrew Douglas Alexander Thomas, *Earl of Elgin and Kincardine* 1983
Burnett, Sir John Harrison, *Principal and Vice Chancellor, University of Edinburgh* 1987
Cameron, Lord John, *Senior Judge of the College of Justice in Scotland* 1981
Caplan, The Hon Lord Philip Isaac, *Senator of the College of Justice in Scotland* 1996
Casson, Sir Hugh Maxwell, *President of the Royal Academy* 1980
Clark, Ian Robertson, *Executive Member of the Board of the British National
Oil Corporation* 1979
Clark, Robert, *Chairman of the Stock Conversion and Investment Trust PLC* 1984
Crawford, Sir Theodore, *Emeritus Professor of Pathology in the University
of London* 1979
Currie, Sir Alastair Robert, *Emeritus Professor of Pathology in the University
of Edinburgh* 1987
Dakrouri, Mohamed Ibrahim, *Chairman of MISR American International
Bank, Egypt* 1985

Delors, Jacques, *President of the Commission of the European Communities* 1986
Dewar, Donald Campbell, *Secretary of State for Scotland* 1998
Dick, Sir John Alexander, *previously Sheriff Principal of Glasgow and Strathkelvin* 1987
Eringen, Ahmed Cemal, *Professor of Continuum Physics and Civil Engineering*
    in Princeton University 1981
Ewing, Winifred Margaret, *Member of the European Parliament* 1995
Finniston, Sir Harold Montague, *Director of Sears Holdings Ltd* 1978
Flowers, Brian Hilton, *The Right Honorable Lord Flowers of Queens Gate*
    in the City of Westminster and Vice Chancellor of University of London 1987
Fox, Sanford J, *Professor of Law, Boston College Law School, Massachusetts, USA* 1997
Fraser, Lady Marion Anne, *Chair of the Board of Christian Aid, and Her Majesty's*
    High Commissioner to the General Assembly of the Church of Scotland 1995
Fraser, Sir William Kerr, *Permanent Under-Secretary of State, Scottish Office* 1982
Gill, Lord Brian, *Senator of the College of Justice in Scotland, Chairman*
    of the Scottish Law Commission and Judge 1998
Glick, David, *Emeritus Professor of Pathology at Stanford University Medical Center* 1980
Goldstone, Richard Joseph, *Member of the Constitutional Court of South Africa* *1997*
Gordon, Gerald Henry, *Sheriff of Glasgow and Strathkelvin* 1993
Gowans, Sir James Learmonth, *Secretary and Deputy Chairman of the*
    Medical Research Council 1988
Gray, Sir William Stevenson, *previously Lord Provost of Glasgow, and Chairman*
    of Scottish Development Agency 1980
Grossart, Angus Mcfarlane McLeod, *Managing Director of Noble Grossart Ltd,*
    merchant bankers 1985
Higgins, Rosalyn, *Member of the International Court of Justice* 1997
Hills, Graham John, *Principal and Vice Chancellor, University of Strathclyde* *1985*
House, Jack, *Author and Journalist* 1978
Irvine, Alexander Andrew Mackay, *The Right Honorable the Lord Irvine of Lairg,*
    barrister and Lord High Chancellor of Great Britain 1997
Jawara, Sir Alhaji Dawda Kairaba, *President of The Gambia* 1990
Johnston, Thomas Lothian, *Principal and Vice Chancellor of Heriot-Watt University* 1989
Kelly, Michael, *Lord Provost of the City of Glasgow* 1984
Kerr, Sir John Olav, *Permanent Under-Secretary at the Foreign and*
    Commonwealth Office 1999
Koiter, Warner Tjardus, *Professor of Mechanical Engineering in University of Delft* 1978
Lang, Anton, *Member of the National Academy of Science, USA and Professor*
    of Botany and Plant Pathology in Michigan State University 1981
Lind, William, *Secretary, Business Archives Council of Scotland* 1988

Longuet-Higgins, Michael Selwyn, *Royal Society Research Professor in the University of Cambridge* 1979

McClintock, Frank Ambrose, *Professor of Mechanical Engineering in Massachusetts Institute of Technology* 1981

MacCormick, Donald Neil, *Regius Professor of Public Law in the University of Edinburgh* 1999

McCrone, Robert Gavin Loudon, *Secretary of the Industry Department for Scotland and Chief Economic Adviser, Scottish Office* 1986

Macfarlane, Sir Norman Somerville, *a Member of the University Court* 1988

Macgregor, Ian Kinloch, *Chairman and Chief Executive Officer of American Metal Climax Inc* 1978

MacInnes, Hamish, *mountaineer and author on mountain rescue techniques* 1983

Mackay, James Peter Hymers, *Baron Mackay of Clashfern, Lord High Chancellor of Great Britain* 1994

McKay, Johnston Reid, *Assessor of the General Council on the University Court* 1985

Meehan, Francis Joseph, *Diplomat in the US Foreign Service and United States Ambassador to the German Democratic Republic* 1986

Millan, Bruce, *previously Member of the Commission of the European Communities* 1995

Milson, Stroud Francis Charles, *Professor of Law and Fellow of St John's College, Cambridge* 1981

Mooney, Peter, *YDH Dato'Kurnia Bakti Diraja, Advocate and Vice Chairman of the Bar Association of Malaysia* 1989

Muluzi, Bakili, *President of the Republic of Malawi* 1997

Neil, Matthew, *Secretary and Chief Executive of Glasgow Chamber of Commerce* 1983

Noble, Sir Fraser, *Principal and Vice Chancellor of the University of Aberdeen* 1981

Oakley, Charles Allen, *Member of the University General Council and Editor, Glasgow Chamber of Commerce Journal* 1986

O'Brien, Conor Cruise, *author and editor* 1990

Penrose, The Honorable Lord George William, *Senator of the College of Justice in Scotland* 2000

Pindborg, Jens Jorgen, *Professor and Chairman of Department of Oral Pathology, Royal Dental College, Copenhagen and Head of Dental Department, University Hospital, Copenhagen* 1979

Pontecorvo, Guido, *Honorary Consultant Geneticist, Imperial Cancer Research Fund, London* 1978

Prejean, Sister Helen Theresa, *human rights campaigner and author* 1995

Renton, Air Commodore Helen Ferguson, *Director of the Women's Royal Air Force* 1981

Risk, Sir Thomas Neilson, *Governor of the Bank of Scotland* 1985

Rodger, Alan Ferguson, *Baron Rodger of Earlsferry, Lord Advocate*   1995
Ross, William, *Member of Parliament for Kilmarnock Division, Ayr and Bute*   1978
Sayles, George Osborne, *previously Professor of History in the Queen's University,*
 Belfast and the University of Aberdeen   1979
Shaw, Sir John, *Governor of the Bank of Scotland and Chairman of the*
 Scottish Higher Education Funding Council   1998
Smith, Elizabeth Margaret, *Baroness Smith of Gilmorehill, Chairman of the*
 Edinburgh Festival Fringe Society   1998
Smith, Sir Robert Courtney, *Chartered Accountant*   1978
Smith, Thomas Brown, *Member of Scottish Law Commission*   1978
Smith, William Leggat, *Chairman of the Board of Governors of Glasgow School of Art* 1987
Stevenson, Sir Simpson, *Chairman of the Greater Glasgow Health Board*   1982
Stone, Sir Alexander, *Chairman of Combined Capital Ltd, Glasgow*   1986
Stuart, Lord Alexander John Mackenzie, *first British judge to be appointed*
 to the Court of Justice of the European Communities   1981
Sutherland, James, *President of the International Bar Association*   1985
Taylor, William Leonard, *Chairman of the Glasgow Citizens' Theatre*   1991
Thomson, Adam, *Chairman of British Caledonian Airways*   1979
Thomson, Thomas James, *Chairman of the Greater Glasgow Health Board*   1988
Veil, Simone, *previously President of the European Parliament*   1995
Walton, David, *Chairman and Joint Managing Director of the Scottish*
 Metropolitan Property PLC   1985
Watson, William Alexander Jardine, *Ernest P Rogers Professor of Law in the*
 University of Georgia School of Law, USA   1993
Williams, Glanville Llewelyn, *previously Rouse Ball Professor of English Law*
 in the University of Cambridge   1980
Williams, Sir Alwyn, *Principal and Vice-Chancellor*   1988
Wright, Sir Robert Brash, *previously Honorary Clinical Lecturer in Surgery,*
 President of the Royal College of Physicians and Surgeons of Glasgow and
 President of the General Medical Council   1981
Xiang, Huan, *Member of the State Council Institute of International Relations,*
 Jeijing, China   1986
Younger, George Kenneth Hotson, *previously Secretary of State for Scotland*
 and Secretary of State for Defence   1992

Doctor of Letters

Andrews, Keith, *Keeper of Prints and Drawings at the National Gallery of Scotland* 1980
Barrow, Geoffrey Wallis Steuart, *Sir William Fraser Professor of Scottish History
 and Palaeography, University of Edinburgh* 1988
Berend, Ivan Tamas, *President, Hugarian Academy of Sciences, Hungary* 1990
Brown, George Mackay, *author and poet* 1985
Burri, Alberto, *abstract expressionist painter*
Carson, Robert Andrew Glendinning, *Keeper, Department of Coins and Medals,
 British Museum* 1983
Coppock, John Terence, *previously Ogilvie Professor of Geography at the
 University of Edinburgh, Secretary and Treasurer of the Carnegie Trust for
 the Universities of Scotland, and founding editor of the International Journal
 of Geographical Information Systems* 1999
Currie, David Anthony, *Lord Currie of Marylebone, Professor of Economics,
 London Business School* 1998
Daiches, David, *previously Director of Institute of Advanced Studies in the
 Humanities, University of Edinburgh* 1987
Deane, Phyllis Mary, *Emeritus Professor of Economic History, University of Cambridge* 1989
Donaldson, David Abercrombie, *painter and limner to Her Majesty the Queen,
 in Scotland* 1988
Eco, Umberto, *author and Professor of Semiotics in the University of Bologna,* 1990
Elton, Geoffrey Randolph, *Professor of English Constitutional History in the
 University of Cambridge* 1979
Forsyth, William, *film director* 1984
Gordon, Hannah Campbell Grant, *actress* 1993
Greene, David William, *Senior Professor, School of Celtic Studies,
 Dublin Institute for Advanced Studies* 1979
Havel, Václav, *President of the Czech Republic* 1998
Havergal, Giles Pollock, *Artistic Director of the Citizens' Theatre, Glasgow* 1982
James, Phyllis Dorothy White, Baroness James of Holland Park, *author 'P D James'* 1995
Kenny, Anthony John Patrick, *President of the British Academy* 1990
Klein, Lawrence Robert, *Benjamin Franklin Professor of Economics,
 University of Pennsylvania* 1991
Kyi, Aung San Suu, *co-founder of the National League for Democracy
 in Burma and Nobel Peace Prize Winner* 1997
Lindsay, John Maurice, *author, poet, journalist and editor* 1982
Lochhead, Elizabeth Anne, *poet and playwright* 1992
Low, Bet, *artist* 1999
Macgregor, Robert Neil, *Director of the National Gallery in London* 1998

Maclean, Alistair, *author* 1983
Maclean, Sorley, *poet* 1996
McClelland, Ivy Lilian, *previously assistant lecturer and reader in Spanish* 1989
McIntosh, Angus, *Emeritus Forbes Professor of English Language in the University of Edinburgh* 1994
McNeill, William Hardy, *Robert A Milliken Distinguished Service Professor of History, University of Chicago* 1987
Meade, James Edward, *Emeritus Professor of Political Economy, University of Cambridge* 1985
Morgan, Edwin, *poet and critic* 1990
Moscovici, Serge, *Directeur des études, a l'École des Hautes Études en Sciences Sociales, Paris* 1982
Murdoch, Dame Iris, *novelist and philosopher, Honorary Fellow of St Anne's College, Oxford* 1990
Paolozzi, Eduardo Luigi, *sculptor and author* 1980
Philipson, Sir Robin, *President of the Royal Scottish Academy* 1990
Prebble, John Edward Curtis, *author* 1997
Quirk, Sir Charles Randolph, *President of the British Academy* 1988
Reston, James, *Vice President of the New York Times* 1983
Seuren, Pieter Albertus Maria, *Professor of Theoretical Linguistics, University of Nijmegan* 1996
Singer, Hans Wolfgang, *Emeritus Fellow at the Institute of Development Studies, University of Sussex* 1994
Smart, Roderick Ninian, *Professor of Religious Studies in the University of Lancaster* 1984
Smith, Iain Crichton, *author and poet* 1984
Solow, Robert Merton, *Professor of Economics at the Massachusetts Institute of Technology, and winner of Nobel Prize for Economics* 1992
Steiner, George, *Extraordinary Fellow, Churchill College, Cambridge, Professor of English and Comparative Literature, University of Geneva* 1990
Stone, Lawrence, *Dodge Emeritus Professor of History in Princeton University, USA* 1993
Sutherland, Sir Stewart Ross, *Principal and Vice-Chancellor of the University of Edinburgh* 1999
Tapies, Anthony, *artist* 1990
Warnock, Helen Mary, Baroness Woeke in the City of Manchester and Mistress of Girton College, *Cambridge* 1988
Watt, Donald Elmslie Robertson, *Emeritus Professor of Scottish Church History in the Department of Mediaeval History, University of St Andrews* 2000
White, Kenneth John Dewar, *Professor of Twentieth Century Poetics, The Sorbonne, Paris* 1991

Doctor of Music

Alexander, Joan, *singer*	1978
Babbit, Milton Byron, *composer and William Shubal Conant Professor of Music in Princeton University*	1980
Bent, Margaret, *musicologist and Senior Research Fellow at All Souls College, Oxford*	1997
Davies, Sir Peter Maxwell, *composer*	1993
Glover, Jane Alison, *conductor*	1997
Legge- Schwarzkopf, Elizabeth, *singer*	1990
Musgrave, Thea, *composer*	1995
Penderecki, Krzysztof, *composer*	1995
Wilson, Thomas Brendan, *composer and Emeritus Professor of Music*	1991
Xenakis, Iannis, *composer*	1990

Doctor of Science

Abdul Rahman, Dato' Haji Abdul Hamid Haji, *Vice-Chancellor of the National University of Malaysia*	1988
Arbuthnott, Sir John, *Principal and Vice-Chancellor of the University of Strathclyde*	1999
Arima, Akito, *Professor of Physics in the University of Tokyo*	1984
Bader, Alfred Robert, *founder of the Aldrich Chemical Company*	1999
Ball, Johnny, *producer and presenter of popular mathematics and science television programmes and Rector of the University of Glasgow*	1997
Black, Sir James, *Professor of Analytical Pharmacology, King's College School of Medicine and Dentistry, University of London*	1989
Bleeker, Gabe Meinte, *Emeritus Professor of Ophthalmology, University of Amsterdam and founder and Director of the Netherlands Ophthalmic Research Institute*	1989
Bremner, John McColl, *Curtiss Distinguished Professor in Agriculture, Professor of Agronomy and Biochemistry, Iowa State University*	1987
Burnell, Jocelyn Bell, *Professor of Physics at the Open University*	1997
Calman, Sir Kenneth Charles, *Chief Medical Officer, Department of Health, London*	1996
Campbell, Fergus William, *Professor of Neurosensory Physiology, University of Cambridge*	1986
Chadwick, Peter, *Professor of Mathematics in the University of East Anglia*	1991
Clark, Douglas Henderson, *previously Consultant Surgeon in the Western Infirmary, and President of the Royal College of Physicians and Surgeons of Glasgow*	1983
Coats, David Jervis, *Senior Partner in Babtie, Shaw and Morton, Consulting Engineers*	1984

Doerffer, Jerzy Wojciech, *Professor and Rector of Gdansk Technical
University, Poland*   1983

Donald, Ian, *Regius Professor of Midwifery*   1983

Doyle, Peter, *Group Research and Technology Director, Imperial Chemical Industries*   1992

Dunitz, Jack David, *Organic Chemistry Laboratory, ETH-Zentrum, Zurich*   1999

Fichera, Gaetano, *Professor of Higher Mathematical Analysis, University of Rome*   1987

Frame, Sir Alistair Gilchrist, *previously Chairman of Rio Tinto Zinc Corporation Ltd*   1990

Gould, Stephen Jay, *Professor of Geology and Alexander Agassiz Professor
of Zoology, Harvard University, USA*   1994

Gurdon, Sir John Bertrand, *John Humphrey Plummer Professor of Cell Biology,
University of Cambridge and Chairman of Wellcome Cancer Research
Campaign Institute, Cambridge*   2000

Hamer-Hodges, Mary Elizabeth, *Medical Director of St Andrew's Clinics for
Children, Sierra Leone*   1997

Hart, Julian Tudor, *general practitioner and epidemiologist, Glyncorrwg,
South Wales*   1999

Hawthorne, Victor Morrison, *Emeritus Professor of Epidemiology, University
of Michigan, USA*   1996

Hillhouse, Robert Russell, *previously Permanent Under Secretary of State,
Scottish Office*   1999

Huxley, Sir Andrew, *President of the International Congress of Physiology,
and President of the International Union of Physiological Sciences*   1993

Kee, Chin Fung, *Tan Sri Professor Emeritus of Engineering, University of Malaya*   1986

Kendrick, Stanley B, *Deputy Chief Scientific Officer, Admiralty Research
Establishment, Dunfermline, Fife*   1986

Lin, Ting-Shen, *President of the Tatung Institute of Technology, Taiwan*   1992

Mackensen, Gunter, *Professor of Ophthalmology, Dean and Prorektor in the
University of Freiburg*   1982

McGirr, Edward McCombie, *Emeritus Muirhead Professor of Medicine*   1994

McGregor, Ian A, *Director of West of Scotland Regional Plastic and Oral Surgery
Unit, Canniesburn Hospital, Glasgow*   1986

McGregor, Sir Ian Alexander, *President of the Royal Society of Tropical Medicine*   1984

McKillop, Thomas Fulton Wilson, *Chief Executive of AstraZeneca PLC*   2000

Moffat, Sir Cameron, *previously Surgeon General/Director General of the
Army Medical Services*   1991

Murray, Robert, *Consultant in Occupational Health*   1993

Ogilvie, Bridget Margaret, *Director of the Wellcome Trust*   1995

Paul, John, *former Director of the Beatson Institute for Cancer Research*   1989

Penrose, Sir Roger, *Rouse Ball Professor of Mathematics, University of Oxford*   1996
Pierce, Gordon Barry, *Professor of Pathology in the University of Colorado*   1984
Phillips, Sir David, *Professor of Molecular Biophysics and Fellow of Corpus
  Christi College, Oxford*   1990
Prance, Sir Ghillean Tolmie, *Director of the Royal Botanic Gardens, Kew*   1999
Robson, Sir Gordon, *previously Director and Professor of Anaesthesia at the
  Royal Postgraduate Medical School, London*   1991
Romanes, George John, *Dean of the Faculty of Medicine, University of Edinburgh*   1983
Rossman, Michael G, *Hanley Professor of Biological Sciences in Purdue
  University, Indiana, USA*   1993
Salam, Abdus, *Professor of Theoretical Physics, Imperial College of Science
  and Technology, University of London*   1986
Saunders, Dame Cicely, *Chairman of St Christopher's Hospice*   1990
Scriver, Charles Robert, *Professor of Paediatrics and Human Genetics (Biology)
  at McGill University, Canada*   1993
Serre, Jean Pierre, *Titulaire de la Chaire D'Algebre et Geometrie,
  College de France, Paris*   1983
Sharp, Phillip Allen, *The Salvador E Luria Professor in the Centre for Cancer
  Research at Massachusetts Institute of Technology*   1998
Shoda, Paul Taizo, *former Executive Vice-President, Mitsubishi Heavy Industries
  Ltd, Japan*   1988
Soergel, Volker Hermann Alfred, *Professor of Physics, Ruprecht-Karls-Universitat Heidelberg* 1994
Sokoloff, Louis, *Chief of the Laboratory of Central Metabolism, National Institute
  of Mental Health, Bethesda, USA*   1989
Steinberger, Jack, *former Senior Physicist at the European Organisation for
  Nuclear Research, Geneva, and Professor of Physics at the Scuola Normale
  Superiore di Pisa*   1990
Stevens, Thomas Stevens, *Emeritus Professor of Chemistry, University of Sheffield*   1985
Stewart, Sir Frederick Henry, *Emeritus Professor of Geology in the University
  of Edinburgh*   1988
Stewart, William Duncan Paterson, *Chief Scientific Adviser to the Cabinet Office
  and previously Secretary of the Agricultural and Food Research Council*   1991
Stoker, Sir Michael, *President of Clare Hall, Cambridge*   1982
Wells, Alan Arthur, *Director General of the Welding Institute, Cambridge*   1982
Williams, Peter Orchard, *Director of the Wellcome Trust*   1992
Wroblewski, Andrzej Kajetan, *Professor of Physics and Rector of the University
  of Warsaw*   1992

Doctor of the University

Annand, Louise Gibson, *artist*	1994
Baird, Susan, *Lord Provost of the City of Glasgow*	1990
Barclay, David Rowat, *businessman*	1998
Barclay, Frederick Hugh, *businessman*	1998
Begg, Robert William, *President of the Royal Glasgow Institute of Fine Arts and former Chairman of the Trustees of the National Galleries of Scotland*	1990
Donald, Colin Dunlop, *member of the University Court*	1992
Gemmill, Robert, *member of the University Court*	2000
Giay, Luis Vicente, *President of Rotary International*	1997
Gillespie, John Spence, *Emeritus Professor of Pharmacology and previously Dean of Faculties*	1998
Goodwin, Sir Matthew Dean, *previously Chairman of Hewden Stuart Ltd*	2000
Gordon, James Stuart, *Lord Gordon of Strathblane and Chairman of the Scottish Radio Holdings and a Member of the University Court*	1998
Gray, Alexander, *solicitor*	1990
Gulliver, James Gerald, *businessman*	1989
Ikeda, Daisaku, *founder of Soka University and President of Tokyo Fuji Art Museum, Japan*	1994
Lader, Philip, *American Ambassador to the United Kingdom*	2000
Lindsay, David Cameron, *Member of the University Court*	1994
McCormick, John, *Controller of BBC Scotland*	1999
MacKay, Thomas Andrew Wilson Neilson, *President of the British Psychological Society*	2001
McKenzie, Peter, *previously Consultant Physician, Belvidere Hospital, Honorary Clinical Lecturer, and Oral Historian*	1992
MacMillan, Alexander Ross, *previously Chief General Manager of the Clydesdale Bank and a Member of the University Court*	1989
MacPherson, John Hannah Forbes, *previously Chairman of the Glasgow Development Agency and Member of the University Court*	1996
Mason, Sir David Kean, *Emeritus Professor of Oral Medicine*	1998
Stepek, Jan Wladyslaw, *benefactor to the University*	1997
Stirling, James Fraser, *architect*	1990
Sutherland, Hugh Brown, *previously Director of the University of Glasgow Trust and Emeritus Cormack Professor of Civil Engineering*	1991
Suzman, Dame Helen, *politician, Republic of South Africa*	1990
Williams, Lady Edythe Joan, *Service to the University*	1988
Wilson, Richard, *previously Rector*	1999
Wolfson, Leonard Gordon, *Lord Wolfson of Marylebone, Chairman of the Wolfson Foundation*	1997

Doctor of Veterinary Medicine and Surgery

Campbell, Roderick Samuel Fisher, *Emeritus Professor of Tropical Veterinary and Animal Science, James Cook University, Townsville, Australia*	1999
Crosbie, Annette Ross McLeod, *contribution to animal welfare*	2000
Piller, Gordon James, *previously Director of the Leukemia Research Fund*	1997
Porter, Alastair Robert Wilson, *previously Secretary and Registrar of the Royal College of Veterinary Surgeons*	1994
Shelrick, Daphne Marjorie, *founder and administrator of the David Sheldrick Wildlife Trust, Kenya*	2000
Svendsen, Elisabeth Doreen, *founder and administrator of the Donkey Sanctuary, Sidmouth, Devon*	1992
Weipers, Sir William, *previously head of the Veterinary School, Glasgow*	1982

The following is a list of official degrees awarded up to 31 March 2001.

Master of Arts

Baillie, John, *Johnstone Smith Professor of Accountancy*	1983
Craik, Sheila M, *Senior Assistant, University Library*	1993
Curtis, Eric W, *Curator, Glasgow Botanic Gardens*	1991
Harris, John L F, *Catering Officer*	1979
Hood, David, *Senior Administrative Assistant to the University Court*	1987
Kane, Thomas, *Court/Senate Steward*	1999
Mcphail, Barbara, *Administrative Assistant*	1982
Meighan, James Alistair Spence, *Personnel Officer*	1987
Roberts, John, *Clerk to the Faculty of Veterinary Medicine*	1989
Smith, George, *Dental Instructor*	1987
Whiteford, Ruby A, *Clerk, Students' Representative Council*	1990
Whyte, Pauline H, *Lecturer in Accountancy*	1985

Master of Science

Marshall, William, *Senior Chief Medical Laboratory Scientific Officer, Glasgow Dental Hospital and School*	1996

Select Bibliography

This bibliography is a selected list of volumes on the history of the University. The University Library has a large holding of works on the history of Scottish education and the University of Glasgow's role in the Nation's education.

W I Addison	*A Roll of the Graduates of the University of Glasgow From 31 December 1727 to 31, December 1897* (Glasgow, 1898)
W I Addison	*The Matriculation Albums of the University of Glasgow From 1728 to 1858* (Glasgow, 1913)
T Annan	*Memorials of the Old College of Glasgow* (Glasgow, 1871)
Anon	*Munimenta Alme Universitatis Glasguensis. Records of the University of Glasgow: from its foundation till 1727* (Glasgow, 1854)
Anon	*The Book of the Jubilee: In commemoration of the Ninth Jubilee of the University of Glasgow, 1451 - 1901* (Glasgow, 1901)
Anon	*The Book of the Fifth Centenary* (Glasgow, 1952)
Anon	*The Centenary of the Glasgow University Engineering Society* (Glasgow, 1991)
Anon	*The Centenary of the Glasgow Veterinary College and University Vet School* (Glasgow, 1962)
Anon	*The Curious Diversity. Glasgow University on Gilmorehill: the first hundred years* (Glasgow, 1970)
Anon	*Record of the Ninth Jubilee of the University of Glasgow, 1451-1901* (Glasgow, 1901)
A L Brown and M S Moss	*The University of Glasgow, 1451 - 2001* (Edinburgh, 2001)
J A Coutts	*A History of the University of Glasgow. From its foundation in 1451 to 1909* (Glasgow, 1909)
J Durkan and J Kirk	*The University of Glasgow 1451-1577* (Glasgow, 1977)
T A Fitzpatrick	*No Mean Service. Scottish Catholic Teacher Education 1895 - 1995* (Bearsden, 1995)
J Geyer-Kordesch and R Ferguson	*Blue Stockings, Black Gowns and White Coats. A brief history of women entering higher education and the medical profession in Scotland* (Glasgow 1995)
I R Hamilton	*The Five Hundred Year Book to Commemorate the Fifth Centenary of the University of Glasgow, 1451 - 1951* (Glasgow, 1951)
T B Henderson	*The History of Glasgow Dental Hospital and School, 1879-1979* (Glasgow 1979)

R T Hutcheson and H Conway — *The University of Glasgow, 1920-1974: the memoir of Robert T Hutcheson* *(Glasgow, 1997)*

R T Hutcheson and C A Oakley — *The Fleeting Years. A collection of drawings of incidents and personalities at Glasgow University* (Glasgow, 1951)

J D Mackie — *The University of Glasgow, 1451-1951: a short history* (Glasgow, 1954)

D J Martin — *Auchincruive: The history of the West of Scotland Agricultural College, 1899-1990* (Darvel, 1994)

M S Moss, J Munro, and R H Trainor — *University, City and State - The University of Glasgow since 1870* (Edinburgh, 2001)

D Murray — *Memories of the Old College of Glasgow* (Glasgow, 1927)

J B Neilson *(ed)* — *Fortuna Domus: A Series of lectures delivered in the University of Glasgow in commemoration of the Fifth Centenary of its foundation* (Glasgow, 1952)

C A Oakley — *A History of a Faculty: Engineering at Glasgow University* (Glasgow, 1973)

C A Oakley — *Union Ygorra. The story of the Glasgow University student over the last sixty years* (Glasgow, 1951)

C M Primrose — *St Mungo's Bairns: some notable Glasgow Students down the centuries* (Glasgow, 1990)

J G S Shearer — *Town and Gown Together: two hundred anf fifty years of extra-mural teaching at the University of Glasgow* (Glasgow, 1976)

W Stewart *(ed)* — *University of Glasgow Old and New* (Glasgow, 1891)

A S Thom — *From the Days of the Horseless Carriage*

R Y Thomson *(ed)* — *A Faculty for Science. A unified diversity* (Glasgow, 1993)

D M Walker — *A History of the School of Law* (Glasgow, 1990)

Appendix 1 - Chairs in Order of Foundation

Dates in brackets indicate the year of foundation of the lectureship on which the chair was based. The exceptions are Humanity and Greek where the date is the earlier occurrence of the title "Professor" being attributed to a regent.

1637	Medicine and Therapeutics (Regius Chair)
1640	Divinity
1682 *(1618)*	Humanity
1691	Mathematics
1704 *(1581)*	Greek
1709	Hebrew and Semitic Languages
1712	Law (Regius Chair)
1716	Ecclesiastical History
1718	Anatomy (Regius Chair)
1727	Logic and Rhetoric
1727	Moral Philosophy
1727	Natural Philosophy
1760	Astronomy (Regius Chair)
1807	Zoology (Regius Chair)
1815	Obstetrics and Gynaecology (Regius Chair)
1815	Surgery (Regius Chair)
1817 (1747)	Chemistry (Regius Chair)
1818 *(1704)*	Botany (Regius Chair)
1831 *(1766)*	Materia Medica (Regius Chair)
1839	Forensic Medicine (Regius Chair)
1839	Physiology (Regius Chair)
1840	Civil Engineering (Regius Chair)
1861	Conveyancing
1861	Divinity and Biblical Criticism
1861	English Language and Literature (Regius Chair)
1874	Clinical Medicine
1874	Clinical Surgery
1883	Naval Architecture and Ocean Engineering (John Elder Chair)
1893	Pathology
1896 *(1892)*	Political Economy (Adam Smith Chair)
1903	Geology
1893	Modern History

1907 *(1902)*	Mining (James S Dixon Chair)
1911	Medicine (Muirhead Chair)
1911	Obstetrics and Gynaecology (Muirhead Chair)
1911	Pathology (St Mungo-Notman Chair)
1911	Surgery (St Mungo Chair)
1913	Scottish History and Literature
1917 *(1828)*	Ophthalmology (Tennent Chair)
1917 *(1895)*	French Language and Literature (Marshall Chair)
1919 *(1887)*	Modern Languages (William Jacks Chair)
1919 *(1894)*	Mercantile Law
1919	Immunology (Gardiner Chair)
1919 *(1898)*	Chemistry (Gardiner Chair)
1919	Biochemistry (Gardiner Chair)
1920	Natural Philosophy (Cargill Chair)
1921 *(1898)*	Electrical Engineering
1921	Mechanical Engineering (James Watt Chair)
1923	Public Health (Henry Mechan Chair)
1924	Child Health (Samson Gemmell Chair)
1924	Hispanic Studies (Stevenson Chair)
1924 *(1902)*	Italian (Stevenson Chair)
1925	Accountancy (Johnstone Smith Chair)
1928	Music (Gardiner Chair)
1934	New Testament Language and Literature
1934	Old Testament Language and Literature
1934	Systematic Theology
1939	Christian Ethics and Practical Theology
1947 *(1907)*	English Language
1947 *(1908)*	Geography
1947	Psychology
1948	Applied Physiology
1948	Roman Law (Douglas Chair)
1948	Psychological Medicine
1948	Engineering (Mechan Chair)
1949 *(1894)*	Education
1949	Applied Economics
1951	Dental Surgery
1951	Oral Surgery
1951	Orthodontics

1951	Small Animal Clinical Studies
1951	Veterinary Pathology
1952 *(1878)*	Jurisprudence
1954	Agriculture
1955	Genetics
1955	Mathematics (Simson Chair)
1955	Mediaeval History (Edwards Chair)
1955	Economic History
1956	Equine Clinical Studies
1956 *(1881)*	Celtic
1957	Mechanical Engineering (Rankine Chair)
1958	Virology
1959 *(1942)*	Orthopaedics
1959	Infectious Diseases
1959	Dental Prosthetics
1960 *(1909)*	Politics (Edward Caird Chair)
1960	Administrative Medicine
1960	Industrial Relations
1960	Veterinary Medicine
1961	Natural Philosophy (Kelvin Chair)
1961	Chemistry (Joseph Black Chair)
1962	Veterinary Physiology
1962	Experimental Medicine (MacFarlane Chair)
1962	Political Economy (Bonar-Macfie Chair)
1964	Microbiology
1964	Pathological Biochemistry
1964	Pharmacology
1964	Geriatric Medicine (David Cargill Chair)
1964	Neurology
1965	Public Law
1965	Cell Biology
1965	Fine Art (Richmond Chair)
1965	Politics (James Bryce Chair)
1965	Sociology
1965	English Literature (Bradley Chair)
1965	Botany (Hooker Chair)
1965	Zoology (John Graham Kerr Chair)
1965	Biochemistry (Cathcart Chair)

1965	Physiology (Buchanan Chair)
1965	Statistics
1965	Town and Regional Planning
1965	Anaesthesia
1965	Dermatology
1965	Civil Engineering (Cormack Chair)
1965	Electrical Engineering
1965	Architecture
1966	French Language and Literature (Stevenson Chair)
1966	Chemistry (Ramsay Chair)
1966	Mathematics (Thomas Muir Chair)
1966	Geography
1966	Computing Science
1966	Medical Cardiology (Walton Chair)
1966	Oral Medicine
1967	Neurosurgery
1970	Hannah Chair
1970	Management Studies
1971	Dental Primary Care
1971	Postgraduate Medical Education
1971 *(1912)*	Social Policy and Social Work
1972	Archaeology
1972	Drama (James Arnott Chair)
1972	European Law (Jean Monnet Chair)
1973	Clinical Physics
1973	Accountancy
1973	German Language and Literature
1973	Medical Genetics
1974	General Practice (Norie-Miller Chair)
1974 *(1917)*	Slavonic Languages and Literature
1974	Business Policy
1974	Organisational Behaviour
1974	Cardiac Surgery
1974	Medical Oncology (Cancer Research Campaign Chair)
1975	Veterinary Anatomy
1975	Accountancy
1977	Child and Adolescent Psychiatry
1978	Psychology

1978	Veterinary Parasitology
1979	Modern History
1980	Surgery
1983	Computing Science
1983	Electronic Systems
1983	Astrophysics
1984	Mathematics (George Sinclair Chair)
1984	Professional Legal Practice
1985	Commercial Law (Alexander Stone Chair)
1985	Law (John Millar Chair)
1985	Political Economy (Daniel Jack Chair)
1985	Radiation Oncology
1986	Accountancy (Ernst and Young Chair)
1987	Geophysics (Britoil Chair)
1987	Medicine (Burton Chair)
1987	Mechanical Engineering (Wylie Chair)
1988	Business History
1988	Computing Science
1988	Protein Crystallography
1988	Pharmacology
1988	Housing and Urban Studies
1988	Nursing Studies
1988	Human Nutrition (Rank Chair)
1988	Biotechnology (Robertson Chair)
1989	Applied Geology (James S Dixon Chair)
1990	Rheumatology (McLeod/Arthritis and Rheumatism Council Chair)
1990	Law and Ethics in Medicine (International Bar Association Chair)
1990	Land Economics and Finance (Mactaggart Chair)
1992	Community Care Studies (Nuffield Chair)
1992	Study of The Child (St Kentigern Chair)
1994	Molecular Medicine
1994	Palliative Medicine (Macmillan Professor in the Dr Olav Kerr Chair)
1994	Computing Science
1994	Psychology
1994	Clinical Psychology
1995	Metaphysical Philosophy
1995	Spanish (Ivy McClelland Research Chair)
1995	Geography

1995	Accountancy
1995	Transfusion Medicine
1995	Aerospace Systems (Shoda Chair)
1996	Housing and Urban Studies
1996	Urban Economic Development
1997	Russian and East European Studies (Alexander Nove Chair)
1997	Veterinary Informatics and Epidemiology
1997	Social Policy (Strathclyde Region Chair)
1997	Banking Law
1997	Biostatistics/Biometrics
1997	Applied Dynamics
1999	Health Policy and Economic Evaluation (William R Lindsay Chair)
Pending	Accounting
Pending	Accounting
Pending	Clinical Neuropsychology
Pending	Corporate Strategy
Pending	Environmental Economics
Pending	Finance
Pending	Health Promotion Policy (Health Education Board for Scotland Chair)
Pending	Learning Disabilities
Pending	Marketing
Pending	Mechanical Engineering
Pending	Modern French Studies
Pending	Psychiatry
Pending	Scottish Literature
Pending	Social Work
Pending	Strategic Management

Appendix 2 - Changes of Name of Established Chairs

Original Name	New Name	Year of Change
Accountancy (Arthur Young Chair)	Accountancy (Ernst and Young Chair)	1990
Anaesthetics	Anaesthesia	1973
Anatomy and Botany (Regius Chair)	Anatomy (Regius Chair)	1818
Animal Husbandry	Animal Husbandry and Veterinary Preventative Medicine	1968
Animal Husbandry and Veterinary Preventative Medicine	Equine Clinical Studies	1995
Applied Physics (Cargill Chair)	Natural Philosophy (Cargill Chair)	1945
Bacteriology (Gardiner Chair)	Immunology (Gardiner Chair)	1990
Civil Law (Douglas Chair)	Roman Law (Douglas Chair)	2001
Conservative Dentistry	Dental Primary Care	1995
Dental Surgery	Oral Surgery	1977
Drama	Drama (James Arnott Chair)	1996
Economics (James Bonar Chair)	Political Economy (Bonar-Macfie Chair)	1990
Government (James Bryce Chair)	Politics (James Bryce Chair)	1970
History	Modern History	1956
Mathematics	Mathematics (Thomas Muir Chair)	1973
Medical Paediatrics (Samson Gemmell Chair)	Child Health (Samson Gemmell Chair)	1947
Medieval History	Medieval History (Edwards Chair)	1989
Midwifery (Regius Chair)	Obstetrics and Gynaecology (Regius Chair)	1992
Modern Romantic Languages (Marshall Chair)	French Language and Literature (Marshall Chair)	1966
Natural History	Zoology	1903
Oncology (Cancer Research Campaign Chair)	Medical Oncology (Cancer Research Campaign Chair)	1985
Organic Chemistry (Gardiner Chair)	Chemistry (Gardiner Chair)	1942
Oriental Languages	Hebrew and Semitic Languages	1893
Palliative Medicine (Dr Olav Kerr Chair)	Palliative Medicine (Macmillan Professor in the Dr Olav Kerr Chair)	1997
Physiological Chemistry (Gardiner Chair)	Biochemistry (Gardiner Chair)	1958
Political and Social Philosophy (Edward Caird Chair)	Politics (Edward Caird Chair)	1970

Political and Social Theory (Edward Caird Chair)	Political and Social Philosophy (Edward Caird Chair)	1965
Practical Astronomy (Regius Chair)	Astronomy (Regius Chair)	1893
Practice of Medicine	Medicine and Therapeutics	1989
Spanish (Stevenson Chair)	Hispanic Studies (Stevenson Chair)	1959
Theory and Practice of Heat Engines (James Watt Chair)	Mechanical Engineering (James Watt Chair)	1952
Theory of Physic or Institutes of Medicine (Regius Chair)	Physiology (Regius Chair)	1893
Urban Studies	Housing and Urban Studies	1990
Veterinary Surgery	Small Animal Clinical Studies	1969

Appendix 3 - When Degrees First Awarded

Degree	Year
BA: Bachelor of Arts	1450s-1560, 1774-1861, 1983
BAcc: Bachelor of Accountancy	1971
BAH: Bachelor of Animal Health	1997
BCommEdCommDev: Bachelor of Community Education and Community Development	1995
BD: Bachelor of Divinity	1866
BDS: Bachelor of Dental Surgery	1952
BEd: Bachelor of Education in Primary Education	1922
BEng: Bachelor of Engineering	1987
BES: Bachelor of Engineering Studies	1997
BFLS: Bachelor of Financial and Legal Studies	2000
BMedSci: Bachelor of Medical Science	1998
BMus: Bachelor of Music	1925
BN: Bachelor of Nursing	1982
BSc: Bachelor of Science	1873
BSc (Eng): Bachelor of Science (Engineering)	1983
BSc in Engineering: Bachelor of Science in Engineering	1893
BSc (Dent Sci): Bachelor of Science (Dental Science)	1993
BSc (Med Sci): Bachelor of Science (Medical Science)	1996
BSc (Nau Sci): Bachelor of Science (Nautical Science)	Resolution pending
BSc (Sci): Bachelor of Science (Science)	1983
BSc (Vet Sci): Bachelor of Science (Veterinary Science)	1994
BTechEd: Bachelor of Technological Education	1991
BTheol: Bachelor of Theology	2000
BVMS: Bachelor of Veterinary Medicine and Science	1954
DClinPsy: Doctor of Clinical Psychology	1995
DD: Doctor of Divinity	1709
DDS: Doctor of Dental Surgery	1981
DEng: Doctor of Engineering	1989
DLitt: Doctor of Letters	1896
DBA: Doctor of Business Administration	Resolution pending
DMus: Doctor of Music	1970
DSc in Dentistry: Doctor of Science in Dentistry	Resolution pending
DSc in Engineering: Doctor of Science in Engineering	1980
DSc(Med): Doctor of Science in Medicine	Resolution pending

DSc: Doctor of Science	1890
DUniv: Doctor of the University	1988
DVM: Doctor of Veterinary Medicine	1963
DVMS: Doctor of Veterinary Medicine and Surgery	1982
DVS: Doctor of Veterinary Surgery	1977
LLB: Bachelor of Laws	1771
LLD: Doctor of Laws	1709
LLM: Master of Laws	1976
MA (SocSci): Master of Arts (Social Sciences)	1970
MA: Master of Arts	1450s
MAcc: Master Accountancy	1975
MB ChB: Bachelor of Medicine and Bachelor of Surgery	1897
MB: Bachelor of Medicine	1865
MBA: Master of Business Administration	1970
MCC: Master of Community Care	1992
MD: Doctor of Medicine	1703
MEd: Master of Education	1966
MEng: Master of Engineering	1968
MFIN: Master of Finance in International Finance and Financial Institutions	Resolution pending
MLitt: Master of Letters	1970
MM: Master of Midwifery	1996
MMus: Master of Music	1988
MN: Master of Nursing	1985
MPH: Master of Public Health	1982
MPhil: Master of Philosophy	1970
MRes: Master of Research	1999
MSc: Master of Science (Economics)	1965
MSc: Master of Science (Medical Science)	1982
MSc: Master of Science (Organisational Development Practice)	1982
MSc: Master of Science (Science Education)	1982
MSc: Master of Science (Veterinary Science)	1982
MSci: Master in Science	1997
MSW: Master of Social Work	1993
MTh: Master of Theology	1967
MVM: Master of Veterinary Medicine	1985
PhD: Doctor of Philosophy	1921

Degrees and Qualifications no longer awarded by the University of Glasgow	Year
BA (Planning): Bachelor of Arts in planning	1985
BL: Bachelor of Law	1874
BLitt: Bachelor of Literature	1953
BPhil: Bachelor of Philosophy	1968
BSc (SPT): Bachelor of Science in Speech Pathology and Therapy	1983
BSc in Agriculture: Bachelor of Science in Agriculture	1895
BSc in Applied Chemistry: Bachelor of Science in Applied Chemistry	1914
BSc in Architecture: Bachelor of Science in Architecture	1923
BSc in Pharmacy: Bachelor of Science in Pharmacy	1906
BSc in Public Health: Bachelor of Science in Public Health	1892
BSc in Pure Science: Bachelor of Science in Pure Science	1920
ChB: Bachelor of Surgery (single degree without MB)	1819-1822
CM: Master of Surgery	1817
DCL: Doctor of Civil Law (one degree only)	1745
DDSc: Doctor of Dental Science	1973
DSc in Public Health: Doctor of Science in Public Health	1892
MAppSci: Master of Applied Science	1977
MDS: Master of Dental Surgery	1961
ChM: Master of Surgery	1817
MAdmin: Master of Administration	1970
MUnivAdmin: Master of University Administration	1990
DPhil: Doctor of Philosophy	1895

Degrees awarded in conjunction with Glasgow School of Art	Year
BArch: Bachelor of Architectural Studies	1973
BA in Design: Bachelor of Arts in Design	1993
BA in Fine Art: Bachelor of Arts in Fine Art	1993
BEng: Bachelor of Engineering (Product Design Engineering)	1987
BSc: Bachelor of Science (Product Design Engineering)	1987
MArch: Master of Architecture	1993
MEng: Master of European Design (Product Design)	1987
MFA: Master of Fine Art	1993

Degrees awarded in conjunction with the Scottish Agricultural College	Year
BSc in Applied Plant and Animal Science: Bachelor of Science in Applied Plant and Animal Science	1993
BTechnol in Agriculture: Bachelor of Technology in Agriculture	1998
BTechnol in Food Production and Land Use: Bachelor of Technology in Food Production and Land Use	1994-1997
BTechnol in Countryside Management: Bachelor of Technology in Countryside Management	1999
BTechnol in Food Technology: Bachelor of Technology in Food Technology	2000
BTechnol in Food Production, Manufacturing and Marketing: Bachelor of Technology in Food Production, Manufacturing and Marketing	1994-1999
BTechnol in Leisure and Recreation Management: Bachelor of Technology in Leisure and Recreation Management	1994
BTechnol in Rural Recreation and Tourism Management: Bachelor of Technology in Rural Recreation and Tourism Management	1994

Degrees awarded in conjunction with the Royal Scottish Academy of Music and Drama	Year
BEd in Music: Bachelor of Education in Music	1983-1993
BA in Dramatic Studies: Bachelor of Arts in Dramatic Studies	1983-1993
BA in Musical Studies: Bachelor of Arts in Musical Studies	1983-1993